£4

FAR FROM A LOW GUTTER GIRL

FAR FROM
A LOW
GUTTER
GIRL

The forgotten world of state wards:
South Australia 1887-1940

Margaret Barbalet

Melbourne
Oxford University Press
Oxford Auckland New York

FOR MY PARENTS, ANNE AND JOHN HARDY

OXFORD UNIVERSITY PRESS

Oxford London Glasgow New York Toronto
Delhi Bombay Calcutta Madras Karachi
Kuala Lumpur Singapore Hong Kong Tokyo
Nairobi Dar es Salaam Cape Town
Melbourne Auckland
and associates
Beirut Berlin Ibadan Mexico City Nicosia

National Library of Australia
Cataloguing-in-Publication data:

Barbalet, Margaret, 1949–
    Far from a low gutter girl.

    Bibliography.
    Includes index.
    ISBN 0 19 554379 3.
    ISBN 0 19 554380 7 (pbk.).

    1. Guardian and ward – South Australia – Case studies.
    2. Domestics – South Australia – Case studies. I. Title.
362.7'3

Designed by Pamela Brewster
Typeset in Hong Kong by Graphicraft Typesetters
Printed in Hong Kong by Nordica Printing Company
Published by Oxford University Press, 7 Bowen Crescent, Melbourne
Oxford is a trademark of Oxford University Press

'I don't think I am cared for here they often tell me that I am a low girl and was picked up from the gutter which hurts my feelings very much. I don't think I deserve such a name as that as I consider myself far from a low gutter girl.'

Mary Smith, 1902

ACKNOWLEDGEMENTS

This book was written with the aid of a grant from the Australian National Advisory Committee, International Women's Year, my debt to whom is gratefully acknowledged. I am indebted also to the South Australian Archives for their unfailing helpfulness both in correspondence and while I was in South Australia. I am grateful too, to the South Australian Department for Community Welfare for allowing me access to their records.

I would like to thank Brian Dickey for his suggestions and encouragement while I was writing the book, and Dorothy Johnston, Jack Barbalet, and Elizabeth Tombs who read the manuscript with great care; however, as the book was written alone, any errors remain mine.

I would also like to thank my son Tom, my family, and the many friends in Adelaide, Bathurst, Canberra, and the United Kingdom who encouraged me along the way. I am grateful also to Anne Clugston who typed from a very untidy manuscript.

Most of all, I would like to thank all the unknown and anonymous wards of the state who put pen to paper.

Margaret Barbalet

CONTENTS

PREFACE

In 1981 there were over 20 000 children under state guardianship in Australia.

This book is about girls who became state wards in South Australia. It begins in 1887, the year the State Children's Council, an honorary board of ladies and gentlemen, was established to oversee the boarding-out of children in large numbers throughout the state. Such children were supervised by a new government department, the State Children's Department. The account ends in 1940 because that was when the world began to change for women, particularly in South Australia where there had not been large-scale industrialization. There was also a gradual change in the way state wards were treated after there had been an extensive inquiry into the system in 1939, and this seems to make 1940 a doubly logical end point.

Most state wards were fostered, that is boarded-out with families other than their own. At thirteen, the boys became farm-labourers and the girls domestic servants. A breakaway from this, particularly for boys, began in the late 1920s but the system really only changed after World War II. A study of the few hundred girls who were wards of the state (about 400 to 800 in any one year) therefore has very wide implications. Thousands of women throughout Australia's history have been domestic servants. A considerable amount is known about them, but – and it is an enormous distinction – we know it from above, from the outside, from the employers' point of view. We know barely anything about the women's thoughts, their experiences, their complaints and joys.

These pages show their days and vicissitudes in their own words. They were working-class women and children: domestic servants and foster-children. From these hundreds of ordinary women comes a mosaic of experiences of everyday life, a life as full of hope and desperation as any more elevated, and as important. From these hundreds of 'shards' one can reconstruct a world.

The servant-employing class in Australia, just as in England, talked and wrote about the frequent crises in the kitchen, cook's departure, the maid's impudence, or how to manage the 'general'. Accounts like this abound. But letters from wards themselves to the Department that controlled their lives break apart the stereotypes perpetuated by employers, reporters, and cartoonists. The other side of 'the servant question', the sensibilities of working women, and of those even more 'invisible souls', poor children, are revealed.

This is not a case study of state wards and no recommendations or prescriptions are to be found here. Nor is it a book about social welfare programmes, although the history of the State Children's Department is treated in the last chapter. It is an investigation of the experience of female state wards, 'state girls' as they sometimes called themselves, and not a study of poverty or of the dependent poor, although there is obviously a need for a future statistical study of the dependent poor in South Australia, the state that was supposed to be different. This book is not a complete study of social welfare in South Australia; others are doing that. But I hope this account of the experiences of dependent girls will make a valuable contribution towards the social history of Australia.

One omission from this study is any discussion of wards who were black. They came under the umbrella of the State Children's Department from 1911 onwards. In many ways their lot was hardest: poor, female, state ward and black, in a white Australia. Scattered references to them could not in the end be just, so they are omitted as they need a full scale study of their own. And because this study is about children boarded-out, it deals only in passing with institutions in chapter 8. Readers with little time should immediately turn to this chapter – a monograph on philanthropy and class in South Australia. It is chapters 1–7, however, which recreate the world of foster-children, ordinary children whose families had in some sense failed.

The 'raw materials' were the Correspondence of the State Children's Department and Files relating to children under departmental supervision and released in the 1940s and 1950s. Both these record groups are found in the South Australian Archives. Between a third and one half of the Correspondence of the State Children's Department, 1887–1927, was studied in detail. The files occupy almost 20 metres of shelf space and run alphabetically; Files 'A' to 'F' were looked at in detail.

State wards in difficulty, often on isolated farms, wrote to the Department with their grievances; some were semi-literate, many were angry. The question of whether they were accurate and objective looms large, but is not quite as difficult as it may at first appear.

First, the sheer number of letters means that the common experience can quickly be distinguished from the bizarre or unusual. Girls who wanted a change, any change, had to complain to the secretary, hence, to balance the picture, letters of contentment and adjustment have been included in this book in greater number than they occur in Departmental records. Second, wherever possible, the word of a girl is backed up by an inspector's account or by checking an administrative decision on whether a girl was removed, a foster-mother cautioned, or a wage raised. Third, girls were obliged to be accurate to some degree, since their letters might result in investigation by Departmental inspectors. In many accounts by girl or mistress there is a considered calmness, 'second thoughts' following a row the day before. Others are written in the heat of the moment, despatches from the domestic front, moments vividly recorded. Both are part of the record. It should be noted that real names are never used in this book for state wards, foster-parents and employers, although they are for Departmental officers, teachers, and police, and that in general all correspondence is quoted as in the original.

Appendixes at the back of this book, and tables throughout, list the reasons why children became wards, some differences between boys and girls, how many absconded, how many were insane, how many girls became pregnant, and the reasons why so many were returned from foster-homes and employers. These precise indications of number lie behind the text rather than interrupting it.

There are good reasons for regarding the letters from girls as treasured historical evidence, a rich seam from the clay of all those forgotten and lost lives that made Australia. Working-class lives written or recorded when pulses have long since slowed, often smooth over details, minimize difficulties, or forget. And as John Burnett has pointed out, the working-class diarist was 'engaging in an activity which set him apart from the majority of his fellow men and that to this extent he was not a strictly representative figure'.[1] As the twentieth century advanced women were even less likely than men to record their lives. By the accident of a centralized welfare bureaucracy, state wards had to record their lives until their release from the control of the state at twenty-one years of age. Their lives after that are not recorded and would be impossible to trace except by invasion of privacy and Herculean labour. Periodically the welfare bureaucracy published figures that seem to indicate that most wards merged anonymously into the community and were not known to the police in later life.[2]

All Australian states treated state wards in much the same way as South Australia. So this book, while centred on the experience of state wards in South Australia, applies in many ways to the thousands of ordinary working lives that shaped the Australia of the past.

INTRODUCTION

In any one year between 1887 and 1940 there were likely to be between 860 and 1 840 wards of the state, and slightly less than half this number were females. Table 1 indicates the parental circumstances of all children who became wards of the state in the first six years of the boarding-out scheme which began in 1887. This shows clearly that absence of a parent was the most common reason for committal, particularly absence of the father. A sobering number of children (19 per cent) had simply been abandoned or orphaned, a similar number (23 per cent) had one parent in hospital, gaol, or other institution.

Behind these figures lie the harsh realities of poverty and dependence in nineteenth-century South Australia. Families might be able to obtain meagre rations from the Destitute Board. In old age or ill-health some of their number could resort to the Destitute Asylum on Kintore Avenue. They might depend to some extent on private charity. For destitute pregnant women there was the Lying-in-Home. But there was no old-age pension, no widows pension, no deserted wives pension, no child endowment. Not for forty years after 1887 were children able to be boarded-out with their own mothers, and not until 1942 were widows allowed a pension.

Mothers often tried desperately to prevent their children becoming state wards. The North Adelaide police wrote of one woman in 1891:

The children must necessarily be neglected by the fact of their father for whose arrest a warrant is now in existence for having deserted them is still at large, the maintenance of her children depends upon whatever she can earn by washing which is nothing short of a miserable existence.[1]

Single women had an almost impossible task to try and keep a family, and their poverty might become conspicuous.

The secretary of the State Children's Department might write, in this case to the police in 1901:

I am informed that the children of a woman named Smith living in Tatham St, off Franklin St are neglected by their mother and that they are allowed to run the streets at all hours of the day and night. Will you be good enough to favour me with a report.

Back would come the report:

Foot Constable Hogan reports having made enquiries and finds that Mrs Smith referred to in attached is living in No. 11 Tatham Terrace off Franklin Street. She

Table 1 Parental circumstances of all children committed by the State Children's Council 1887-92

Mothers / Fathers	Absent	Institutionalized	Poor	'Improper'	'Inadequate'	'Respectable'	Total
Absent	214	147	88	80	18	90	637
	19.3%	13.2%	7.9%	7.2%	1.62%	8.13%	57.5%
Institutionalized	28	16	10	19	—	9	82
	2.6%	1.4%	0.9%	1.7%		0.8%	7.4%
Poor	22	—	44	3	—	—	69
	1.98%		3.8%	0.27%			6.2%
'Improper'	16	6	3	45	2	6	78
	1.4%	0.5%	0.27%	4%	0.18%	0.54%	7%
'Inadequate'	—	—	—	—	1	—	1
					0.09%		0.09%
'Respectable'	50	20	—	13	3	154	240
	4.5%	1.8%		1.17%	0.27%	13.9%	21.6%
Total	330	189	145	160	24	259	1 107
	29.8%	17%	13%	14.4%	2.1%	23.3%	100%

Source: State Children's Council, *Annual Reports*.

TABULAR CATEGORIES:	COUNCIL CATEGORIES:
Absent	Dead, unknown, deserted, in another colony, looking for work, in the country
Institutionalized	In gaol, destitute asylum, lunatic asylum, hospital, refuge, or lying-in home
Poor	Poor, crippled, in service, poor and honest, unable to work due to . . ., divorced
'Improper'	Drunkard, bad character, disreputable, prostitute, intemperate, very low, keeps a brothel, a married woman of loose ways
'Inadequate'	Married again, eccentric
'Respectable'	Fair circumstances, respectable

One parent absent	68% (38% absent fathers)
One parent institutionalized	23%
One parent poor	15%
One parent improper	17%
One parent inadequate	2.16%
One parent respectable	31.1%

N.B. Because more than one child from a family was sometimes committed, some parental circumstances of course appear more than once in this table.

is a widow having buried her husband on the 28th Ult. She has seven children the eldest 13 years old and the youngest 18 months. She has no means but receives rations from the Government. The eldest girl went to a situation with a Mrs Fox of Flinders Street on the 18th inst, the children look as if they are well fed but are badly clad and are not kept clean. Mrs Smith is spoken of by her neighbours as steady but is of untidy habits. She states that if she could put 3 of her children into the Industrial School she would be able to provide for the 3 youngest herself. From all that I can learn from the neighbours – this man was addicted to drink and left his family Absolutely destitute even of furniture . . .[2]

On subsequent visits the constable found conditions worsening, the children running about the streets in a 'filthy manner', and so some of the children became state wards.

In other instances a father might not be able to cope if his wife were inadequate.

I am a poor man often have to go to work from home and then the poor children suffer. I have known them to go a fortnight without being undressed and if I bring anything home for her to make for them she only destroyes it and they go about like blackfellows.[3]

Destitution visited the city and country towns. The Kapunda police reported in 1891:

there is no doubt that the person referred to is very poor, she is a widow and has one child to care for, and I have been informed that she got but very little work to do, as there are so many char women in the place, that there is not work for them to do. There was a subscription list about for this woman not long since to try and get enough to send her to Broken Hill to try and get work there.[4]

Some children were rescued from 'moral danger'.

the house of Mrs Venturi in Divett Place is not only a house of Assignation but also a brothel it being the house of two prostitutes name Betty Flynn and Fanny West who take men home with them.

I am further informed that three young persons . . . live there. I am naturally anxious to know if the information received is true and shall be greatly obliged if your officer may be permitted to report on the matter.[5]

As far as religious belief was concerned it is significant that of the children who became wards in the period 1887 to 1892, far more (28.5 per cent) were Roman Catholic than Roman Catholics in the South Australian community as a whole (14.72 per cent). Church of England (37.6 per cent) compared rather more with the general population (27.86 per cent), followed by 10.3 per cent Wesleyan (15.34 per cent), Baptist 4.5 per cent

(5.50 per cent), and Presbyterian 4.3 per cent (5.68 per cent). A letter from Archbishop O'Reily in 1896 regarding the difficulty of finding enough respectable Catholic foster-homes, further illuminates the position.

The Catholic body draws the bulk of its members from amongst the working class; of the remainder but comparitively few are well to do. As a consequence when homes are looked for for Catholic destitute children in Catholic households, the search is not a readily successful one.[6]

It seems likely that these poor Catholic families were of Irish descent but the labour necessary to verify this has not yet been done.

Table 2 indicates that at least 81 per cent of all the children who became state wards in the years 1887 to 1892 were sentenced until they were sixteen years of age or older.

Table 2   Length of sentence of children committed 1887–92

	1887	1888	1889	1890	1891	1892	Total	Per cent
Six mths	5	5	–	–	–	–	10	1
One yr	8	11	20	7	5	5	56	5.7
Two yrs	5	3	4	–	3	1	16	1.6
Three yrs	1	2	2	–	–	–	5	0.51
To 13 yrs	–	–	1	–	1	2	4	0.4
To 14 yrs	2	1	4	1	1	1	10	1
To 15 yrs	–	–	1	–	1	1	3	0.3
To 16 yrs	21	69	96	63	105	81	435	44.9
To 17 yrs	–	–	–	1	–	–	1	0.1
To 18 yrs	15	55	63	58	92	69	352	36.3
Surrendered	–	–	4	13	11	16	44	4.5
Admitted temporarily	–	–	2	4	8	18	32	3.3
Total	57	146	197	147	227	194	968	100

Source: State Children's Council, Annual Reports.

Sex differences emerge when considering the ages of children sentenced. As Table 3 indicates, 46 per cent of the boys were sentenced between the ages of ten and fifteen whereas only 30 per cent of the girls were. This would seem to fit a pattern of sex-determined juvenile delinquency from which Western industrialized society has only just begun to diverge.

In order to test the persistence of the statistical findings from the period 1887–1892, a 5 per cent sample of all children committed in the period 1918 to 1928 was taken. The main difference to emerge was the decline in the number of 'absent' mothers. The number of 'absent' fathers remained at 38 per cent. Far fewer children (6.6 per cent) had both parents dead or deserted than in the 1890s (19.3 per cent) and fewer (52.7 per cent) had one parent 'absent' than in the earlier period (68 per cent).

Table 3   Ages of all children newly committed 1889–92

	Boys	%	Girls	%	Boys & Girls	%
Under 1 week	—	—	3	.9	3	.39
Under 6 weeks	2	.46	4	1.2	6	.78
Under 1 year	17	3.92	25	7.5	42	5.49
1–2 yrs	16	3.69	22	6.6	38	4.96
2–3 yrs	28	6.46	15	4.5	43	5.62
3–4 yrs	21	4.84	20	6.02	41	5.35
4–5 yrs	26	6.0	24	7.2	50	6.53
5–6 yrs	20	4.61	14	4.2	34	4.44
6–7 yrs	20	4.61	16	4.8	36	4.70
7–8 yrs	20	4.61	19	5.7	39	5.09
8–9 yrs	27	6.23	19	5.7	46	6.01
9–10 yrs	36	8.3	15	4.5	51	6.66
10–11 yrs	46	10.6	27	8.1	73	9.54
11–12 yrs	48	11.08	11	3.3	59	7.71
12–13 yrs	43	9.9 (46%)	10	3.0 (30%)	53	6.92 (39%)
13–14 yrs	37	8.5	16	4.8	53	6.92
14–15 yrs	13	3.0	14	4.2	27	3.52
15–16 yrs	13	3.0	22	6.6	35	4.57
16–17 yrs	—	—	22	6.6	22	2.81
17–18 yrs	—	—	14	4.2	14	1.83
Total	433	100	332	100	765	100

Source: State Children's Council, *Annual Reports*.

Table 4   Parental circumstances of a 5% sample of all children committed 1918–28

One parent absent	52.7%
One parent institutionalized	6%
One parent poor	45%
One parent 'improper'	13.4%
One parent 'inadequate'	20.6%
One parent 'respectable	34%

Source: *Court Mandates committing Children to the Custody and Control of the Council 1918–27*.

T.H. Kewley in *Social Security in Australia*, shows that throughout the 1920s there was an impetus towards, but a consistent failure to enact, social security legislation.[7] This emerges as an important difference when analyzing who became wards of the state in the 1920s. Far more children (45 per cent) had one parent who was simply described as poor, than in the earlier period (15 per cent). Families in desperate need still had to rely on rations from the Destitute Asylum and, depending on their skill and resourcefulness, could apparently obtain clothing from various sources, but their lack of cash income (at least before the passing of the Maintenance Act in 1926) meant that merely obtaining day to day necessities was a hard struggle. As a Department inspector noted in 1920,

What Mrs Schubert [a deserted wife] really needs is hard cash as she has the bulk of her clothing given her from various sources – Certainly it is not all one could wish but she makes it do somehow. As cash seems out of the question I beg to recommend she is helped with clothing.[8]

The family without a breadwinner was seen as being on the edge of an abyss. With family to support, the burden of earning and parenting was seen as too heavy to permit proper supervision of growing children.

Mother a widow in poor circumstances. Home humble and fairly comfortable. I fear that having to go to work Mrs Coates cannot give her children the care they need. Also have such a tiny home and yard that it is a great temptation to get into the streets.[9]

This was also the case for fathers.

Mr Watson's first wife died and during his widowhood the family went to pieces growing wild and disobedient. This was especially so in the case of Maggie . . .[10]

Some families broke down because one parent was inadequate or mentally deficient, others because of the pressures left by World War I.

Although only 13 per cent of the South Australian population were Roman Catholic in the 1920s they made up 30 per cent of the population of state wards. This was now well-known to the Department, the *Annual Reports* for 1910 and 1915 having carefully noted that Catholics were over-represented among state wards. During the same period, wards who came from Church of England families (27 per cent) were roughly comparable to their numbers in the population (33 per cent), as were Methodists (16:24 per cent), Presbyterians (3.3:4.9 per cent), and Baptists (4:4.65 per cent).

During the 1920s the basic wage was revealed as barely adequate for even the average-sized family, and large families must have been poor in many instances.[11] Many questions are yet to be answered about the nature and survival of large families, especially those without a breadwinner in the decades before Australia enacted significant social security legislation.

In regard to age at the time of committal, the statistics are largely the same as for the period to 1892, except that children could now be sentenced until twenty-one years of age. Between the ages of fourteen and eighteen, just over 36 per cent of all wards were committed. It is not possible to ascertain length of sentence, but long sentences were at this time favoured by the State Children's Council.

After the passing of the Maintenance Act in 1926 the numbers of state wards, not unexpectedly, fell. In 1925 there had been 1 773, by 1935 there were only 1 042 children. But the children whose mothers received assistance under the provisions of the Maintenance Act while not removed from their mothers, were still liable to be visited like 'children boarded-out'.[12] And the social welfare bureaucracy continued to grow.

CHAPTER 1

The Childhood
of State Wards
1887–1914

Mr. and Mrs. Smith have both been a good Father and Mother to me ever since I
have been with them and I should be very sorry to leave them now. I am going to
receive my clothes and pocket money as if I was their own child.[1]

before going to school Mrs. West said to me 'this is not the place for the Skimmer'.
I had washed it the previous evening and left it in the kitchen instead of the Dairy.
I did not reply to Mrs. West. She had a stick in her hand. She struck me a great
many times. I screamed. I then went to school. I told Sarah Evans at the
school . . . Mrs. West was dressing Ernie. She said his stockings were not properly
darned. I said nothing. I went into the kitchen. Mrs. West following and took a
stick – honeysuckle about 2 ft long from the safe and hit me she struck me many
times over the back and head. I cried. I went to school. I was late. Sarah Evans
said she heard me crying.[2]

Between these two extremes, the happy and the brutal foster-home, lies
the middle ground, the typical experience that this chapter will seek to
capture.

Whatever the reasons for a girl becoming a ward of the state, if she were
an ordinary healthy girl under thirteen years of age she would eventually
find herself arriving at a foster-home to be introduced to her foster-family
by an inspector from the State Children's Department.

The Department took considerable trouble to find good foster-homes
since the home was the essential ingredient in their formula of reformation. All applications for foster-children had to be accompanied by the
certificates of a clergyman, magistrate, 'or other responsible person'.
Children boarded-out were supposed to be 'properly fed and clothed (in
accordance with Regulation 31) sent regularly to Sunday and day school,
and trained up to be honest, truthful, and modest, respectful to their
teachers and others, and obedient to their foster-parents'.[3] Not more

1

The home was the essential ingredient in the early reformers' schemes for poor children and it was most important that the foster-home have a respectable atmosphere.

than four state children were to be placed in any one home, and there were supposed to be no boarders or lodgers other than state children.

The locality of the foster-home does not seem to have been very important in these decades. Despite a distrust of the city, foster-homes were likely to be found in the suburbs as well as in the country.

In 1887 a lady visitor for a southern suburb of Adelaide described the sort of foster-homes she had visited that year and her report was quoted approvingly in the Department's Annual Report. She reported that the homes were, with one exception, 'substantial stone houses' with four to six rooms. She added that they were in 'healthy situations', meaning that they were not low-lying, the importance of which, in an era without deep drainage, cannot be underestimated. She then went on with unruffled upper-class confidence:

The general condition of the population of Goodwood, which consists mainly of trades-people and artisans of the better class and in fairly steady work, produces a class of homes which appears to me specially adapted to the boarding-out system, being mostly detached houses, well fenced, and surrounded with gardens or large yards, and in the occupation of a respectable body of people.[5]

It was even thought in these heady early years that the 'tone' of the homes themselves was being raised by having a foster-child and lady visitors.

Once the basic structure of the foster-family's house was found to be sound (with particular attention being paid to the airy healthy aspect of the bedroom), a great deal of attention was paid to the morality of the family. It was not necessary that the family be a 'nuclear family'. Not only wives, but also widows, single women, and extended families were quite acceptable provided that the home had a respectable atmosphere. In one instance an application was declined not only because a house had merely two rooms, but also, and more importantly, because 'the Ryans are not people to whom one would entrust the care of girls'.[6] In another instance the Department's secretary wrote to the police stating that he had heard 'rumours' concerning a foster-mother, a married woman, who lived in Flinders Street. The police informed him that she was 'a respectable hard-working woman and supports herself and Family by taking in sewing. There is no record against her and nothing is known against her character by the Police'.[7]

Children, it was firmly believed, should grow up in a state of innocence. The secretary encapsulated this belief when he wrote concerning some children who were appearing in plays at the Theatre Royal in 1911; he thought it 'not suitable for children of tender years' because they became 'precocious, too much self-possessed, too much men and women – shall I say too bold'.[8]

It was generally regarded as important that the foster-mother be a 'kind' or 'motherly' person, but the difficulties in ensuring this were immense. Although training and firmness were expected of foster-parents, physical violence was not permitted. Corporal punishment was to 'be administered as seldom as possible, and shall be only resorted to when absolutely necessary for discipline and not for first offences, unless of a grave nature'.[9] This did not mean that physical violence did not occur, it did. The problem lies in estimating how much mistreatment was never reported.

Children were supposed to be visited every six weeks by a member of a district visiting committee. In addition, public school teachers were required to report on each state child every three months. Despite this, one of the recurring criticisms directed against the State Children's Council was that the children could not say what they really felt about foster-homes to the visiting committees.[10] This is discussed fully in Chapter 8.

Casual cruelties perpetrated against children that *were* discovered make quite chilling reading. One girl ran away from her foster-mother, who protested:

in answer to the charges . . . that the girl was never got up before 6 am seldom or

3

never milked the cows or fetched them in the morning. Did whip her with a willow stick for telling lies and being disobedient but never did so severely. The girl seldom or never came home [from school] before 5 pm. Her principle work was nursing the baby.[11]

Apart from the Department, the only persons entitled to take any action to protect a state girl were police officers. Any girl who found conditions in the home intolerable was supposed to take refuge in the nearest police station and wait until the Department in Adelaide had

The transformation in appearance of which the State Children's Council was so proud: from dirty and neglected street children to well-clad, well-fed foster-children, dressed in their best outfits for the serious occasion of a photograph.

been notified by wire. Any other escape from the home was regarded as absconding.[12]

Sometimes a neighbour might intercede on a girl's behalf. One girl, after several beatings, ran to the house of a nearby minister who wrote to the Department stressing that he had 'some difficulty' in getting the girl to accompany him back to her foster-home. He urged that she should be removed from the home and added that he had had to 'promise her, that if she were beaten again she might come and stay with me, till she could go to Adelaide'.[13]

The above paragraphs are not an argument that a majority of state wards were treated badly, but an indication of the difficulties that often faced a child trying to report unhappiness or cruelty.

Some wards, of course, had very happy childhoods. They were placed as infants and never knew themselves to be state children; others had very loving foster-parents. They were a minority however, but although their happiness was accidental and not due to the policies of the Council, they are very much part of the record:

I like living here very much and I would not like to go away from them and I am very happy and comfortable. It is the nicest home I have been to yet for a long time . . . I take the mailbags up to the post office for Mr. Milem and then come home and get tea.[14]

I have had a nice time in the holidays I went to Middleton beach for a day and I went out in the hills for a day and I am going to Victor Harbour next week for a day.[15]

There is also much evidence of foster-parents' attachment. One foster-mother wrote that her charge had had pneumonia,

and it had left her lungs weak. Dr. Street advised me to watch her closely for some months: I am doing so she is not strong but seems fairly well . . . I hope we shall not have to part with her for she is a clever companiable [sic.] child, and is really attached to us.[16]

Foster-mothers frequently realized afresh after a child had been seriously ill how much they loved the child. Others showed their affection by painstakingly teaching girls who were backward in school work.[17]

There were yet other girls, very much in the minority, who grew up unaware that they were wards of the state and acquired middle-class accomplishments. One mother wrote:

Eleanor is always asking me to get her an instrument (an Organ or Piano) as I have no way of getting it I want please to know if you would let me have £20 or 25 that would buy an organ and pay for music lessons so far she has only played the harp, but that is not much use to [her] in connection with the Sunday school work she says she would rather have the money spent on an instrument . . . [18]

It was often not the neatest home or the best managers who formed the strongest attachments. The Department's inspectors developed a fine appreciation of the sort of home where things might be untidy but the foster-parents were fond of and affectionate towards the children. One inspector visited a home where a young girl had been living for seven years and commented that:

Mrs Hughes is a somewhat rough woman in her speech and manner and her house is by no means an example of order and neatness as her health is somewhat indifferent and she is not methodical in her ways, but she is kind and affectionate and I think a thoroughly good woman. Ruth is much troubled at the idea of leaving here when she is 13, and there were tears in her eyes when I saw her a few weeks ago and she spoke about it. [19]

Other girls were more fortunate, one being returned to her foster-mother when the latter promised to 'train her up and learn her to work' as her employer was at present doing. The foster-mother explained that she had had the girl for a long time without any subsidy at all and now she had gone 'something seems missing every day'. [20] Behind these genuine attachments there is also an appreciation that the girl would now be more useful. Having finished school she could assist around the house and look after the younger children in much the same way that a natural daughter of the house would be expected to do if family circumstances would support her at home.

The State Children's Council was aware that it was not good for children to have changes in foster-parents. As early as 1887 they commented in the annual report how 'disheartening' it was to have so many children returned as unsuitable or for misconduct, going on to add that 'nothing so hardens a child as frequent visits to the Industrial School'.

Two-thirds of state wards were not committed as infants but between the ages of four and sixteen. In over 80 per cent of cases they were committed until they were at least sixteen. Most girls were placed out as foster-children or as servants; only a minority remained in institutions (see Appendix 4).

The reasons why children were returned are detailed in Table 5. Despite all the care taken in finding homes, 19.5 per cent of all children placed out were returned in any one year. It is obvious that children were in a somewhat inequitable position. Table 5 shows that of all children returned, 45 per cent were returned as a result of their guardian's dissatisfaction, whereas only 14.7 per cent were returned because the home was unsuitable. A number (10 per cent) were returned because they absconded; this number included fewer girls than boys (see Appendix 4). A surprising number (12 per cent) were returned because of illness, death, or economic difficulty on the part of guardians.

Even more important, perhaps, than the reasons for return was the fact of it: the instability it brought to children's lives. Most children would experience more than one foster-home and service-home, and some experienced as many as six or seven. One of the greatest certainties of childhood is knowing the permanence of one's relationship to one's parents, be they poor or rich, capricious or fair. To be a state child was usually to have something infinitely less: a home and 'parents' that might change or disappear forever. Then for a while one would be in an institution again, without parents, and then a new home and new parents would be found. This is the central distinction which marks the childhood of most state girls.

Table 5 Principal reasons for children being returned 1887-92

Reason for return	No.	%
Misconduct	231	25.9
Child unsuitable	171	19.2
Home unsatisfactory	131	14.7
Absconded & captured	90	10.1
Guardian unable to keep	48	5.39
Mutual dissatisfaction	29	3.2
Ill-health or death of guardian	34	3.8
Home broken up	26	2.9
Other	129	14.5
Total	889	100

Table 6 Percentage of children returned 1887-92

Total number placed out 1887-92	4557
Total number returned	889

19.5% of all children placed out were returned in any one year
8.8% of all children placed out returned due to guardian's dissatisfaction
4.8% of all children placed out returned (including absconders) due to child's dissatisfaction.

Source: State Children's Council, *Annual Reports*.
These tables refer to *all* state children, that is those at service as well as those under thirteen who were boarded-out.

Sometimes a child would be returned by a genuinely regretful foster-parent:

owing to my husband securing a position in New South Wales I shall be leaving Naracoorte about 22inst therefore am obliged to return to your care the little girl Pearl Lovell. I am really sorry to part with her but under the circumstances I am obliged to do so. She is a very good little girl suits me well but I am obliged to go away from Naracoorte.[21]

Sometimes foster-parents would be hard: 'She has been a very naughty girl we are quite glad to be rid of her. She is not fit to mix with other children'.[22] And sometimes, a peculiar nineteenth-century mixture of both:

when I am away Laura is unmanageable she will not heed what anyone says to her in fact I am the only one she is obedient to and I have had a lot of trouble with the child but think for the comfort of my family I had better send her away . . . She does not want to leave me and I am sorry to part with the child but the change may be for her good. I shall always feel an interest in Laura and hope she will try to be a good girl.[23]

Foster-parents had little to fall back on when a child disappointed them. They could not easily reassure themselves, as could a natural parent, that the child was merely 'naughty' or 'going through a phase'. They might resort to blaming the child's ancestry. One foster-father wrote:

in my opinion it is heredity or the accident of birth. As a child she was not shy nor could I say she was forward though the tendency to forwardness was there. I am sure that her conduct is not the result of her training. She is treated exactly as if she were a child of my own. She sits at the table with the rest of the family, and no difference is made between her and the others . . . but she will loiter on the way home from school, though repeatedly told to hurry home. Since the inspector's visit I have heard that she was very naughty during the absence of Mrs. Oldfield and I on our holiday.[24]

He then went on almost casually to reveal that:

Until a few months ago I kept from her the knowledge that she was not my child but just then her wilfulness was so manifest that I told her that she was a state child and that unless she behaved better I should return her to the state. I feel confident that her wilfulness is inherent and not the result of training. I have now fully decided that unless she alters very materially before the next visit of the Inspector, I will return her to you . . .[25]

A few weeks later this girl was returned, her foster-father adding that she 'does not try to please either my wife or myself'. Thus, in a tragic contradiction, a system designed to help children resulted in the rejection of this girl by the people she had known all her life as 'parents'.

There was not necessarily even a combination of attachment *and* discipline in the lives of state girls; they were supposed to be prepared for hard lives during their childhood. Anne Barter, for example, was transferred to a new foster-mother in February 1900 in order that she be more strictly controlled. The inspector wrote:

Mrs. Kenton understands children. She is kind but firm and requires obedience from all children under her care. I do not think Anne Barter will display her tantrums before Mrs. Kenton. She is just at a tiresome age now and it will not do to allow her to act on her own.[26]

Behaviour that would just have to be endured by natural parents was often the catalyst for a state child's return from a foster-home. One foster-mother wrote from a country town in 1906:

I have had such trouble with Susannah, Sunday morning I send her to Church with my Mother this is Tuesday morning and I have not seen her since, instead of going to Church she went to somebodys Mulberry tree spoiled her dress and would not come home . . . I was hoping she would be better now she has been with me two years but she is such a story teller you cannot believe a word that she says . . . I think she will be better in firmer hands than mine.[27]

Attachment was the missing factor in the equation of bringing up children under the state. It was considered enough that foster-parents be kind, conscientious and, it was to be hoped, affectionate; they were not asked if they could become attached to a child. Ironically, the fear of losing a child back to the Department may have prevented many foster-parents from forming strong bonds with the children under their care. It often prompted requests to adopt a child.

Until the mid 1930s there was simply no adoption of children as we know it today. To 'adopt' a child in the years 1887–1913 meant only that foster-parents ceased to be paid a subsidy for a state child. They usually also had fewer visits from inspectors of the Department. Permission for a child to be adopted had to be obtained from the child's natural parents where they could be contacted, and naturally it was sometimes refused, which led to much worry and uncertainty for the foster-parents. A foster-mother of Kenton Valley wrote to the Department:

if there is any fear at all of the child being taken from us I will adopt her at once as I am sure Mr Young would rather adopt her than have her removed as we have had all the trouble with her since a baby and now she is attached to us and she can toddle around . . . of course we are living in hope of some of our own some day, but [she] has a place in our hearts being such a little tot.[28]

It was not unknown for a state child to ask her foster-parents to adopt her, as one girl did in 1909:

I find it a very comfortable home. And I will be able to help her with the little ones, a work which I like doing very much. Mrs Jones lets me go every Sunday morning to Sunday School and then I stop to the (11 o'clock) Church Service which I like very much. Oh Mr Grey I hope there will be nothing to stop me from staying here I am pleased to say that I have not got any bad marks in my (book) yet.[29]

Older girls might be asked to write to the Department and give their opinion about whether or not they wanted to be adopted.[30] Their answers tended to be full of information about how they liked the daily routine, the practicalities of family life.

Parents might write of a toddler with emotion but they, too, were more likely to be quite 'sensible' about the qualities they wanted in an older child. The Macclesfield Visiting Committee wrote of one girl that

she is a good intelligent child, strong, healthy, fair size for her age – not promising to be tall seemingly adapted for household duties but should she get longer at school would suit any sort of business, she is honest truthful and sensible.[31]

The girl herself wrote:

my Aunty will keep me as long as she can she says that I am too young to go among strangers yet. She told me to ask you if you would give up all claim to me and let her keep me as her own child.[32]

Quite different experiences might lie behind the wish to adopt. The first letter below is from a woman applying to adopt a girl she had not even met. The other is from a couple who wished to adopt a child they had looked after for some time.

I am anxious to entirely adopt a girl (if possible an Orphan) as my own if not as my own, I would always feel afraid I should lose her in some manner perhaps at the time I would most need her . . .[33]

I may mention that we are very much attached to the child and that it is our most earnest wish to look upon her as our own daughter – the child is also very much attached to us, and quite regards us as her own parents.[34]

One foster-parent wrote that her heart was intwined with three foster-children. She wished to adopt from motives of simple affection. Others with a pragmatic approach saw adoption as 'a splendid chance for the child', adding not any airy words about love, but just the practicalities:

'She would be well trained and educated and put to a good trade and well provided for'.[35]

Even if a child were adopted by foster-parents, natural parents would in some cases be able to petition to have the child returned to them. They sometimes succeeded, and this was the flaw in the whole system. It meant that the natural parents suffered, the foster-parents suffered because they could never be completely certain that a child was theirs, and of course the unfortunate state children suffered most of all as the system militated against stability of relationships.

The Department had to decide whether children could remain with foster-parents. There were some cases where the issue was clear-cut, where, for example, the child had never known her natural parents. Inspector Wheaton wrote of one girl whose foster-parents had pleaded that they 'could not part with her now': 'She is a fine beautiful girl and I have no reason to doubt their affection towards her, she is treated as their own in every respect and to remove her would be a great blow'.[36] She added that the girl was unaware that she was not the natural child of her foster-parents. But there were other cases where the issue was not so easily decided. In those cases where foster-parents were aware of the possibility that a loved child might be removed from their care even if 'adopted', there is clear expression of how unsatisfactory they found the system. One woman wrote unequivocally:

I understand if I adopt her from the State that she can then be removed at any time, and her mother could claim her any time. This is not what I want. I want to know if I could get her as though she were my own child, she is extremely quick, and if I adopted her I would do for her the same as my own.[37]

Other inspectors wrote of a childless couple who were 'in constant fear' of losing the baby girl in their charge and 'anxiously awaited' the secretary's decision about whether they could keep the baby. Theirs was one of the clear-cut cases: twenty years later the girl was still unaware that she was adopted.[38]

To some extent the Department used the willingness of parents to forgo the payment they received for boarding children as an indicator of their sincerity in wishing to adopt. The appropriate attitude was shown by a Mrs Johns who in 1907 kept a respectable boarding-house in Pitt Street, and supplemented her income by doing 'plain sewing' for the Department. She was prepared to take on her niece 'at a personal sacrifice to herself as she is a widow and a poor woman'.[39]

But it was not adoption in the modern sense. Girls were returned to institutions years after they were adopted, sometimes even for reasons of economy. A Strathalbyn farmer spelt out his reasons all too succinctly when he returned a state girl. He was, he explained baldly, unable to continue operation on the farm ... on account of the want of sufficient capital I am obliged to abandon the lease and sell off the stock etc. As it will cause some considerable monetary loss I am desirous of economising expenditure in the future and am writing this to ask if your Council will permit me return the child ... to the care of the state.[40]

Given the unsatisfactory nature of adoption and the successive foster-homes that many girls had it is no wonder that a thin but unbroken thread of interest in natural parents could be maintained despite tenuous contact with them. The rules of the Department stated clearly that relatives:

shall not have access to children placed out, except in the case of a child becoming seriously ill, or under special circumstances with the sanction of the Council; but, on application to the Secretary, they may be informed as to the health and general well-being of their children.[41]

Letters, too, had to be sent through the secretary who would forward them only if he considered them suitable, which meant that contact with natural parents was difficult. Despite this, foster-parents could not be a substitute except in rare cases.

Foster-mothers were performing a special task for which they were paid. Mothering is usually an unselfconscious activity and one without payment. State children were fostered with 'good' mothers because of a failure (often primarily economic) of their own family structure. No matter how much a foster-mother tried to treat an older state girl 'as one of her own', the girl would still be known to the world, her new mother, and herself as an outsider. She would be sent out to her foster-home with a regulation outfit in a special box and unless she had been especially fortunate this box might contain no personal property at all; no photographs, no books, no trinkets, no letter-cards, no pressed flowers.

GIRLS OUTFIT (IN A BOX) 1887

2 pairs boots	2 nightdresses
2 hats	2 pinafores
2 dresses	3 handkerchiefs
2 chemises	1 jacket or ulster
2 petticoats	3 pairs of stockings
2 flannel petticoats	Hairbrush, small and large comb
2 pairs drawers	1 bible or prayer book
2 flannel vests	

Philanthropy in the nineteenth-century sense often prevented anonymity for state children. All district visiting committees, for instance, were expected to hold an annual picnic for the state children of the district. As one secretary reported enthusiastically in 1896:

The Annual treat for the State Children was held on the Show grounds on Wednesday 2 inst all but 3 children were present in most instances robust and happy, through the kindness of Local Sunbeams 30/– worth of presents were purchased for distribution amongst the kiddies which with the good things provided by the Ladies of the Committee, ... made up quite an enjoyable afternoons outing, at the close of the day Mrs Jones wife of Dr P.R. Jones kindly

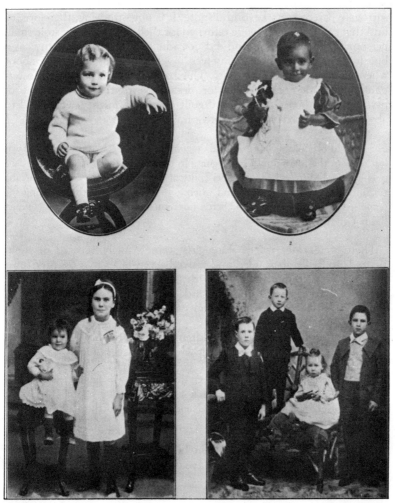

Children boarded-out were supposed to be 'properly fed and clothed ... sent regularly to Sunday and day school, and trained up to be honest, truthful, and modest, respectful to their teachers and others, and obedient to their foster-parents'.

presented to each child from the Dr a brand new shilling which topped up the day's enjoyment.[42]

The sufferings of childhood are rarely articulated and it is particularly true of the early years of the boarding-out system. It is from actions often regarded as ungrateful and unpredictable that one can discover childhood malaise. The detrimental effects of frequent changes in carers and repeated spells in institutions without the presence of a parent or surrogate parent seem beyond dispute. It is not surprising, therefore, to find that some state girls were returned for theft. They usually stole small personal items or money, and did not admit to the theft in many cases but in order to protect themselves invented elaborate stories about where they obtained the money. This baffled and angered both foster-parents and the Department for decades until the development of psychological theory. Shame and guilt over theft might lead a child to abscond. One foster-mother wrote grimly:

She went to School this morning and on coming out at 12.30 went away and was last seen on the Main South Road going in the direction of Adelaide.
The School Mistress had found her guilty of stealing six pence worth of darning cotton from another girl's bag and when accused of doing it this morning she confessed to the theft . . . you had better not return her to us again as this conduct has not given satisfaction.[43]

There were cases where state girls were wrongly accused of theft. Bernadette Reilly absconded and walked seven miles to a country town police station rather than face the punishment her foster-mother threatened for stealing a wedding card. In the event, she was believed by the police who wrote to the Department for her and thus helped establish her innocence.[44]
Another problem that led to children being returned by foster-mothers was bed-wetting. One foster-mother wrote in exasperation:

we cannot under any circumstances keep the girl . . . as she has an affliction that the poor girl cannot help herself but that it is very annoying and not pleasant to us, her weakness is she wets the bed and has done so three times this last week . . .[45]

Such an 'affliction' led to children being returned by a succession of foster-mothers – hardly likely to have done anything other than worsen the problem.
In many cases, however, a girl who was happy in her foster-home could avoid being returned for a misdemeanour if she wrote an appropriately contrite letter to the secretary of the Department. Many girls showed a sophisticated awareness of what the secretary wanted to hear: the fuller

14

their repentance the greater the likelihood of forgiveness. One girl wrote after running away:

My dear Mr. Grey,
    Please Mr Grey will you let me stop with Mrs Henry I forgot I promised you that I would not go away the time before. If you will forgive me this time I will never do it again. Mrs Henry says that I shall have to go back unless I don't go away any more and if you will let me stay I will never go away any more. My brother did not write to me and will you let him write please if I am a good girl.[46]

Sometimes a girl would be fully aware of her 'misdeeds', but in other cases letters would be written in bewilderment and confusion. The strongest reason for good behaviour was the fear of being removed from a happy foster-home. The threat of being taken away might even be used to extract a confession from a rebellious girl, with no regard to the insecurity such threats might engender. One girl who was fostered in a country town in 1903 was given 'another chance' after she wrote that: 'I will try to please in future please don't take me away, I will keep the room and my box tidy and I promise you won't hear any more complaints. If you do I will leave at once'.[47]

Some children could not bring themselves to confess small misdeeds and ran away rather than face an angry foster-mother. In March 1908 Alice White was sent to her convent school with three shillings 'to get some groceries coming home in the evening', but the large sum of money proved too much of a temptation and she did not go to school at all. Her foster-mother informed the police and then set out

walking the district till now 10 o'clock at night. I regret my letter of Feb 11th was not forwarded to you. So that she might have been taken back and saved us all this worry and anxiety, the Sisters advised me long ago to send her back as she was demoralising the children at school in getting them to wander and stray from home.[48]

This led to Alice being returned.

Although state girls had to attend school until they were thirteen, the work expected of them while they were still at school was not slight, indeed it might even make an economic contribution to the foster-family. In many cases state wards only performed the work around the house or farm that their contemporaries did in an age when working-class children were usually kept busy. In 1913 it was not regarded as unusual for children to be away from school to help pick seasonal fruit crops with their families.[49] Neither was it uncommon for both sexes to have to work with parents even if this did interfere with school attendance. (In fact, until 1915, children did not have to attend every day but only a certain minimum of days per year.) One mother wrote asking that her adopted niece be allowed to have wash day at home to help her. The child was nine years old.[50] In another case a prospective foster-mother wrote of a child: 'I think I will give her a trial although I think she is rather small but Mrs Bartlett assures me she is a nice little girl and can make herself very useful',[51] while another wrote:

I want a good handy girl to just help me to clear away the breakfast and get the children ready for school a girl from 11 to thirteen and no older and she can go to school and I will do the milking my self . . .[52]

Sometimes girls were returned because they could not be 'useful':

she is a good little worker, but she is not the girl for me and she is so careless. Only last night, because there were two young men here, she was keeping her eyes fixed on them and listening for every word that was said she put a lighted candle right underneath a bunch of grass that was in a vase we both looked around just to see it all in a flame.[53]

This foster-mother requested another girl, not so young, to 'go errands and do little things'.

To some extent expectations of a girl were determined by personal and physical maturity. Girls who were childish for their age or frail were sometimes kept at school later than thirteen, whereas girls who were strong and mature were sometimes removed from school a little early. One foster-mother wrote:

We find it is impossible for us to send her to school any longer as our income will not allow it she has grown almost into a woman now and it is very expensive for us to keep her as we have a family of our own and Mr. Keel is only receiving 6/6 per day which is not enough to keep a family on; so if you have no objections we are going to take her from school and let her learn to sew.[54]

Work in itself was not thought to be degrading or a hardship to children. There can be no doubt that most working-class children in Victorian times were expected to be 'useful' even in the most loving families. Everything depended on the type of work and for whom it was done. Something of these sentiments lay behind the letter an angry foster-mother wrote to the secretary in 1891 in answer to the charge that her foster-children were overworked. She began by discussing milking:

I may state in the first place milking is 'not' hard work. My own children have milked from the age of 5 or 6 years and preferred it to other work. We always give Mary the easiest and quickest . . . they *always* have been in ample time to get to school early. I *never* keep them later than half-past eight that is allowing them an hour to go to school where I can go in half an hour . . . I never send Mary on an errand but she is always gone three times as long as she ought to be ... she would rather milk than wash-up the breakfast things ... a girl of 11 years to milk 4 quite easy and almost dry cows ...[55]

Mary was not removed from her care.

In another case in the same year, a visiting committee described the work a girl had been doing as:

carrying a few buckets of water every morning for some time before going to school and that the lady with whom she lives goes half way to help her. She also said that she would discontinue doing so when the rain comes to fill their own tank. She likes the place very much. She seems well and happy.[56]

In this case it is easy to see that the labour, though heavy, was not performed in isolation, and it was temporary work carried out for a reason that a farm child could easily understand.

But there were homes where a child was clearly treated more harshly than contemporaries thought just. An anonymous letter-writer complained about the work expected of Addie Kerr who was eleven years old. According to the inspector who visited, Addie

rises at 5.15 am goes for the cows, milks 2 cows, sets the breakfast, washes up, goes to school. She returns to her dinner in the middle of the day and washes up before going back to school. When school is over she gets morning wood and feeds two pigs goes again for the cows milks two of them, sets the tea and takes the cows back to the paddock. After tea, she cleans her boots, washes up the tea things darns her own stockings Mrs Hartmanns and a child's socks does her homework and goes to bed at 9.30 pm.[57]

On another occasion this child had had to carry a 25-pound bag of meat for nearly a mile. The inspector concluded that Mrs Hartmann had been 'extremely selfish and neglectful'.[58]

Other girls were clearly treated as nothing more than drudges. In 1907 a ten-and-a-half year-old girl was placed with a foster-mother at Lyndoch in a large, apparently suitable house. There were grown-up sons but no other children of her age in the family. There was one servant in the house and the girl had to help her before and after school hours with the housework. The local school-teacher finally told the inspector from the Department that the girl

is often late and sometimes is kept home for trivial excuses. The child says that she rises at 6 o'clock and works till school time and when she returns in the afternoon she works again cleaning knives and boots and helping to get tea and wash up and that she goes to bed about 9.30 pm. On Saturday she also washes over the kitchen floor. She is a very thin child and painfully shy, in fact rather dull mentally and I find difficulty in ascertaining whether she is happy here. She says she often gets the strap on the hands and shoulders. She has her meals in the kitchen with the servant. There are no children for her to play with and as far as I can tell no time or very little in which to play. I am sure she is taken for the sole purpose of helping with the work and that there is no home atmosphere and little if any love to help in a child's development.[59]

In the wider community many children began contributing to the family income long before they left school by collecting bottles, running errands or minding babies. Dorothy Roysland, one of ten children, with her younger sister.

18

In other instances it was more difficult to decide whether a child was merely being used by the foster-parents. It was an era when a great deal of baby-minding was expected of older girls in large families, but even with this work there were limits. A neighbour wrote in October 1896 to the Department about one state girl being overworked:

> She is not strong enough to be always nursing those two babys, she has always either one or the other when she is home from school and they are very heavy it tires a grown-up person to be always nursing babies ... she is as good as a grown-up person in the house so I don't like to see her put upon ...[60]

Letters were also written by concerned outsiders about children being physically punished or 'getting a good many knocks'.[61] The Department's attitude against physical punishment distinguished between discipline and brutality. They were prepared to overlook a slap or two' if administered in the heat of the moment for a sufficiently serious reason such as an 'immoral offence' or 'telling lies',[62] but their rules did not allow beatings or prolonged physical punishment for a child's carelessness or slowness at household chores.

Childhood could be measured regularly and accurately in the matter of school-work. In South Australia primary education had become compulsory for all children (except Aboriginals) in 1875. (It was not free until 1892. Between 1875 and 1892 fees were fixed at 4 pence to 6 pence a week although poor children did not have to pay.) There were standards and grades against which state children could be measured. They were often 'found wanting' for a number of reasons. The most common was that state girls had simply not attended school at all in their earliest years and were thus 'backward in every way'.[63] The Mother Superior of a Dominican convent to which one girl had recently been sent, commented:

> she is one of those children to whom a teacher finds it impossible to impart knowledge. This must have been also discovered by her former teachers for when she came to us at 9 years of age from the Port Adelaide Public School she was not able to keep pace with the lowest division of the infant class.
> Her deficient eyesight was for a long time a drawback.[64]

One can only guess at the extent to which being known at school as a state child led to lowered expectations on the part of teachers. In one case a state girl stole some books from the school cupboard and after at first inventing stories about where they were, she confessed her theft to her teacher and to the head teacher. The latter thought the whole incident 'rather magnified', but the child's own teacher thought her conduct unsatisfactory; she was to him 'the most troublesome girl in her class'.[65] In some cases state girls themselves would appeal to their foster-parents to keep them on at school after thirteen years of age so that they could reach a higher grade. One bright girl had in two and a half years reached the fourth grade at school and according to her teacher was 'very anxious' to pass the compulsory standard. In this case the teacher was openly in favour of the girl and commented that:

if you knew her as I do you would think her quite worthy of allowing her to stay this little extra time at school as she having [sic] worked so well since she has had the opportunity of being at school at all.[66]

Another teacher was even more forceful. She taught a small school in the mid north and had a state girl fostered with her. She wrote to the secretary asking for another year's schooling:

She has made great progress with her studies during the past year and therefore I think it would be a great pity to deprive her of the privilege she now has ... She is not a strong child and therefore is unfitted for 'service' yet – And so she is so anxious to persue her studies I think the opportunity should be afforded her, especially as she is now residing in the school house and would receive every assistance from myself. And another reason is, that in the near future, 14 not 13 will be the compulsory age for a child to leave school. And so it should be as few children at that tender age are fit for work.[67]

A number of state girls were granted extra schooling because at thirteen they were thought to be not 'strong enough' to go to service in an 'ordinary place'.[68] And yet a balance had to be struck: too much schooling led to some girls being unacquainted with 'every hint of housework', according to their foster-mothers.[69] Thus while on one hand the delicate or small girl might be kept at school for another year until she was strong enough for the rigours of housework, other girls were trained in domestic skills, 'an hour or so daily' before they turned thirteen.[70] Occasionally there were other reasons why a state girl at thirteen was not sent out to service. A few girls were delicate, crippled, and one or two subject to 'fainting fits' or spells of hysteria.[71]

Only two or three girls in this period really distinguished themselves at primary school. One girl was allowed to sit for an examination which might have provided her with a scholarship to high school, but competition was fierce and she did not get one.[72]

The State Children's Advancement Fund had been founded in 1908, and among other purposes it was intended to help children who showed 'special ability' to pursue their education, perhaps even to university. But this fund achieved little. In 1912, £2 12s 6d was spent on tuition for a state girl. In 1914 the fund was stated to be emerging 'from the chrysallis', but it was still a small amount of money.[73]

Most girls began their working lives at thirteen, but not without protest from teachers and foster-parents. It seems that many people felt that thirteen was simply too young to be sent out to service and that the Department was acting harshly even by the unsentimental standards of the nineteenth century.

Sister Joan of the Sisters of St Joseph at Sevenhills in the mid north wrote forcefully to the secretary in 1909 (in a way that not many foster-parents would have dared) about several girls:

they really want another year in school they are not fit for service it would be a charity to give them a longer time, you gave Evelyn Flanagan and Dora Connelly till fourteen these want it just as much ... they are all good children but want a longer time.[74]

And a foster-parent wrote a long letter in 1910 asking that her foster-daughter be allowed to stay on as a domestic servant. This letter illuminated many of the differences between being fostered and living with one's own family: a natural family would only through sheer economic necessity send away a small immature girl of thirteen. The foster-mother wrote concernedly:

I have not much work to do but the girl suits me very well, and I am so used to her now and she is so happy that I don't like to see her go to strangers she is a very good girl but a very childish girl as really you would not take the girl for 14 but I suppose it is owing to her having no education but I have always treated her as my own and I try to teach her to read and write ... I keep the girl more for company as I have only myself and my aged mother most of our time I will do all her sewing as usual only her church dress and that I always put out ...[75]

There were other foster-parents who had no children of their own and found that faced with separation from their foster-child they preferred to pay the child a wage and keep her on service terms rather than see her go away to what they called 'hard rough work'.[76] Others wrote that they found that their ward became 'in a great state at the idea of having to leave us', and appealed to the secretary against the child's lot.[77]

On the other hand some foster-parents, perhaps trying to be more realistic, tried to prepare their foster-child for a life of hard work. One woman wrote:

Laura is a splendid little worker if anyone is kind to her. I have taught her to do everything. She can blacken a stove wash iron and clean a room very neatly. I have given her a good home training the same as my own daughters.[78]

The Department may have had more success if it had not sent out girls who were quite so young. Very often a mistress would find that a young girl could not do any heavy work

21

such as one would get from a general servant she is useful to us in this way for taking care of the Children and any light work about the house but she cannot possibly do any washing or cooking she is a delicate girl we have to employ a woman every week to do the washing . . . [79]

From statistics in the annual reports of the State Children's Council it appears that only four girls were sent out to occupations other than domestic service in the years 1887–1913. What alternatives were available to the State Children's Council other than sending out almost all girls to be domestic servants? Domestic service suited the Department because it enabled girls to be supervised and carefully controlled by their mistresses, but apart from this there was no real alternative in pre-World War I Australia.

K.R. Bowes, discussing the 1890 maritime strike in South Australia, states:

Rarely in normal activities of the day would people see a building large enough to give employment to 50 workmen. Normally they would see three or four toiling in an open forge, or pass by a dozen working in a shed. This is the industrial community of Adelaide in 1890.

Writing of the expansion between 1889 and 1890 he goes on to say:

All these factories, with the exception of three or four large printing works and a couple of coach-building firms in Adelaide, employed on the average less than 10 men. That these were regarded as typical South Australian factories is shown by the acceptance by the Shops and Factories Commission of 1892 of the definition of a factory as a place where four or more persons were employed . . . [80]

Women's employment lagged decades behind that of men. The clothing industry was dominated by the 'sweating' system. The apprenticeship system for women was

obsolescent and abused. Girls were engaged as apprentices in some trades most particularly dressmaking and after years on a very low, or perhaps even no wage, when the time came for it to be increased they were often put off with some spurious explanation – the real reason being obvious to all. [81]

That work in factories was unpleasant and badly paid is well-documented in the evidence of the 1892 Shops and Factories Commission [82] and in the reports of the Factory Inspectors. The report of the Commission pointed out that in South Australia there was no protective legislation at all to curb the hours worked by women and children. The Commission's evidence contains details of the sweating of workers and the bad effects this had on their health. Mrs E. Rogers, whose husband was ill and who worked 'for the sweaters', stated in answer to a question about girls having their health ruined:

I could mention six now whose lives are worked out through working so hard at the shirt trade. It is hard work to make a dozen shirts in a day, and some have to work, oh so hard. One girl is at home now, and is being attended to by the doctor. She had to make a dozen shirts in a day to get her wages. [The girl got 12s 6d per week if she made 12 shirts a day.][83]

A girl who worked in a 'factory' making shirts testified:

You get tired all over; but you had to go on if it were possible for you to work at all.
Q.5972. One lady has told us that when a delicate person got tired it was in the lungs. Do you find that so – I think I get tired in my feet.[84]

One is reminded of the 'Song of the Shirt' by some of the testimony of Mrs A.A. Milne:

I would say that, for a fact, there are men, women, and children working at this the whole day on Sunday. They never have a rest. If not working at shirt work they are doing domestic work, cleaning up their homes, etc. I know of three cases where they have to do it. There is one young girl only 19 who has so overworked herself that the doctors say that they can do no more for her.[85]

In 1904, with the recommendation of Wage Boards, the first step was taken towards legislation which would eventually protect women working in industry. But in South Australia women were only very slowly absorbed into the factory workforce; real change came with World War II. After 1900 there was a thin trickle of jobs open to women, mainly in dressmaking, millinery, shops, fruit and preserve factories, and later in commerce. By 1911, teaching commercial subjects had become such a profitable business that Muirden College was able to move to 'New and Up-to Date Buildings' in Grote Street, Victoria Square, where day and evening instruction in shorthand, bookkeeping, and other subjects was available and where there were 'Special Classes for Ladies in all Business Subjects'.[86]

Domestic service, always unpopular, became more so as the new century's opportunities appeared. State girls, as much as anyone else, disliked working as domestic servants and many tried to get other jobs. Dressmaking was the occupation most hoped to enter:

My Apprenticeship ending this month I should with your permission like to leave Mrs Carters and take in Dressmaking on my own account I am quite able to get a living by it now. Mrs Rex has offered to give me a room free of charge and I think I shall get along nicely.[87]

By 1911, teaching commercial subjects had become such a profitable business that Muirden College, Adelaide, was able to move to new premises in Grote Street where there were 'Special Classes for Ladies in all Business Subjects'. A typing class at Muirden – including gentlemen – in 1911.

Arrangements for learning dressmaking had to be carefully made:

Victoria Kay is anxious to learn dressmaking and cooking and tells me she has an older companion who will accompany her. I think it is a good idea and I am quite willing that Vicky should go (if it meets with your approval) providing she will always catch the 9.30 pm train from Adelaide. The lesson is from 7–9 pm so that should allow her plenty of time . . . Our house is right next to the Plympton Station, so Vicky would be quite alright at this end . . . [88]

At the end of the three months I would like to learn dressmaking. Mrs Porter knows the head dressmaker at Marshall's and also at Foy and Gibsons and she said she would speak for me if I like, so I wanted to ask if you think the Council will have any objection to it if I have a nice respectable home to board in, I feel as if I would like to take up some lighter work than I have been doing. [89]

The second of these girls found that as a dressmaker's assistant in 1913 she would only be paid 4s a week for twelve months, a wage she described as 'useless'. She then asked the secretary if he would write her a letter of introduction to one of the larger department stores, as Marshalls and John Martins had recently advertised for assistants.

The letters written to the store and to the girl illustrate well the dangers the Department saw in allowing state girls to work anywhere other than in private homes:

The bearer Miss O'Hara is one of the State children. She is anxious to secure employment as a shop assistant in one of the drapery firms of this town, she especially mentions your establishment.

You will be doing the child a favour, and I shall be personally obliged if you can find room for her where she will be safe as a young girl can be among so many assistants, as your firm employs. So far she has been a good girl, and I think has every intention of continuing to be so.

To the girl he wrote:

I should like however, if you go to either of these places to mention that you will not find yourself free from restriction, nor I fear from temptation. I have every confidence in your goodness of intention, but the danger of all such inducements to wrong is their very insidious nature. If a person asks you point blank, and without preamble to do something we know to be wrong there is very little difficulty in saying no ... but when the approaches of evil are sweetened with what appears kindness or even affection, often one finds that the salary one gets is very inadequate.[90]

A small minority of state girls wanted to be nurses. This was badly-paid arduous work but it carried a social cachet far removed from domestic service. Jasmine Smith wrote in 1907:

I have a great desire to become a trained nurse, and have wondered if in any way you could help me.

It is not a mere fancy. I have thought seriously about it for some time. Having been in the Hospital once for a short period I have some idea of what a nurse's duties are. I know how much you strive to help us children and feel confident that you will do all in your power to help me in this matter.[91]

Jasmine Smith did successfully complete her training at the Royal Adelaide Hospital.

Some girls found a niche that satisfied the Department and yet avoided the stigma and drudgery of domestic service. This small group of 'refined' girls gradually became companions doing 'light housework'. The other area where girls tried to gain employment was as 'nurse girl', which meant they would be employed primarily to look after children:

I really can't stand this any longer I have had enough for once in my life. I have seen in the paper plenty of people want a nurse-girl. I know you wont like my writing but I cant help it.[92]

she does not like housework and she will not do it . . . But she has one quality I have always appreciated and valued very much and that is her gentle quiet manner so unlike the generality of colonial girls . . . She seems determined to be a nurse girl . . . her quiet gentle manner would be valuable with children if she were in a nice family . . .[93]

Domestic service was the reality that confronted the vast majority of state girls on their nineteenth birthday, despite their youth, in defiance of their dreams, and notwithstanding the views of some articulate foster-parents who thought it 'a shame' to send a girl out before she was fourteen.[94] Most state girls *did* go out to service at thirteen, an age when their upper-class contemporaries were just putting up their hair and wearing longer skirts. Childhood for state girls was short and abruptly terminated.

From now on most would be servants in the houses of their 'betters', serving a sort of apprenticeship while fully controlled by the mistress of the 'service home', and indirectly but firmly by the Department.

CHAPTER 2

Domestic Service
1887–1914

Removed from childhood at the age of thirteen or fourteen, into paid employment and apprenticeship with strangers, there can be no doubt that many girls found life hard.

Kathleen Fox, in service for the first time, wrote to the secretary of the State Children's Department in 1890:

I would rather be back in the school again than at service. I think that it is because I have not been to Service before . . . You said it was better for me to write and let you know than it was to run away . . . I get eight shillings a week it is a good thing that I do because I brake so many things and I have to replace them again.[1]

Ada West wrote secretly to her sister complaining about the monotony of service: 'In this hole of a place I see the same thing day after day and nothen to look forward to I must wait pashintly and the time will come some time'.[2] The time she was looking forward to was, of course, the time of her release from the Department's control at twenty-one.

The State Children's Department tried to avoid discontent among girls in service by having inspectors visit every three months and by matching the state girl with the home but this attempt could never entirely eliminate dissatisfaction. Girls had to gain experience and the Department could not afford to be too particular beyond ensuring basic standards. These included trying to see that the work suited the girl's age and experience, and determining that the home was completely respectable, with proper sleeping accommodation for the state girl. Particular attention was now paid to the *position* of the room to be occupied by the young female servant. A state boy might sleep in an outhouse or sleepout, but a state girl had to be in a well-protected room with no doors opening to the outside or on to a verandah. This care reflected the Department's realism about the danger of sexual exploitation of state girls by the men of the household.

State girls could be returned to the Industrial School if they did not suit the mistress of the household. They might be too small and unlearned,[3] or they might 'take advantage' of a mistress whose health was 'very much broken up'.[4]

However, there were great advantages in employing a state girl: her abilities would have been assessed before being sent out and, more importantly, she could not leave as other servants might, precipitating a domestic crisis. Even so, some women when applying for a state girl would specify that they wanted a girl without relations 'so that we will not have to part with her just as she is getting into our ways'.[5] But most simply wrote specifying the age of the girl they wanted and assuring the Department that they would endeavour to give a girl 'training and care'.[6]

Different aspects of the household determined how hard a state girl had to work. One was the sort of mistress, whether easy-going or querulous. A decisive factor was the niche in the household that the girl was expected to fill and another variable was the size of the family. The degree of mechanization in the kitchen was also important. Richard Twopeny, in *Town Life in Australia*, commented of the 1880s:

> As a rule, the kitchens are terribly small, and in summer filled with flies. How the poor servants manage to exist in them is more than I can understand . . . Biddy has to content herself with a table, dresser, safe, pasteboard and rolling pin, and a couple of chairs.[7]

A girl in a typical 'place' would have a day like this:

> she gets up in the morning sets the breakfast milks 3 cows feeds one pig, one calf, comes in washes up the breakfast things she then has the drawing room, pantry and kitchen to clean for the day sometimes cooks a little dinner for me and the children Mr Black he is very seldom home for dinner we keep no men in the evenings she helps with the children milks 2 cows, waters the fowls and then lay the tea table washes up, lastly she is supposed to mend her clothes.[8]

Where a girl was expected to perform a wide range of tasks it was very easy to be made to work too hard. Anything extra could tip the balance in an unstructured work situation. Hilda Symes wrote to the Department at the turn of the century because she considered her health was being ruined by having to work in a house with stairs. She stressed that the doctor had told her she should

> leave here on account of the stairs and this is a very hard place, I hope that you won't think that I am unable to work and keep me in the school as I don't feel that bad and I know that if I got a place where there were no stairs my leg would not get any worse as I have always had to work but I never been in a two storey house before and I feel sure if I got a place without stairs I would be all right so don't keep me in the school please Sir as I hate being out of work. I dare say they will tell you

I want a rest but I don't I want to go out to a place . . . I'm quite able to work and will only be miserable without it . . .[9]

There can be no doubt that service was tiring work. One woman, returning a state girl, wrote that she had wanted, instead of a youngster, an older girl who could virtually take her place while she recovered from illness. A girl

who could wash iron bake bread and milk, this one says she cannot do either. I put the washing off till the girl would arrive as I was too ill and after all I had to do it myself . . . I wanted one to take the heavy work off me . . . We are but 4 to do for yet to keep all clean its too much for me.[10]

Differences in physical strength meant that some girls began the heavy jobs such as washing at a much younger age than others. How well a state girl could do such difficult work depended on both age and experience. Some girls had gained experience from their foster-mothers or at the Industrial School but most were completely untrained, which led, an inspector considered, to many of them having to be

Different aspects of a household determined how hard a domestic had to work. One was the size of the house and another was the degree of its ornamentation. The sort of drawing-room that needed a lot of dusting – Chief Justice Way's House in North Adelaide in the 1890s.

so constantly corrected and scolded that many of them abandon all attempt to improve.

The girls as a rule complain very little. I find the mistress usually has much fault to find probably with justice, but the girl is often dumb, and so one cannot help her as one would.[11]

The number of other servants in the household, especially the presence or absence of a cook, also determined a girl's duties. Most young girls began as an assistant to the cook or to their mistress. Under constant supervision and criticism state girls began their apprenticeship. One mistress wrote:

today it was a quarter past twelve before she had the Breakfast things washed up. She works in fits and starts. I have been ill for over a week.

She is quick in her movements but has no system in her work. She has only 4 to cook for and then besides herself to wash for and no children to bother her and it does not seem to matter she is getting slower instead of quicker . . . [12]

Another girl, having been told to heat water in a saucepan to wash breakfast dishes,

got a saucepan that meat had been cooked in to put it on with all the grease and I told her to wash it out Mabel took it out and brought it back just the same and then she was scolded or growled at as she calls it . . .

As some explanation her mistress advanced the view that:

Mabel was very cross because my daughter went to a social and did not take her she told me that she was writing to Miss Bayley [and was] underhanded about it she even gave it to the workman and never said a word about it.

I am sure she is not overworked my daughter and myself both work and my Husband separates the milk and we send the cream to Adelaide . . . [13]

If the family had a large enough property to graze cows, milking and all the washing and careful cleaning of churns and separating equipment that was part of the task was an extra duty that added considerably to a state girl's chores.[14] Milking could be tedious and tiring. Mabel East gave her side of the story in 1901:

I have all the work to do and no one to help me there is nine cows to milk night and morning . . . you can think how miserable it must be to have no one to speak to only the daughter and mistress growling at me all the time . . . I hope you won't be cross with me because I can't help writing to you . . . [15]

Nevertheless Mabel did stay on at her place and gradually liked it better.

To be a 'good milker' was a very desirable quality in a state girl and immediately made her employable even if she still needed 'a little teaching in housework'.[16]

The second major task that could mean a state girl worked extremely hard was washing. Before households acquired a hot water service and a washing machine, washing was an enormous task which meant the female servants and the mistress too in many cases would rise before dawn and toil until dusk. Some households sent their washing 'out', others had a washerwoman come in to do it – usually an older woman, a widow, or a single woman with children to support. A description of washing day can show why there was such a division between state girls who were strong enough to do the wash and those who were not.[17]

The household wash was an enormous task that meant the female servants (and the mistress too, in many cases), would rise before dawn and toil until dusk.

First of all, fires would have to be built to heat the water for the tub or copper; sometimes a whole cake of lye soap would have to be shaved into boiling water; the clothes would be sorted into piles of different sorts of whites, coloureds, work clothes, and rags; flour would be stirred into cold water and then thinned down with boiling water for starching; and the dirtiest spots on clothing would be rubbed on a board and then boiled or in the case of coloured clothing just rubbed, rinsed, and starched. Heavy, steaming loads of clothing would have to be lifted out of the copper on poles, put through the mangle, rinsed, blued and starched, and put to dry on the lines which would then have to be winched high enough. Tea towels would be spread on lavender bushes or on the grass, old rags hung to dry on the fence, and the family underwear hung discreetly on lower lines between the larger items. Finally, the rinsing water would be used for the family's weekly baths or to water the garden, and the hot soapy water to wash the verandahs.

For many households, the crucial factor in continuing to employ a state girl was whether or not she was strong enough to help with the washing. A housewife from Maylands, an eastern suburb, wrote in 1904 to tell the Department that she would

prefer to do my own housework as I feel it is too much responsibility to keep Louise here and the expense after her wages of putting the shirts and collars out seems quite unnecessary besides her being slow. I feel I would rather be alone and put the washing and ironing out.[18]

But though it was hard work there were limits. A girl might complain if she had to continue washing as late as 11.30 p.m. In a household which could only afford one or two servants it was thought better to employ both a young girl (who would be paid very little) to look after the children and a strong older woman who could cook and help substantially with the washing.[20]

Baking bread and making butter were other chores greatly adding to the state girl's duties, even if the butter was only made once a week and the bread twice.[21]

The number of children in the family (and how a state girl got on with them) also contributed to a place being 'hard' or 'easy'. In many ways caring for the children and housework were mutually contradictory tasks and if there were a great many children (over six for instance) the work not only increased, but doing it efficiently became almost impossible for a girl who was the only servant.

Being 'good with the children' was an endearing quality in state girls and sometimes meant that a girl would be kept despite dissatisfaction. One woman wrote that she had 'put up with everything' because her two little children were attached to the state girl and she 'looked after them well'.[22] In other cases girls were returned because their not getting 'on too well' with the children was the final straw.[23]

At thirteen or fourteen years of age state girls were very often only a few years older than the rest of the household. Called upon to fulfil an 'elder daughter' role, state girls often objected to the number of young children in a household. The amount of work expected of such girls was not light. As one woman explained:

we are only five in family we have no workmen in the house so there is not much washing up. She does nothing for the children except clean their boots and that's only about once a week unless they are going out. She cleans the knives once a week and then not done well and I like them cleaned oftener But put up with it.[24]

A home was considered very hard if there were, for instance: '9 children, the eldest 13. Annie did all the washing and cooking and milked three cows. She is not in good health and most likely has felt not able to work lately'.[25] Some state girls were sent back to the Industrial School the moment a daughter of the house left school and could help in the house, their dismissal underlining the niche they had occupied.[26]

Other girls thought that having to do boots for all the children of the family was one task too many. It was a dirty lengthy process, but it was the element of personal service that most girls disliked. They felt they were employed to be servants to the household, not to its members. Lizzie Smith thought that her mistress

thinks because I am a State girl she can do anything with me Mr Gray she would not done do it to another girl, and I have to clean all the boots for everyone that is there, they pitch the boots outside the door, and when I went back at Christmas time there were six pairs of boots belonging to one son, and I said when I saw them (I was going through the kitchen) any one would think I was 'boots' instead of a girl. She always has two or three pairs every day. I have them every day and young Mrs B. (she does not have so many) and Mr Marr but he goes to business and I do not mind that, and this other creature puts his boots out and he never as much [as] says thank you . . .[27]

And Rose Johnston thought that having to do boots for several boys should not be her work. She wrote to the Department in 1905:

On Sunday morning Mrs Edwards asked me why I had not cleaned the two eldest boys boots and I replied that Mr Edwards had told me that I wasn't to clean them again as the boys were big enough to do them Mrs Edwards said I was to clean them and she didn't care what Mr Edwards had said. It went from one thing to another she called me several nasty names and I said that I would write to Mr. Gray . . . I went to pass her at the door when she lifted her hand and struck me on the face . . .[28]

A hard day's work could also become drudgery if a girl was working in a very large house. Ruth Beale asked to be removed from her situation in 1912 because the house she was working in had fifteen rooms, some of which were used as classrooms for a private school.

Of these one is a large boxroom which is seldom touched, four of them are large class rooms which have to be swept and dusted each day, but scrubbed only once a quarter. In the kitchen one gas and wood stoves bath and the washhouse is convenient. The house is partly underground so there is a good deal of running up and down stairs. From the kitchen to the dining room is the length of the verandah and three steps up. The girls beds and mattresses were out in the yard. The beds have been scalded, kerosened and sprinkled with insect powder. The mattresses are of unbleached calico filled with flock. The seam of one is unstitched and the flock escaping. A girl could mend it in less than five minutes. The girls' bedroom is large and cool but smelt offensive. The washstand had not been attended to since Tuesday . . . Miss Vera Johns says that her eldest sister has been managing lately, and she is sharp and irritable. In future she will undertake to be the only mistress . . . will engage a washerwoman to make the work lighter.[29]

Housework was often monotonous hard work; too hard, many state girls argued. Margaret Kelly for example, wrote to the Department, saying:

I know some people that would like to have me and I think I could better myself in a lighter place. I have tried to do my best but I find that the work is too hard. I have already complained to the inspector but have heard nothing further. There are 5 young children; the eldest being 8 years old and the youngest only 8 months. I have to do for them and the housework as well as I am but 14 years old I find I cannot manage it. I have been with Mrs. Nichols 4 months and have only been out 3 times. hoping you will let me have an early reply.[30]

In this case an inspector decided that the work was too hard and that she should be removed to a lighter place.

Provided that a girl could complain to the Department (and this was sometimes far from easy), real hardship in the service home was taken seriously. Clarice Harrison complained

of being obliged to carry up about 14 buckets of water from the cellar daily. Mr Hall stands at the top of the narrow cellar steps and takes the buckets from her and empties them. Last winter for a time she brought up many more than this, on one occasion the number reached 60. She has always done it willingly and her complaint today came as a surprise to him. His heart is too weak for him to . . . carry them himself but he will have a pump refitted to draw off the water in future.[31]

Many mistresses seem to have misjudged the amount of work that a young girl with limited training would be able to do. A woman might write of her state girl's duties being 'decidedly light' but then describe what the girl actually had to do. In the case below, the girl had no cooking to do but still worked

in the kitchen and washes (which takes her from 5 in the morning till ½ past 4 usually in the afternoon anyone else here gets done before dinner or at dinner time, she rises from her breakfast and washes till its done then I often have to either wash over the men's clothes or put them back into the wash . . .[32]

This girl was removed by the Department. Another girl, who was working at Semaphore in January 1911, had to rise at 6 a.m.,

Sweep kitchen and back verandah. Get 2 breakfasts 1 for 7 and 1 a little after. Sweep back door and front verandah. Get breakfast for 5 persons for 8 o'clock. Sweep sitting room and dust it. Scrub room every day. Sweep and dust hall. Sweep and dust dining room. Get lunch at 12.45 and beeswax floor. Get dressed iron from 3 to 5. Get tea for 7 persons. Wash up for cook read and iron till 10 pm then bed. Now rise at 5 and bed at 9 pm [because it was summer].

Have headaches Dr Hone says suffer Constipation and indigestion. Has meals in kitchen.

Breakfast at 8 am interrupted by calls and to wait at table finish at 8.30. Lunch 1 o'clock. 20 past go to work again. Tea at 6 pm. Some times eat as washing up. Does no washing. Scrub every room in house once fortnight. 9 rooms.[33]

Other girls found that if everything went according to plan they could get through the work but if one more burden was added they could not cope. Thus one girl wrote in desperation:

would you please take me away from Mrs Graycar because there is 5 little children and Mrs Graycar is not very well and I have to do all the work myself and I cannot do it. I do not go to bed till about 10 o'clock every night an up a six in the mornings working . . .[34]

This girl battled on, however, and was able to cope again when her mistress recovered her health.

Some girls could not cope, especially if relief was not in sight. The dismissal or disappearance of other servants not only caused frequent crises for employers, but also meant that a state girl might suddenly have to shoulder a much larger share of the household work. Many girls then reached the point of despair.

There were also girls who had kindly and considerate mistresses. Letters about such women are just as much part of the record, less in number though they may be.

Mrs James will kindly keep me at the rate of three shillings per week which I am quite satisfied at that they are very good to me and I know it is both a good home and good people I am very glad to say I can give them a good name they are so kind to me ain't I glad I can stop [in her present service home] it cheered me up and drove away the tears and made me quite happy see what it is to have a good home and it is your children that knows it Mr Whiting . . . it would brake my heart if you was to take me from it . . . and I know you would [not] be so cruel as to take me from my good home as I am happy now . . .[35]

I love the children and Mr and Mrs Andrews very much I don't think I should have been able to get a better place than what I've got now . . . I hope I shall never have to leave Mrs Andrews for she treats me just like one of her own children.[36]

A girl's transfer might induce her mistress to write to the Department explaining how well they had got on:

We shall be very sorry to lose Charlotte as she is a very good girl and suits us in every way being clean tidy and kind to the children . . . we treat her as one of the family . . . [37]

I am indeed sorry to part with Hilda as she has continued all through to give satisfaction and I can only report well of her. A friend of mine . . . would like to take Hilda and Hilda hopes she will be permitted to go. [38]

Affection for a state girl who was leaving led a few households to try and find a place for the girl with relatives. If this was not possible they might try to ensure that she remained in the district where she could occasionally visit her original service home. [39]

It is easy to see that where girls were happy in a household it was primarily because their mistress was likeable. A woman who could write: 'I am not a woman that will sit down and let a girl do the work. I always done the heavy part of the work', [40] would be a person whom a girl could grow to like. The readiness with which a girl was accepted into the family's activities, instead of being treated like an inferior, usually depended on the attitude of the mistress of the house. The letters below speak for themselves.

Today I went to Chapel with Mrs Samuel and two of the children and the baby stayed home with its father. They are such sweet little things at first it was mummy for everything but now I can undress and dress them the baby is two years this month and the eldest is 6 yr this month. I have made a big cake had great success I boiled a lot of fig jam and pasted it down she told Mr Samuel that she thought I did well being the first week here they seem very nice people they [are] so jolly Please Mam would you kindly get one of the girls to copy out some nice recipes for Mrs Samuel says she likes to see girls try she asked me if I ever made a coffee cake and told her I had not so she told me what she put in it and left me. I made the cake and it turned out splendid and so light . . . [41]

I have felt happy this last twelve months since I have been in the Mount but I am sure I do not now I have received such news [that she might have to leave] . . . I am quite happy with Mrs Rett I said I would stay with her the next twelve months if she is willing but I would not think of taking more wages if she is to send more to the Department I will take less because she is not like a Mistress she's more like a mother. I have parents but I [would] rather stay with her. [42]

A state girl's wages were generally raised on her birthday and this often led to acrimonious correspondence, the mistress claiming that the girl was not worth the extra shilling, and the Department threatening to remove the girl unless the extra amount was paid. In other cases a family might claim they were not able to afford anything extra but still would not want to part with the girl. In that case the girl herself would be asked by the Department if she was willing to stay on at the lower rate of pay. Some girls decided to remain despite low wages; their letters revealed their contentment:

I feel quite happy in my present place and I feel quite thankful to think I was sent to such a nice place. I do not wish for any higher wages than I have been getting because it is a very easy place and I would not take higher wages I do not think any girl has a nicer place than I have and I would be very sorry to be taken away and I will try to do my best to please Mrs Connell.[43]

A quality which particularly warmed employers to a state girl was if she remained (or perhaps even became) modest and respectable while living with the family. One employer approvingly stated that 'in the whole of the nine months Connie has been in my service she has been a respectable hard-working girl',[44] while a girl wrote:

I am still doing my best to please my Master and Mistress and find my Mistress very strick and particular in housework but I don't mind as I think it is all for my own good. If they had only wanted a girl years ago and you sent me to them you would never of seen me in the school again a moore kinder Master and Mistress good [sic] not be found, if you do what is right . . . Mrs Gale said that her house could be my home as long as I lived and they would be a Mother and Father to me, they are that now, I have only 4 months to serve and then I will be 19 years old . . . this home as made me a different girl all together Mr Gale and Mrs Gale are such good living people . . .[45]

A readiness to be patient and helpful about a state girl's shortcomings, admitting that 'there are faults in us all', helped lessen the social distance between the servant and the family.[46] Occasionally a mistress took such an interest in a girl that she taught her the rudiments of reading and writing:

I supplied her with a slate etc and two evenings a week have given her instruction in Arithmetic, reading and writing. All arithmetic has been completely forgotten; reading and writing have been kept up fairly. She is utterly ignorant of the value of money.[47]

Sometimes a girl even received a present from her mistress:

she had to go to Walleroo for a fortnight and I had to be housekeeper while she was away she was so pleased when she came home she said everything looked lovely and she has given me enough stuff to make a new dress for a present.[48]

Some girls were fortunate enough to have mistresses who helped them with sewing or used their husband's business connections to have the price of a sewing machine 'considerably' reduced for them.[49]

While some girls had good relationships with their mistresses, more seemed to find only tension. There were many reasons why. There might be too much speculation; talk that 'rumours' about a girl's background were 'true'. There might be complaints that a state girl was too rowdy for a refined household, as one girl wrote:

It strikes me she does not want me She is so funny she is not very sociable at any time she now thinks she and her husband would like to be alone. Well you see when she was a girl she was quiet hardly a word out of her well you see I am a very lively temperament so I cannot help but be a bit rowdy so I suppose I am to lively she is such a gloomy person . . . I am used to a lot of life being with a lot of girls I deer say I may be a little Childish but of course that is my nature I am not one of those who have come from some big well brought family . . . she said I am not a thief Sir or a girl that runs after men . . . [50]

Theft was for many mistresses a transgression they could not overlook. Girls who stole usually took small amounts of money and spent it on jewellery or food. Occasionally they spent it on other things. One mistress wrote in 1896 about missing milk money: 'I told her that the milkman could not have charged the second time if she had done so [i.e. paid him]; she then said she spent it – and bought a book "A Scarlet Sin"'.[51] Some girls stole food from the pantry and ate it, but this was viewed in a different light than theft of money, clothing, or jewellery. A mistress might find

a pair of Combinations one gone, new Combs trimmed with Tarsen lace a stripped Flannelette Petticoat with a shaped Calico band on and a pair of white Gloves only been washed once also a packet of p.c. [postcards].[52]

Being wrongly accused of stealing could lead to much ill-feeling.

My opinion is that Miss Johns has given them away with the other books and has forgotten but she said they were stolen either by me or by Jenny Fox but as long as I have breath in me to say I am innocent I will and I am sure Jenny Fox is a little more above than stealing books, and besides what would we wants books for. When Miss Johns first missed the books she sneaked down into our room and Nettie happened to be in it at the time Miss Johns was coming down the stairs. Miss Johns was sneaking down and when she saw Jenny she stopped and said, Look here Jenny I want those books . . . I am not going to have it thrown up to my face every time Miss Johns gets in a hasty temper . . . my life is a perfect misery ever since I came to this place.[53]

Many women wrote to the Department that temper was a girl's 'worst fault', but they would also mention that the girl was good at her work or kind to the children.

> Since I wrote to you I told Sarah Coates that I was sending her away on Tuesday and the girl has made herself really sick and ill with crying and fretting – I could not bear to see the poor girl so heartbroken that I told her I would write and ask you if I might give her another trial and that has brought back some life to her – I had no idea she was so attached to me – Her temper is the only fault I have to find with her . . . [54]

Slow or slovenly work in the kitchen and around the house led to the largest number of complaints. Domestic efficiency had to be learnt. But state girls were not running their own house, so they had none of the satisfactions that came from being a good manager and housewife. And there were few other rewards for efficiency. Girls could look forward to few outings except a weekly visit to church. Sometimes there might be the delight of a picnic or a visit to the beach. Girls were expected to be content with a quiet life, plenty of repetitive work, and direction from other servants or their mistress.

Under these circumstances it is no wonder that many girls were careless. Girls were said to 'work in a dream' or to be 'neglecting' their work, or they might be loath to get out of bed in the mornings, all human failings but ones which made them unsuited to the life of a domestic servant.[55] Efficient, energetic girls who could work unsupervised were what most women wanted. Mrs Norman of Kadina wrote in 1905:

> Her average time to wash the dishes is 1½ to 2 hours and not clean at that if left to herself. All her work is proportionately slow, I find her untruthful, and thoroughly lazy. All she did for me after breakfast Friday and Saturday morning was to wash breakfast dishes peel potatoes and one other five minute item. She seems quite strong and eats most hairtly.[56]

There were often complaints about the way state girls quarrelled with the children of the house. One girl infuriated her mistress by threatening the children that she would write to the secretary and have them put in the reformatory.[57] Others were 'always quarrelling' with the little boys of the household.[58] This may sound petty but state girls had to work while children almost their own age splashed in the water they had carried up to bedrooms, or dawdled over food they had laboriously cooked. Or they might crowd into the kitchen and comment on a state girl's work, wounding her self-esteem. Children might also interfere with the satisfactions housework could bring. Dora Evans wrote in 1913:

> the work is to much and to hard I have all the washing for nine and ironing and

the cooking and housework thir are six children they are very rude to me Mrs Withers said I must feed the baby and I have objected to do it I think I do my share of the work she ought to do hers thire is three floors to be washed every day and 6 children to be scrub every week . . . I would like to live with someone that is more fond of thire Home Mrs Whithers allows the Children to Pull the things about just as they pleas and there is no satisfaction for my work at all I don't mind working hard Mr Gray but I do like to see some satisfaction for it.[59]

Disputes with children could even lead to a girl running away.

Girl reported to police at 2 pm Reported employer nagged and kept her at work until midnight . . . on the whole I do not think Eva had very much reason for leaving her employment – but reading between the lines I consider that she had been made the butt of any disagreement in the family – there being 9 children – the oldest being only 13 years of age – the girl being of a very sensitive disposition, takes notice of, and feels keenly any unkind words.[60]

Related to these disputes was the state girl's almost complete lack of privacy. Food, clothes, accommodation, and even personal items such as soap were supplied by the household. A girl's room would be inspected, not every day, but often enough for her to have very little life that was hers alone and free from scrutiny. All this in an era when rectitude, the power to receive people only when you were 'dressed' and to avoid others knowing anything except a carefully presented exterior were essentials for the middle class. State girls were not expected to have any secrets. No wonder that some resorted to lying. One mistress wrote:

I will tell you her fault which after two years experience I am convinced I can never correct. She is not truthful. When it suits her purpose to do so she never scruples to tell a cool deliberate lie and she feigns as cleverly as a well-trained actress. However take away this unpardonable fault and she is rather a good girl very kind and unselfish to the little children, fair in her work, respectful to her mistress, in no way impudent whatever.[61]

Lying was one of the most common complaints.[62] Not all girls, however, resorted to it.

A more perilous way to resist all that went with being a servant was to act like a 'lady'. There were many complaints that girls 'turned sulky' when they were reprimanded.[63] One mistress went so far as to charge that 'the State girls want to be kept as ladies and not do any work',[64] while another family asserted that their state girl was 'a good hard-working girl but rather inclined to presume on her position and wants keeping in check'.[65] Intellectual curiosity was not wanted in a servant. One state girl who 'acted like a lady' infuriated her mistress:

Directly I leave her doing anything and go to another part of the house she sits down in the arm chair and reads, I put away papers and books as much as possible but it is of no use we are constantly at all hours of the day finding her reading instead of doing her work.

She is good and kind to the children or else [I] should never have kept her . . .[66]

One very common complaint was untidiness. This ranged from the girls who were liked: 'I shall be very sorry for Lena to leave me but I cannot make her tidy and clean – but she is honest and obliging – I hope she will get a good place',[67] to those who were feared because their habits were held to be part of their immoral nature.[68]

There were some girls whose dirtiness obviously resulted from deeper psychological malaise: 'One of her dirty habits is to wear her underclothes a fortnight and bring out clean things to wash another to never wash in the morning on rising'.[69] Allied to this was the practice of stealing food, hiding it, and eating it secretly.[70] This often seemed strange when the same girls would refuse food at meal times. One woman wrote:

we ask her will she have some cake at meal times she will say no thanks and when the cake is put away in the safe she will go and eat nearly the half of one and last night Mrs Ryan told her to get the child's milk and afterwards watched her take drink after drink from the bottle and the jug and then make it up with water and when she brought the bottle up for the child it was 3 parts water to the 1 part milk.[71]

What was not understood was the strain of eating with one's employers and social superiors or the pleasure a servant might feel eating alone, unobserved, and undisturbed.

In the self-contained world of each household, it was very common for an argument to start over such trivial incidents and then rapidly develop into a row if the servant lost her temper. A state girl complained in 1891 of one such argument:

just now Miss Sinclair comes in and said I took the spoon out of the sugar and put [it] into the fruit she was going to have for dinner she said I had been eating it, both of them blame everything they can on to me I feel inclined to run away I have never been happy from the first day I came here . . . Miss Sinclair said after dinner that I did not take the fruit she said Bill must have taken it but I am going to send this letter all the same . . .[72]

And in 1896 a mistress wrote her side of a similar story:

everything I tell her to do she turns round cheeks grumbles and I have to tell her twice or three times before she does it, I tried my best to get on with her but unless I let her have all her own way there is no living on the place where she is . . . We

Servants were expected to be deferential, although many resented wearing a uniform and having to address their employers as 'Madam' and 'Sir'.

told her to attend the Sunday School and Chapel as our trap is going regularly, but she says she'll go just when she pleases . . .[73]

Sometimes the rows resulted from girls not being subservient enough; they were supposed to accept instruction without thinking themselves 'too big to be told'.[74] There were doubtless girls who would have provoked anger in the calmest of women, but also tyrannical employers, women who were perpetually irritable, critical, or suspicious. One state girl wrote:

it is no use of trying she had five girls in three months before I came and one told me that she would not go to another place like it again . . . I made the bread as she told me but I mixed it so stiff and she said I wanted kicking till I was black and blue and a little while ago I brought my clothes off the line and I just put them in the Pram for a few minutes while I went outside when I came in she threw them on the floor and said she would burn them if I put them there again . . .[75]

A very common source of tension was breakages by a servant. If these could clearly be shown to be a girl's fault she was supposed to pay for them out of her wages. Determining how the item had been broken could be a very difficult matter and feeling might run high.

In reply to your letter informing me of Mrs Wyatt's claim I beg to inform you that I did not break the butter dish the bedroom water bottle I broke by accident. As to the cheese dish the girl broke the handle off before I went there the other part I broke by putting the washing machine in its place. The bedroom basin was cracked and had a piece out of it she said she would not charge me for it as I slipped and broke it.[76]

To an outsider, quarrels often appeared to be the result of hasty tempers on both sides. A member of the Gumeracha Visiting Committee wrote in 1896:

Last evening Mary Waters came to me just at dark and reported that Mrs Duigan and herself had been quarrelling and she said she would not remain there any longer for some time past I have found it impossible to get these two to get on together their tempers being both rather violent . . . I find that one is as bad as another.[77]

One girl who reflected, instead of writing in the heat of the moment, was Harriet Tilley;

I know sometime I am rude to Mrs Pike in answering her back but I try my very best in not doing it. I think I will soon get on if I still keep trying I am always sorry of what I said after it [is] done . . . Sir it is getting late and it a washing day tomorrow and I must get up early it is now 9 o'clock. All I hope for mostly is to hear you have a better report of me ...[78]

In response to complaints from a mistress the secretary of the Department would often write to a girl admonishing her:

My dear girl,
  I have just received a letter from Mrs Henderson that is very distressing. You are old enough to know that no one will keep a girl who is useless and who in addition is impudent. It would appear to me I think if I were in your position, much wiser and better in every sense to try to win the esteem and affection of the people with whom you live. Don't you think that is the best way? Will you promise me to try to do better, or must I recall you from Mrs Henderson and send you to an institution where you will be obliged to work all day and get no pay for it at all.
  Please write and let me know what you think of the position.
I am
Your sincere friend[79]

Such letters sometimes meant that a complete break could be avoided, and that a girl might be given 'another chance'.[80] Girls and employers might go on quarrelling and 'making up' for years before the final rupture.[81] If a girl could not agree to be less 'determined', a battle of wills was often inevitable.[82] Ada Cambridge counted herself lucky in 1903 to have avoided 'that servant trouble which seems to keep families in general in constant distress and turmoil'.[83]

During the years 1887 to 1913 it seems to have become less common for a state girl to work in a household where there were many servants and far more likely that she would be the maid-of-all-work in a suburban villa.

Being in a household of servants was a mixed blessing: in many cases girls were at the bottom of a hierarchy of servants and did not get on with them. Others girls were ashamed of being wards of the state and went to some pains to conceal this from their fellow servants.[84] But a large household was likely at least to have an experienced mistress, a woman used to managing servants. These were women who might write of the winter season as a time when their 'friends either do without maids or reduce their wages'.[85] They were a servant-keeping class, one of whom wrote: 'Having kept servants for twenty years some of whom have stayed with [me] four or five years and have married from [here] is sufficient to show that mine is a good home for any girl you may send'.[86]

Such households might find however that a girl was 'too quarrelsome with the other maids' or was too 'insolent to her fellow servants'.[87] The sort of things that could happen were described by a state girl who wrote in 1903:

up here I am always getting growled [at] today has been sunday and it has been the most unhappy day that I could not bear it . . . there is another girl here she has been here a lot longer than I have and of course she is the favourite . . . it is terrible to be where two girls are in the house where one is a favoured and the other is not.[88]

One of the things that made it difficult for girls to conceal their connection with the State Children's Department was the way each girl was sent out to service with a regulation outfit. This was supposed to be kept in good repair by the girl's mistress until the girl was sixteen, when her wages rose sufficiently to cover the cost of her clothes and she had been taught to do her own sewing and mending.

Although wages were set in 1887, the regulations of that year also stipulated that: 'The Council may, however, agree with an employer for a special rate of wages, and make such exemptions as it may deem advisable'. Many mistresses, unable to afford higher wages, would indicate that they would give a girl more time and help with her sewing instead.

I can pay Mary 5/– weekly and give her [a] little assistance with her clothes, such as calico etc. in lieu of the extra 1/– I am quite willing to do so and there by she would lose nothing. She is a nice clean honest girl and my two children are attached to her . . .[89]

Will give her 7/– per week and will do her sewing as I thought by doing her sewing it was a great help to her to save her money as she would have to pay to get her sewing done or buy ready made clothing.[90]

Even if a girl were thrifty her wages were often insufficient to cover the cost of clothing. Through no fault of her own, a state girl might have no clothes left. Alice Green wrote in 1905:

I am sorry to have to write to tell you I am not happy. I have not got any Under Clothing to wear. Mrs Jolley let me run right out. I am of age to buy my own Clothes but I have not got Money to get them made up I had to wear my under clothing for six weeks until the girls gave me a change to wear. That I could be clean. The little boy hit me with the tongs and I gave him a smak on the hand. He called me a mungrel . . .[91]

The Departmental inspector who called found the girl's clothes 'almost in rags' and instructed her mistress to provide some immediately. Another service home led an inspector, Evelyn Penny, to write:

I have visited four different girls in this house . . . have always found the outfits unsatisfactory where Mrs Donald has supplied the clothes, and she has always

45

represented to me that new garments were about to be made or brought. I have never had any opinion of this home ... The clothes, generally washed by the girls themselves have never looked properly clean and have been badly ironed.[92]

A mistress had to take a genuine interest in order to keep a young girl looking respectable. She might have to help one who had no idea of 'purchasing her own outfit as she is supposed to do' or make sure a girl was 'well fitted up with clothes'.[93] The matters that might concern a conscientious mistress are shown in the following letter, written in 1901:

Most of her clothing is about three years old and she having grown wonderfully since they are all too small for her. She was told she did not need stays but her clothes keep falling down, she keeps walking on them, and I'm kept mending for her and then can't keep her tidy without them, besides they are on the list that I must keep in repair.[94]

She then went on to estimate what the necessary items would cost: one flannel petticoat 3s, one pair of stays, 3s, two slip bodies 1s 6d and one pair of stockings 1s, the whole adding up to more than a week's wages for most state girls.

Another woman wrote:

The falatea is very thin and cold for this weather here on such days she is miserably cold in such thin garments. She wants a morning and an afternoon dress, one of winsey the other of good homespun for afternoons.[95]

The occasion of a girl going to a new 'place' either from a previous situation or from the Industrial School or Girls' Reformatory often meant her outfit would be looked at with a critical eye and new garments supplied from those made at the Reformatory or the Central Depot. One girl's outfit was ruthlessly assessed thus in 1902:

Boots 1 leather pair, the other thin 'court' shoes which are not at all strong enough.
Hats Had both when she left the State Dep. Sun (white) none too good. Straw one very shabby indeed, not fit to wear to church. Dresses Best One (Blue serge from State) small and getting shabby for best, the other is a print and that is wearing at sleeves.[96]

State girls spent most of their time in apron and work dress, but they were supposed to have clothes good enough to wear to church. This did not mean anything too fine (many state girls were rebuked by their mistresses for being 'extravagant' or for buying 'useless things'[97]), but they were supposed to have a best dress, hat, and shoes. One sensitive mistress reminded the Department 1900:

she was sent away with two pairs of very heavy boots instead of one pair shoes for best . . . Lottie seems to feel it very much, could you arrange for them to exchange one pair of shoes for the boots they make Lottie look so awkward when she is out and the fact of another girl being differently treated makes her feel it more.[98]

Church was usually the only outing in the humdrum calendar of most state girls' lives and it was important to look one's best. A state girl who needed new glasses wrote: 'If you don't mind I would like you to get frames sothing like one I have got now light ones not big clumsy ones because I have to wear them to Sunday School and chapel'.[99]

Clothing was the only thing that state girls' wages were expected to cover. Time and time again in asking for higher wages girls would emphasize how much their clothing cost, one girl writing 'when we have bought shoes there is not many pennies left'.[1]

In 1908, after twenty-one years, the wages paid to girls over fourteen were revised. Girls of thirteen still received 1s a week, but fourteen-year-olds now got 2s, and fifteen-year-olds 3s. Three quarters of this was paid to the secretary and held in trust by the Department. The wage for a sixteen-year-old became 7s, a seventeen-year-old 8s, an eighteen-year-old 9s, and for nineteen to twenty-one year-olds 10s. This amount included 1s to be sent each week to the Department out of the girl's wage as a form of compulsory saving. It was these accrued savings that girls often applied for after they had left the control of the state.[2] But although these were laid down as the wages girls could reasonably expect, in many cases they were paid less. Wage rises were not automatic and girls were expected to be more skilled if they wanted higher wages.[3]

There were many reasons why employers believed they should not have to pay state girls the regulation amount:

I think the rise should not apply seeing that I keep a boy to milk cows feed pigs and bring the wood in for the girl so that she has not any rough work. The above work many of the girls have to do[4]

If she were capable of filling the position of general servant I should be only to pleased to pay her higher wages. As it is I have to engage a washerwoman every week (4/– a day) and do all the coooking myself and most of the housework while she devotes most of her time to looking after the three children and assisting me as far as she is able with the housework.[5]

If it could be shown conclusively that a girl could not do 'the whole of the work', her wages were a matter for negotiation.[6] One woman wrote indignantly in 1908: 'I do not know of any maid about here receiving 10/– a week with one exception a cook in a large family. The girl I had before Kate came asked 8/– She was 23 a strong general'. She promised she would offer the state girl nine shillings when the shearing began.[7] Physical weaknesses which prevented a girl from undertaking any heavy work, or the inability of girls to work without constant 'watching and teaching', were also reasons why they were not paid full wages.[8] A number of girls would nevertheless elect to stay with a household on a lower wage because they were happy in the home.[9]

The one thing most girls seemed to have dreamed of saving for was a sewing machine of their own. Ostensibly this was for their own personal use but hidden behind the wish to buy a machine was the dream of one day achieving personal status and financial independence through becoming a dressmaker.

As I am now sixteen and providing my own clothes I have decided to write and ask you if I would be allowed to purchase a machine ... only one dressmaker in Hammond now and as she charges a fairly high fee it takes a good deal of my money for the making of my dresses and if I had a machine I could save a lot more than its cost in a very short time as I am a fairly good sewer and can manage a machine very well Mrs Bach also allows me plenty of time to do my own stitching so it would not interfere with my work in any way.[10]

It is a hand machine and I intend giving about £3-10-0 for it I think I would rather have a hand machine than a treadle as I could not very well take a large machine about if I happened to move from here. I can easily sell it and get a treadle when I can afford it better.[11]

Most machines were bought on hire purchase, an agent calling to collect the repayments once a month. This could lead to difficulties. One girl wrote to the Department asking if she could

have a pound as I have been out of a place for a month but have got the promise of the place and if you will let me have it ... The reason I want it is that I have got a Sewing Machine and it has cost me £7.15.0 and I have got it all paid for nearly and they have sent me this letter and he told me on Friday they would take it away if I did not pay for it.[12]

Another wrote to see if her savings could be used to pay

Mr Hindman he is a collector for Wertheim Sewing Machine Company I understand if I could it would save my fourpence every month of course it isn't much but several months and 4d every time I send my money would be a little help to me ...[13]

In the last years before World War I there was an increasing shortage of domestic servants.[14] This may have been due to the rising marriage rate, the slowly increasing opportunities for employment in other spheres, the increasing prosperity which led fewer girls to seek employment, or the good harvests around 1910 which meant that country girls did not need to 'look for a place'. Whatever the cause, it meant that conditions for domestic servants began to improve. And conditions for state girls slowly improved too.

One thing which changed was the matter of free afternoons and evenings. Before 1901 there is not much mention of the maid's afternoon off, though a girl might complain if she felt extremely tired or if she wasn't allowed time to go to church.[15] By 1907, Departmental inspectors had begun to comment on the lack of recreation time allowed to state wards. At the State Children's Convention held in Adelaide in 1907 Miss Penny, a Departmental inspector, suggested that children at service be allowed

some definite time for recreation each week. Girls in shops had their half holidays each week and most of their evenings free. But one rule of the State Children's Department was that children were not allowed out in the evenings. That meant that service children were given no time whatever for recreation. Their mistresses seldom if ever allowed them any time off during the day ... One afternoon each week ought to be officially insisted upon by the Department.[16]

Commenting on one dissatisfied state girl in 1911, an inspector wrote:

The hours of work are long and the work continuous but not more so than in the majority of service homes under present day conditions. It seems to be a necessity of domestic service. May has half a day out once a fortnight from about 12 o'clock till 8.30 pm on Wednesdays and Mrs Kite is willing to give her every other Sunday from 3 pm to 8.30 pm with the Secretary's approval. She has no friends in the Semaphore and would probably go to town.[17]

Some mistresses were liberal. One girl described as having 'a mental capacity below the average' was treated as one of the family, received some 'very nice' Christmas presents and was 'taken out with them every holiday'.[18] Some were suspicious, writing wryly of a girl who 'complained of being tired all day ... and when night came wanted to go to Band of Hope in the town'.[19]

There was such a thing as too much going out – even if the going out was of an entirely respectable kind. One girl who was on probation in 1908 had her outings investigated by Miss Kate Cocks, who wrote:

Her brother, from Broken Hill took her to the theatre last week he has also taken her to a Rotunda Concert and to the market on Saturday evenings.

She has met her sister, several times in the street but has not been to her house since forbidden to do so. She has also been out in the evenings with Anna Graham an ex State girl, but on these occasions Miss Black assures me she has not been late. Miss Black promised me to keep Peg at home in the evenings and to allow her some time off during the day. Peg is willing to do this she is very happy in her situation.[20]

Other girls not so careful received scoldings from their employers for being in 'hours later' than they had been told.

During the week the Duke was in Town I took her in my trap for 3 days, and the day I came home, I told her to be at my Brother's where she stopped at night not later than 1 o'clock. I waited till 1/4 to 2 when I had to leave without her and she came back by the coach next day.[21]

As the twentieth century advanced some state girls were beginning to feel that having to be a servant was an irksome and old-fashioned way of earning a living. They also suspected that they were more restricted than other servants.

I think it is a great punishment for me to be put under government until I have attained the age of 21 years it would be different if I had been put in for bad conduct or misbehaviour but I was put in for some reason and that is because I could not look after myself . . . if Wilma and I have to always go out together . . . If I want to do a little shopping sometimes and I ask Wilma to come perhaps she doesn't want to go out that night and then I have to stop home. I think it is very unjust.[22]

Many girls revealed not only anger but also a shrewd understanding of how the Department thought when they wrote about time off:

you wished me to tell you what I am going to do if I got my afternoons off, well I would want to go into the township to do some little shopping as I don't go in very often or if I never went I would like to have an afternoon to do my mending and several little things like that, mind if I did go out I would be in long before seven o'clock and that I think would be early enough, I know we are not allowed out after dark, and I do not wish to be . . .[23]

Contemporary standards seem to indicate that one free half day a week was not thought excessively liberal. As a witness told the Shops and Factories Commission in 1892,

A. My wife always gives the servant half a day every week to do her shopping, and never allows her out on Saturday night.

Q.12538 Do you know whether all people treat their servants in that way?

A. I am sorry to say that they do not.[24]

50

Having an annual holiday also became an issue after the turn of the century. Before this, holidays seem to have been confined either to holidays with the family or to those times when the service family took holidays and the state girl in their employ was sent to stay with friends or relatives, or if it was thought 'safer', back to the Industrial School.[25] (The latter does not seem to have been thought of as a punishment; one girl actually asked if she could have a holiday there as she had never been 'at the school on Christmas day'.[26] But most girls longed for holidays with friends, relatives, or foster-parents. And they advanced cogent reasons why they should have a holiday: 'it is almost a year since I have seen them ... I need this holiday ... as a result of my accident ... my arms are a good bit bruised'.[27]

so my holidays are due in July but I am going to ask if you would aloud me to go to town on the special eight hours day it is cheap fare then and it is four years since I seen eight hours keep up in Town ...[28]

It would often help a girl to gain a holiday for herself if she could assure the Department that she would be staying with thoroughly respectable people. Having a married sister invite one to her wedding anniversary, for instance, was a very good reason for a holiday.[29] Foster-mothers, too, often invited their former charges to have holidays with them and this was seen as an eminently respectable arrangement.[30]

I feel quite lonely on sunday that I don't know what to do with myself ... could I go for a months holiday for a change. It is so dreadful hot up here that it is nearly roasting me and I am not able to do my work properly and then I get growled at because it is not done properly. It is a change I want and that would set me right.[31]

This girl was writing from her 'place' in the country. Many state wards were sent to work in the country, which some liked but more loathed for its isolation and monotony – a subject more fully discussed in the next chapter.

CHAPTER 3

Country Life
and Other Trials
1887–1940

Country Life 1887–1914

I like it here very much and as I get more used to the daily routine of work I like it better of course after City Life everything seemed at first so strange and quite but now I don't notice it so much . . . I will have to be very patient and not give in at trifles . . . I did not have a very pleasant journey here it was such a nasty day very hot and so dusty that at times we could not see any further than the fence that separates the paddocks from the railway line. After arriving at Kadina I still had 22 miles to go in Coach, it was very shaky and I was so glad to reach my destination I was very tired and I don't think I ever felt more ready for bed . . .[1]

This was Diana Cook's experience of arriving in the country in 1903.

The State Children's Council, in its public statements, made it plain that it believed city life to be a dangerous influence, and preferred a country to a city home for wards of the state. Early reformers had hoped to find country foster-homes for all children,[2] and even when this proved impractical they still preferred a country home to one in the city.[3]

Country visiting committees were continually providing support for this view. They might write of girls being morally improved[4] by working in the country or express sorrow about a girl who was 'determined' to go back to the city.[5] Quite poor living conditions would be tolerated in the country as long as children appeared 'clean and healthy-looking'.[6] The precise advantages of the country home were encapsulated by one woman when she wrote that 'We are living a quiet country life here there are no temptations or indifferent company for her [the state girl] to associate with'.[7] So, girls were sent to country homesteads all over the state. They received free railway travel and virtually always travelled in the company of a member of the Department's staff.

52

Although many girls loathed being sent to service in the country, others loved it. They were pleased with the variety of tasks they had to do and the sense of self-sufficiency and importance life on an isolated farm could bring.

I milk three cows now but they are nearly dry, they will soon be calving again. We are having very hot weather up here some people are carting water already from the river for their stock, but we have not done so yet. Mr Beare had a fairly good crop according to the dry weather we have had . . . thank you for the pretty cards you sent us, we all think the one with the pussy cats driving out is the best. [On New Year's Day] we all went down to The River crayfishing then we boiled the kettle down there, and then had tea, and had some games until sunset, and then I had to take the cows home and milk them, and then we had some games inside we did enjoy ourselves very much.[8]

Sometimes a note of scorn for 'city slickers' might even creep in:

as you are not a farmer I suppose there is not much news up this part to interest you. Our men have just finished their reaping for this season and just in good time too I think as there is apparently a heavy thunderstorm brewing. We have had a most lovely cool summer up here so far . . . Mrs Rodd gave me a nice little gun metal watch and silver chain for good conduct, also a nice leather hand bag for a Christmas box which I think was very kind of her.[9]

Other girls wrote of the freshness of the air early on summer mornings or of the 'nice homely people' in the country.[10] The extension of a girl's sentence until twenty-one years of age might lead her to reassure the secretary that she was a 'good girl' and would stay in the country if released.[11]

There is no doubt that farm work was hard. Farmers' wives, when applying for a girl, would often specify that they must have one who could 'do all the outside work such as the dairying, fowls etc. a good strong girl', one who was used to 'living on a farm' and the 'quiet life'.[12] That it was unpopular work was hinted at by the farmer's wife who complained that she 'could get no one locally. Farmers daughter are all too well off to work outside their own homes'.[13]

Of those who disliked farm work, many girls on farms complained about the hours they had to work. Their complaints were backed up by Evelyn Penny in 1906.

The service girls who are placed out on farms have very long hours especially during harvest time when they usually rise at 5 or 5.30 am and do not finish their work till 10 or 11 at night. I must say in justice to the mistresses that they work even longer hours themselves but one cannot wonder that a girl is slovenly, dirty and slow about her duties after a working day of 16 or 17 hours or that the mistress is impatient and fault finding.

Harvest time in the summer was the climax of the year's labour and everyone on the farm was involved in the work. Harvesting on a South Australian farm at the turn of the century.

I am filled with wonder that the girls complain so little. One girl told me that she always fell asleep before she had finished undressing and hardly found time to wash her clothes let alone mend them and another told me that she had to put all her sewing out although she knew how to do it herself as she never had a moments time for needlework. A girl just out of her time told me in confidence that for two months during the summer she rose at 3 am so as to have the men's breakfast ready for 4 am and was never in bed before half past ten at night.

I can only hope that this is an exaggeration, I was not of course at liberty to question the mistress as to the truth of this statement.

I am impressed with the excellence of the service girls' sleeping accommodation, the majority have nicely furnished airy rooms quite as good as the daughters of the house, and on the farms both boys and girls are generally treated as members of the family have their meals at the same table, and accompany the family to church and amusements but the latter are too often few and far between and work meals and bed seem to make up the tale of the average service boys and girls existence, there is little or no time for recreation.[14]

Girls who did manage to complain that they were working too hard often wrote towards the end of the summer when the harvest demanded such extra effort from everyone on the farm. Mollie Lewis wrote that she felt

clean knock out before half of the day was over and it was so terrible hot up here enough to roast you. They have not got any boy to do the outside work so I have no help to do it milk cows feed calfs cart wood and some times turn the separator. When Sunday comes it is not like Sunday it is as miserable as anything inside all day long just about. If I had enough money I would buy a bicycle and then I would go to church every Sunday.

In this case the Department sent out an inspector who reported that the farmer's wife and daughter took 'an active part in the work of the house', doing all the separating and most of the housework and washing. But this still left Mollie with seven cows to milk night and morning and the cows to be fetched from a distance of about half a mile. But she did not have to cut wood for the stove, and the inspector concluded that while Mollie certainly had 'plenty' to do, she was not working as hard as many other state girls.[15]

The distinction between chopping fire-wood, and merely carrying it, was a central issue. Girls could often get their work on farms lessened considerably if they could prove that they had been doing 'outside' or 'boy's' work.

I did not like staying with Mrs Ophel. I had to round sheep in the paddock besides a lot of other work – bring up the horses and water them ... I liked the housework but not the outside work ...[16]

And a friend might complain if a state girl had

all the five children to mind besides the dinner to cook and house to do then she has to chaff the hay for the cows and she told me she had to help Mr Reel put in a load of sheard hay on New Years morning then she often has to go out and help the working man there put the horses with the drag or Waggon, this is not girl's work ...[17]

As always there was a fine contemporary distinction – which one inspector made:

she tells me that she is often asked to go out to the paddock and she objects and does not think it is a girl's work to winnow wheat kick stones and hoe thistles etc ... But it has been at her own request she has had extra pocket money 13d a day and allowed the privilege of riding a horse.

To look at the girl, she is strong, well-nourished, clean, well-clad and every appearance of being well looked after.

I do not approve of girls being turned into farm hands but in this case I do not think she has much to complain about.[18]

Nevertheless this girl was removed to a nearby farm where she did not have to do such outside work.

One skill, the ability to milk, usually determined whether a girl was a success or failure on a farm. The Department repeatedly faced letters from farmers' wives stating that they had 'no complaint' against a girl except that she could not milk.[19] Milking was a skill and unless a girl acquired the knack the farmer's wife would have to go on doing it, leaving her kitchen unattended at most inconvenient times.[20] Sometimes the farmer's wife would therefore want a girl who could not milk but was capable enough to take over the household while she herself did the milking. One girl described this arrangement as

too much for me. I used to have to go for the cows in the evening. Mrs Cooper used to milk some of the cows and the boy used to help her and I used to go in and get the tea and put the baby to bed, and if it was not done she used to growl at me. As soon as the men went out I had to take the baby. The baby is 12 months old . . . I used to have to carry her round in my arms and set the table.[21]

There were girls, however, who enjoyed milking: 'We milk six cows and separate. Sometimes I milk myself. I am rather fond of milking and don't mind it'.[22]

There can be no doubt that milking cows as well as doing housework demanded a certain amount of stamina which some girls did not have. Yet one mistress wrote indignantly that her state girl had never had to do any heavy work: 'never milked a cow . . . with one or two exception'.[23]

Harvest time in the summer was the hottest time of the year, and for many state girls it was a hard time. There would be extra strains on the whole household as it was the climax of a year's labour on the farm. The following year's prosperity depended on the 'season' and the harvest. State girls were part of the great activity.

the harvest is all over up here and a dreadful harvest time it was for me I used to have to get up in the morning between half-past four and five o'clock to get the men their breakfast by 6 o'clock and it would be nearly 10 o'clock before I would get to bed at night it would be 9 o'clock before they would come to their tea and it was dreadful.[24]

After the harvest was a good time for a girl to ask for a holiday:

if I can go again to visit Mrs Fox at Greenock for a holiday. I would like to go in April I would let you know the exact date of departure if I may go. We all of us like a change after harvest and Mr & Mrs Baker are quite willing to let me go.[25]

she would like to go to Clare with Friends for a fortnight and with your consent I am to spare her as now the busy time is over for a while She is looking rather thin and a change would do her good she has not had a change since she came with me now over 4 years.[26]

The seasons were important to the state girl who became involved in farm life. Rain might be feared or welcomed depending on the cycles of farm life, whether or not the harvest was completed. A girl recently sent to Willowie, wrote in 1913:

it is rather strange to me because I don't know a soul where I am working. It is the Harvest Thanksgiving up here on the 16th of March. Mrs Bean and all are very good to me. It is very hot and sultry up here just now and has been for a few weeks now but hope it will soon break.[27]

It was usually rather a relief when summer was over especially if a girl felt that 'the hot summers are not agreeing with me'.[28]

A bad season could also be very important to a state girl. It might mean that her wages would be reduced or that she would be returned from the farm to the city.

I would like to know what the regulation wages would be for Augusta Shaw for the continuing year as considering this bad season we are having I think five shillings per week is quite as much as she is worth . . . she has been with me for a long time now, and is quite at home, and would not like to be shifted.[29]

we are thinking of sending her back as everything is getting very dull and we are sorry to part with her but I expect we will have to leave the Burra ourselves for the Broken Hill shortly.[30]

Some girls were sympathetic to the plight of such farmers:

Mrs Lee cannot afford to pay three shillings a week when my wages rise next July and I wanted to know as if you would be so kind as to let her pay me the same wages next year . . . Their crops have been so bad this year that they cannot afford it.[31]

Loneliness was the main reason why many girls disliked the country. Weeks might pass before the family went to town or had visitors. Visitors, paradoxically, might only underline the loneliness felt by a girl if she was made to feel a mere servant and not part of the household.

Mrs James is 75 years old, she forgets her young days and she thinks I shouldn't have any enjoyment. The Mount is the only outing I get, I have only been to church twice in the eight months, that isn't my fault.

Sir this is such a lonely place the other girls wouldn't stop here because Mrs James is too strict. I don't know how she will manage when I am gone. I have got to do all outside work . . . I don't like complaining but it isn't nice to be in a place when you are not happy.[32]

I must complayne I feel so lonely out here now, the place is so dull, I have no friends living here they have all gone away to live up the River Murray and I feel rather sorry that I have to stay out here.

Dear Sir I only wish you would take me from my place I have now happeyness out here so I would be glad to here from you that I was going back to town. I would have more company then.[33]

The feeling of being forgotten left many girls feeling angry, even rebellious. Some analyzed their feelings and wrote with insight and deliberation:

I do not for one moment wish you to think that Mrs Johnson is unkind to me, I will admit that I was in an exceedingly bad temper when I wrote to you and hardly know what I said, also I did not mean you to think that I get no time to myself, for I get plenty after my work is finished as Mrs Johnson herself will tell you. But what the trouble really is, is that I feel too lonely and miserable to try and be happy, and that made me paint things blacker than they really are . . . When one thing upsets people they are apt to forget all the nice and kind things that are done and said and only remember the cross words and scoldings.[34]

Others tried to resign themselves to life in the country.

I have a very nice place. And I am going to try my hardest to stay here for twelve months, and then I must come to town to live. It is very lonely here, I sometimes feel it as much as I can bear because I am so far from my young man.[35]

Such feelings could build up until it all seemed too much: 'But I am feeling more and more miserable every day I am up hear . . . why I don't know . . . I don't think country life will see me much longer as it is very lonely indeed'.[36]

Some girls would adjust to loneliness after a time and would gradually grow to like farm life, weighing the good against the bad in a philosophical manner.

I suppose I will stay up here for another two or three years if I get on pretty well. Of course the place is very quiet at times. But still I don't mind now been used to it. I have to milk eight cows and Seperate the milk and feed seven calves and I get up in the morning about half past five or six thats not too early but still it is time enough. I don't say that I am overworked But I always have plenty to do to keep me going. Of coarse I will be getting more wages this month.[37]

And other girls might concede that country life had some merits even if they did not like it wholly; it might have improved their health for example.[38] But for other, particularly younger, girls away from home for the first time, country life was something they could not come to terms with.

I left my dear Aunt to work on a farm and mind children as I thought but I find that it isn't a farm or there aren't any children and that I have to do house-work . . . the people here are kind in their way, but what are they to *me* . . . oh do let me go home if you saw me now you would for my heart is crying for home. Oh why was I such a fool to leave it. This is cruel just like a prison. Oh I ask you and pray to God to let me go home Please Mr Gray grant my wish . . . you may think a child's heart never breaks but it does and mine is.

This girl had already made a number of friends, been taken out for drives, been given pony rides, and been taken to a Continental (an evening dance), according to her mistress. She was not being treated harshly, yet as her letter stated, she was among strangers and she was homesick as a result.[39] It was often especially lonely for a young girl.

I feel dreadfully lonely here we are a mile away from anyone and there is no children and I feel very unhappy I have always been used to Children and I feel quite lost without them I do hope you will let me have a nother place where there is Children and not so far away from anyone I have never had a place like this before I nearly always take to them as soon as I get there but I cant to this It is too lonely. O do let me have another one.[40]

A girl from the city who had 'gone wrong' was often sent to an extremely isolated farm. If she endured this patiently for several years and during that time behaved in a sensible manner, she might be sent to a less isolated situation. One girl who had been managing the house in her mistress's absence had earned a change, according to the inspector who visited her in 1908. She had been left for a month

with Mr Andrews and his two sons aged 7 and 4 years the former is at school all day and the latter out with his father so that Helen has been alone all day except at meal times.
She has found it terribly dull and lonely. Helen has been doing all the cooking housework washing mending and ironing in Mrs Andrew's absence and com-plains of feeling very tired but she looks well and strong.
Helen is very anxious to be moved to another place and I think her request might well receive consideration after her month of loneliness and extra work.[41]

This girl had been filling the place of a 'general', but large country establishments with many servants were sometimes just as hard. The elaborate life of a large country household in the 1890s is well described by Dorothy Gilbert:

Breakfast was a delightful meal, porridge and hot dishes of chops, bacon and eggs, a cut ham on the bone, home-made bread & in winter, toast made as liked at the open fire. The older children had breakfast in the dining-room, the younger were despatched to a suitable meal with their nurses in the nursery . . .

Dinner at night was at seven for which everyone dressed. Men dinner suits, women lacey blouses & flowing skirts & if by any chance it was the Governor visiting, real evening dresses. The meal was a more elaborated lunch, with soup, some type of entree dish, a joint or poultry, sweet, savoury & dessert, the last served with the Worcester china dessert plates and finger-bowls, sitting on beautifully embroidered or hand-painted d'oyleys, and a sprig of sweet-scented verbena or diosma & a gay flower floating in the bowls.[42]

Dorothy Gilbert writes of the servants she remembers with affection but from a distance.

One girl who worked as a domestic in a large house on Hindmarsh Island in 1902 secretly wrote her brother this account of what life in the big house was like for the servants:

it is a farm and a terrible big house it has 16 rooms on it and there is a terrible lot of work to do. They keep another girl and she is nearly 19. We have to get up at 5 o'clock every morning and work till 9 or half past nine at night it is something terrible really more than I can bear we have to work hard all day long they only allow us a quarter of an hour to eat our meals and sometimes there is 5 minutes gone before we can start but they work the time and we have to be finished in a quarter of an hour, or they don't like it . . . they keep a lot of men and of course the make a lot of washing up and I have it all to do by myself, we both have our own work. I have all the dirtiest work to do . . . The men have to milk cows So we have to be [at] work from 5 till 9 . . . we have one afternoon [a] week to sew and no time at night . . . I feel I cannot stand it . . . tell me if you think I had better write to Mr Whiting . . .[43]

A mistress might understand a girl's dislike of the country and help her adjust in various ways.

she gives way to fits of crying declaring she cant stay and afterwards says I think I shall like to stay but to pacify her we promised to write and tell you . . . she says she likes us but is lonely so far from Town. There are 13 people on the premises 6 being females but she does not try to be sociable . . .

In the effort to make her happy we sent the children for a walk Saturday and took her with us to Church on Sunday but she is still the same and it occurs to me that a line from you whom she seems to fear may settle her.[44]

If it was found that a girl was having to milk eighteen cows a day and did not have time for church she would be recalled.[45] Drudgery was not acceptable, but loneliness had to be endured.[46]

Country towns were sometimes disliked as much as the country. One girl wrote of Port Pirie in 1902:

it is terrible the dust and the dirt I think that all I would sooner the Burra, we went to the show yesterday and the ground is just something terrible, I was glad to get off it why the dust even gets in our food when we are eating it . . .

But at least in Port Pirie there might be compensations: 'we went down on the wharf yesterday and it is grand to see them working on the big boats out on the water we quite enjoyed ourselves'.[47]

There is no way of knowing how many girls liked working in the country and how many simply endured it, feeling

just about tired of living where I am . . . I think that every hour is to long to stay in the house I often have a good cry to my self at night when I am in bed and think of you.[48]

Country Life 1915–40

Fewer girls were sent to service in the country in the 1930s. For those who did work in the country very little changed. The arrival of the car lessened the sense of isolation and led to more outings.[49] The telephone also diminished the loneliness. For the farmer, life was undoubtedly easier as a result of increased mechanization, the tractor instead of the 'team'. But the work of the farmer's wife and her 'help' was not much changed. Milking was still done by hand, except on the very largest farms, washing machines were rare, wood stoves almost universal. Everyday. life on the

The arrival of the car lessened the isolation of a country place but in other ways very little changed. Truck at Andamooka station, circa 1910.

farm in the 1930s was in many ways the same as it had been in the early years of the century.

my word it was hot. The temperature was a hundred before dinner ... We took the water bag full of water with us but when we got home it was empty, and so you can guess how thirsty we were. Today in the cowyard to make matters worse the blessed cow kicked me over and hurt my foot. It isn't anything much but it is enough to make me feel miserable. We are milking nine cows and a ½ now, we were milking eleven but we are drying three off. My word Christmas is drawing near now. Are you going to hang your stocking up this year. I am not going to hang mine up because it would be full of grasshoppers instead of Xmas gifts. Dont be at all surprised if you see a present coming along a bit late. Do you think that you could get me a job near you so I can stay home with use. They say theres no place like home and I think its true too. I don't think I will be here long when the harvest is finished and they will finish about the end of this month, and so please try to find me a job before then and ask Mr Burns if I can go home with you ...[50]

The duties required of girls still demanded much stamina. In 1935 Mary Parker had these tasks, in a home she liked although her mistress was a short-tempered woman who sometimes slapped her:

DUTIES
helps with the milking, separator, rough work in the house, scrubbing etc and does the cooking
Washing mornings up at 4.30 am to 5 am.
Other mornings 5.30 am to 6 am.
Wages 7/6 per week[51]

State girls continued to be sent to the country to keep them 'well out of the way of all temptations'.[52] Initial reactions to being sent to the country were often hostile. One girl

stamped her foot at her [mistress] on her arrival in the home and said she would not stay in the country and said that as often as she was sent to the country she would come back again. Other girls did it and they got a town place and she would do the same.[53]

Many disliked the country intensely. One girl wrote in 1918 that she had a good home and her mistress was very nice, but

it is so terribly lonly there is not a house with in miles around and it is so far away from any township. I could never content myself here. I would sooner stay in the reformatory for the 6 months I've got to go much as I dislike the place.[54]

Another wrote to her father in 1934 of a home the Department considered 'very good':

Mrs Porter is fairly nice and kind to me but I don't like working here much all the same . . .

Every morning I get up at ½ past 6 and I generally come to bed at nine. There is quite a number of laughing jackasses around here. Every morning, when I get up, I hear them laughing for all they are worth.

We have got a wireless here and when Mr Porter gets over is illness, we will be listening in to the Blueboys . . .

Well dad it is still the same old cry. I want to come HOME to you all . . .

When I go to get my mornings wood I think of you all, and cry.[55]

Sympathy for the girls' dislike of country life became more apparent. An inspector wrote in 1917, after investigating a girl's complaints:

Of course farm hours are excessively long and the work monotonous and I am not surprised that our girls sometimes complain, the wonder is that they endure farm life as well as they do.[56]

Enduring, however, did not mean that girls did not complain:

I wish that I was back at the home. It is to lonely up her and I am homesick I want to go back to the girls home florence street If you wonte let me go I will run away from this place. You must let me go. You must write and let me know.[57]

I am fretting and crying that much that I can't put up with it here any longer Mrs Paterson said I could cum Back as soon as Nurse Crag can come and get me she wants a girl that will stay with her for years . . .

To the second of these girls the secretary wrote a letter of encouragement urging her to stay and to

Try and be a brave and good girl. Do all you can to help other people with whom you live. You will find that all the fretting and crying will disappear and you will be just as happy as you can be. The truth is that you are home sick.[58]

By the 1930s there was an additional reason why girls hated working in the country: they were well aware that it was an occupation few girls would go to willingly. Domestic service in the city was bad enough; in the country it was detested. The Department was aware of this too. One girl was warned in 1929 that she might be sent to 'a place where she has twice as much work to do – miles from nowhere'.[59] Farmers' wives also recognized how much girls disliked farms. Writing in 1937 of a girl who had become 'impossible', one employer added revealingly that 'she would have returned the girl before but hoped she would improve, also it was hard to get a local girl to go out on a farm'.[60]

> Dear Sir
> I am writing few lines to let you know how I am getting on. I wish that I was back at the home It is to lonely up her and I am homesick I arawant to go back to the girls home florence street. If you wonte let me go I will run away from this place. You must let me go. You must write write and let me know I want to. soon friday

Many girls disliked the loneliness and isolation of country life, as this letter from the country in 1916 makes clear.

Employers were warned that a girl's adjustment to country life would take time and that they should persist in the hope that a girl would 'settle down'.[61]

Being reminded of the pleasures of city life did not help. One mistress reported in 1936 that her state girl had been

unsettled and discontented for a time soon after Raylene Walker came to _____ but has settled down again now.

Raylene told Susan the girls in the city had a much better time than those in the country.[62]

But even if an employer were sympathetic, she might have to eventually conclude that nothing could be done 'as she is so unhappy, and now that I know it and cannot alter it in any way there will only be one remedy and that will be her removal'.[63]

Throughout the years the employment of a servant also continued to be intimately related to the fortunes of the farm. A bad season was often the reason why a state girl would have to be returned.

However, as before, some girls liked the country and were happiest in the bush. One girl, working as a shop assistant in 1935, wrote:

I am writing to ask you if I could have a country job this one is unsuitable. I am unhappy here and I wish to know if I could be shifted from here to a country place. They are hard to get on with and the early hour on Friday morning is making me tired we get up at 4ok and I go down to the shop and scrub it out and on last Sunday we were up all night and Mrs Smith complains then if I don't do things right its only because I am tired . . . but I love country life I did like Golden Grove and you can save better . . .[64]

Many girls, despite their initial despair, grew to like the country and were content to stay. The following letter of complaint was written by a girl who finally decided to stay:

I am very unhappy here. I do not like the place. Mrs Saddler is very nice but I have never liked the country would you write please and let me know when I can go back I would rather work in the school all my life than stop here . . .[65]

And there were brighter sides to life, the usual country pleasures.

If all goes well we will be going to the Tanunda display next Saturday. I think it will be very nice. I am living in hopes that the barley does not ripen to quik or we will not see it, Mr Goutmann has started to cut hay already and the busy time is cumming in fast.[66]

Violence

Letters that alleged physical violence or maltreatment towards a ward by any member of the household were always followed by prompt action whether they came from a country or city home. Trivial misdemeanours by a state girl might develop into a row where violence was inevitable.

The other day just because I broke two cups she [the mistress] was very cross. I told her that I could not help it. And she said that it was only carelessness. she said you have broke no end of things naming some of them among them she named of [sic.] vegetable Dish it was cracked before I came here and I told her that it was. I said that when I went to put the lid on the piece fell out. And she said what did you say, and I never answered her again, so she came in the bedroom where I was and said what did you say, and I told her that I said it was cracked before. So then she got old of me and pinched my arm till it was black and blue, and kicked me about a dozen times, she left two great big bruises on my hip and gave me 9 or 10 smacks in the face and said that she would not be answered back by me or anybody else.[67]

These events were found to be 'to some extent true' and this girl was removed from the service home.

More serious incidents often involved girls being struck not only with the hand.

On one occasion I was removing a small table on which lay some knives and forks, Miss Rice picked up a fork and threw it at me striking me with the prongs on the side of the face leaving a mark for about a week, the wound bled freely. When she saw what she had done she told me to go and get a basin and wash myself. The reason for striking me was because I had left the newspaper on the dining-room table.[68]

On other occasions this girl was hit with a stick by her mistress and she eventually absconded to the Millicent police to whom she told her appalling story. Miss Rice returned the girl two months later, in June 1908.

Other girls were even more severely assaulted for the most trivial reasons. Bertha Clark reported in 1912 that she had gone out

to wash my blouse and she [the mistress] came out and asked me what I was doing. and I said I was washing my blouse, and she said 'You will not wash it now' and pulled it away from me and the water splashed all over her, and she said I threw it over her, and I said I did not Mrs Wright and she said I was impudent, and then she brought the blouse inside and threw it amongst a lot of things used for the ironing - sand paper etc. She threw it there and it was quite wet, and I went to take it from there because it was getting dirty and she said I was not to and I said I would, and she tried to strike me in the face with a hot iron when I said I would not give it to her, and she burned my arm (showed the burns on arm - two places) and I would have got more only I ran into the Street . . .[69]

This girl was removed two months later on the grounds of 'mutual dissatisfaction'. Sometimes assault led other household servants to write to the Department on the girl's behalf.[70] But if physical punishment was the only way to control a girl then it was often permitted, despite a girl's complaints.

She has been caned twice on the hands in the three months she has been here and sometimes for punishment has not been allowed to sit down at the table for regular meals but has been given bread and jam or bread and dripping instead or her meal has been postponed for a few hours ... Mrs Rivers is a very nice woman but hot-tempered and impatient.

Annie has herself a very stubborn temper this is not a fresh complaint I have heard it often before, she sometimes refuses to get up or to do any work and is most sullen and defiant. She does not look like a child that is ill-treated in fact I have never seen her look so well ... Clean and neatly dressed. Mrs Rivers says unless she is allowed to punish Annie in some way she will not be able to manage her at all.[71]

Rather more disturbing than isolated incidents, however, are three separate reports about Mrs Mort, a housekeeper in the mid north in the years around the turn of the century. The first charge was a letter in 1902 from a woman who lived in the house. She alleged that the state girl who worked in the house had been ill-treated by having her nose pulled and her ears boxed. She had also been beaten on the shoulders and back with a strap and a clothes-brush. Mrs Mort was most upset when confronted with these allegations but denied that she had been unkind, saying she would have treated her own children in the same way, except perhaps for pulling the girl's nose. The girl was apparently not removed immediately.[72]

Seven months later, in 1903, another state girl herself wrote to the Department about Mrs Mort.

I took all that I thought necessary to the washhouse. Mrs Mort said I took some things that shouldn't went and then she started knocking me about she hit me across the face and it is all swollen and then she knocked me about the head ...

These events did not lead to the girl being removed. Mrs Mort was merely cautioned, and the girl remained.[73] Nine years later, in January 1912, another state girl wrote to the Department complaining that Mrs Mort had smacked her in the face. The inspector sent to investigate reported that

Mrs Mort said that upon the occasion when Lucy said she pulled her hair, she was very much annoyed as she had frequently told Lucy not to leave her room in the morning with combs and ribbons in her hair but just to coil her hair neatly – on this particular morning seeing that Lucy had again defied her she took the combs from her hair and broke them in pieces and threw them into the fire.[74]

It can be seen from these incidents that the Department continued placing girls in a home where there was a distinct likelihood that they would be assaulted. The home was said to give girls 'an excellent training', but not until this last incident in 1912 was action taken. On 30

January Lucy Troy was returned, and the file states: 'Miss Sara [an inspector] to mark the home unsuitable'.

Illness and Health

The state's provision of medical care for state wards was something less than complete. Even as children, state wards suffered financial loss through ill-health. Wards were supposed to save the banked portion of their wages until they had left the care of the state. But, in fact, if a state girl incurred certain types of medical expense, the cost of these was deducted from her savings by the Department. If a girl wanted a doctor other than the district medical officer she would have to pay from her own wages. Some girls did this.[75]

One girl who was bringing in cows on horseback, hurt her ankle when the horse fell. The local doctor charged £4 for his call, claiming he had gone out of his way to the farm. The girl was unable to pay this amount. Her service home refused to pay and sent her back to the Department, which eventually paid half the bill after taking the other half from the girl's savings.[76]

Other girls had to use part of their savings to pay dental bills. Although some girls needed minor dental attention, more wanted to have all their teeth removed and false teeth fitted so that they would be free from trouble and expense in the future (This was not uncommon in pre World War II Australia; women often 'had their teeth done' before they married to spare expense later.) Toothache could make life a misery:

I am just writing to let you know I have two very bad Teeth they are just starting to Decay I am in Real Misery they are Acking Day and Night I am to Nervoes to go and Have them out I Realy Don't no what to do I can Hardly Hold my head up to Night . . .[77]

Having a new set of teeth involved two procedures. The first part was having the decayed teeth drawn.

my intentions are to have all my teeth out. They have been aching very much this last six months. I intend having them drawn by Mr Eskell. I am therefore going to ask you if you would grant me £2-0-0 out of my Bank money as I would like to pay cash for them being drawn. That amount is then deducted from the price of the false ones.[78]

Girls in service in the country might have to wait for the travelling dentist.

I am obliged to have mine drawn or else suffer great pain . . . My mistress took me

68

to the dentist about six weeks ago . . . most likely I would have to take too lots of gas because my teeth are so scattered and he would not be able to take them out quick enough so I will have to get four teeth put in front in place of the others that are drawn and the cost will amount to £3.0.0 for the gas and teeth altogether and if you could be so kind as to send the money before the dentist comes again he will be here in three weeks . . .[79]

Having all one's teeth extracted was quite expensive. A new set of teeth for the upper jaw, for example, was considered cheap at £4 in 1905.[80] Not all girls could afford to have a new set of teeth the moment they had their own drawn. As one girl wrote to the Department, 'only I feel the want of my teeth I want to know if you will buy them out of my bank money or will I have to save my wages as I want some clothes . . .'.[81] In any case, there was always a waiting period while the gums 'set' after the teeth were extracted. Once obtained, the new teeth were usually admired.

I got my teeth in that evening but we started away before the office opened the next morning so I could not come to show them to you but they fit my mouth nicely and I can eat anything now . . .[82]

The years 1890 to 1913, while benefiting from the medical advances brought by the discovery of antisepsis and the passing of Health Acts, were still years when many state girls were ill for long periods.

Ill-health was often the result of poor nourishment. State girls were sometimes described as 'delicate' and would be prescribed cod-liver oil and extract of malt.[83] Some would be given an extra year in their foster-home so they would become strong enough for domestic service. Girls might suffer from infantile paralysis and be left with one leg shorter than the other.[84] In an age where children walked to school, this usually meant that the girl fell behind in her schooling.

Many girls complained about their health. Apart from 'extra nourishment' doctors might advise 'a change of air'.[85] It was considered rather poor if a girl rarely had anything but bread and jam or bread and butter for breakfast and tea.[86] A girl might write of her blood being in 'a poor state' and add that she needed 'Medicine for the Blood'.[87] Girls might also become 'very unwell at certain times every month' as one mistress put it, and could expect some consideration at such times.[88]

Girls suffered a whole range of minor illnesses ranging from diarrhoea and vomiting from eating too much plum pudding, to a nasal growth.[89] As children they also suffered from accidents peculiar to the household of the turn of the century, such as spraining an ankle while going after the cows or crushing a finger in the laundry mangle.

Little Doris White had the top of her Finger crushed in the Mangle I immediately telephoned Dr Morris - He came up and dressed the finger and instructed me not to touch it until Tuesday morning. You will quite understand how exceedingly sorry I am ... When I was in town yesterday she washed some Dolls clothes and this morning while I was attending to household duties inside she got Kezia to help her mangle them altho' I have repeatedly told her she must not touch the Mangle ... Doris looks a little pale but otherwise she is well and enjoyed her tea just as usual.[90]

Minor illness led to many state wards being returned by employers. A girl might be described as growing 'too quickly' and suffering from 'a slight form of St Vitus Dance', from 'want of blood', or even, in one case, from the 'overpowering' effect of sea air.[91] Recovery from infection was often a slow process. During convalescence a girl might be able to do housework, but not anything as heavy as milking cows.[92]

A significant number of complaints from girls working as servants concerned just two conditions: headaches and sore feet. Headaches might be seen as a direct outcome of the tensions and demands of being a general domestic. While middle-class women were allowed indispositions, 'vapours', and headaches as part of the feminine ideal, working women were supposed to be unrelentingly healthy. But of course they could be overworked.

I have had sick headaches ever since I been here and they have been so bad that I had to cry. I feel half dead when the day is over and I am glad to get to bed. My face was swollen up from my chin to my eye and it was so painful ... I have to milk and get wood and cart it in the wheel barrow because they have not got any boy to do it. It is a very nice place but it is to hard for me.[93]

I find the work here too much for me to do I have not been well since I have been here and of late have had such headaches as to be almost unendurable. It was only this morning that Mrs Thomas told me that she sometimes wondered if my brain did not give way a little at times as I seemed so funny but I only think it is from being over tired and these continuous headaches ...[94]

The other occupational hazard was sore feet. This might be corns and bunions, making one girl write of being able to 'hardly walk'.[95] More commonly, girls seemed to have suffered from swollen, inflamed feet, especially in hot weather. Anyone who has had to work an eight-hour day standing up during the Australian summer will recognize the way this girl felt: 'my feet have been very bad this summer I could hardly put my boots on they where that painful'.[96] Or another, who

has completely given up, as her feet are like raw meat with blue veins running through them and it is cruel to see the girl trying to hobble about the floor on her feet. She really wants proper treatment and to rest them until they are quite healed ...[97]

Conditions such as tonsillitis or an infected scratch, which today heal remarkably quickly when treated with antibiotics, sometimes required months of treatment.[98] And those three killers of children - tuberculosis, pneumonia and diphtheria - took their toll of state wards. Some, more hardy, survived them:

for about four months now I have been under the doctors care about my health he is afraid that if I am not careful I will go like my mother as she died of consumption. I have just had to leave my place as the doctor wants me to get a place where I can be out in the fresh air.[99]

She had been unwell since Tuesday and on Friday Dr Medwell who had been attending her from the first said that she had double Pneumonia. So we engaged a trained nurse (Miss Hill) as we did not want any stone unturned for her good. And on Saturday night the turn came she very nearly passed away - I suppose that we have nothing to do with the Doctor as the expense of the Nurse will come to a good bit.[1]

The availability of a motor car meant that medical treatment could now be sought more quickly, perhaps helping to save a life:

She complained of a bad headache and a sore throat. I gave her opening medicine and gargle for her throat. This morning she was no better so Mrs Reddy took her to Kadina to Dr Powell who ordered her to go to Walleroo to Hospital as she had diptheria. So Mr Reddy hired a motor car and took her to Walleroo Hospital.[2]

Statistics on infant mortality among state children began to be kept in 1911. Before that year, the numbers of wards who died under one year of age are sometimes given. Ten wards under one year of age died in 1898 for example. In 1909 epidemics swept the state, keeping infant mortality high.

It is not surprising that infant mortality among state wards was higher than that of infants in the community but it is surprising that it was so much higher. In 1911, a particularly bad year, it was 55 per cent, while infant mortality in the state was 6 per cent. The following year it was 26.6 per cent for state wards, dropping every year thereafter until it reached a low point of 1.6 per cent in 1917. The Council attributed this to 'the excellent feeding regulations provided by this Department and the careful supervision given to infants under the care of the Council'.[3]

The infant mortality rate in the Industrial School was, as one would expect, higher than that of infant wards in general. There were nine deaths among the infants in 1912. The annual report for 1912 mentioned a continuing 'influx of diseased and ailing infants'. By 1914 the Queen's Home was taking all healthy babies under one year who were committed and the Children's Hospital was taking sick babies, a far more satisfactory arrangement. The infant mortality rate of state children continued to fluctuate, though it never again reached 55 per cent. In 1920 it was 12.5 per cent and 6.7 per cent in the state overall; and in 1940 it was 5.5 per cent, as against 3.5 per cent overall.

Foster-mothers often wrote long accounts of their child's dying, as was the nineteenth century custom.[4]

She was taken ill on Thursday night last about nine o'clock ... a heavy breathing on the chest she was in the cot and I fetched her in my bed and put a mustard blister on her chest and put her feet in warm water and mustard and gave her a spoonful of caster oil and she seemed easier and slept a little and in the morning she eat a egg and a small piece of bread and butter and drank her tea and seemed much better making dolls and playing with the kitten ... [the doctor] sounded her all about the chest and looked down her throat and said she had a bad throat and I was to put her to bed as soon as I get home and I did as I was told and gave her the medecine he ordered ... such a job to keep her in bed ... and about ten on Saturday night she got worse and breathing very heavy so my husband went in for the doctor and he refused to come at night he said he could not do any more if he came he would be there in the morning early ... I could see she was getting weaker with the throughing up ... On Sunday morning she jumped up in my arms and said Mum I am dying. It nearly brakes my heart when I think of her dear little ways ... her sufferings were more than I could bare I had to get a nurse to help me up to the last she was so sensible it seemed something wonderful that she had such sense he said if the lumps kept up in her throat she would get better but if they went down she would soon be gone and it was so ...[5]

Although to me she would never say she felt unwell, only constantly complained of a pain in her side and seemed dull. But I thought she would grow out of it. But sad to say she did not ... she passed away at about half past twelve on the Saturday night. We got her ready and had the funeral to leave her at half past four sunday afternoon. They charged extra to have a decent Funeral ... She had six little girls in white as her bearers and several nice wreaths and seven traps. So we couldn't do any more or treat her any different if she was our own child.[6]

Many girls wrote to the Department for their savings within a few years of leaving the Department's care. Illness had reduced them to abject poverty. A single woman in good health *might* manage to support herself. But wages for women were based on the unspoken assumption that a woman lived at home with her family.[7] Many former state girls, especially those living in lodgings without any family support, found that illness was the last straw.

I have been ill and had to have the doctor twice and I owe him 10/- and I am out of work at present and I can't pay him ... I hate owing anybody a penny much less 10/-.[8]

I have been very ill and under two doctors with my side and have not been able to do any work for over two months in fact I worked that long in agonies of pain then I have the doctors to pay and has not a shoe on my foot . . . I always have to have my boots made to order as I could not where them if not that means 13 shillings and has not yet got a place I tried the convalescent hospital but they said I was too young. My brother having been killed at the outer harbour caused me to spend a good lot more than I would had nothing gone wrong. I had a hat dress, gloves gosmer all to get out of what little I had saved up.[9]

A single girl might also fall into arrears with her rent while ill.

I was in the Hospital with very bad legs, I had (Erytheuma nodoson) or first stages of Rheumatism I am a great deal better although the Doctor told me I was not to resume my duties at the Shop for a week or two . . . while I was in the Hospital I had to keep my room payed so as I would have some where to go when I came out of the Hospital. Well I managed to pay for one week, so now I owe a fortnight without this week and I have not a penny until I go to work . . . I can't expect my landlady to shelter me for nothing when possibly she could let my room . . .[10]

Without savings, illness could reduce a single woman to very dire straits indeed. Generosity to other ill family members was another reason why any savings would be rapidly exhausted.

I do not want to spend all of my money but I want to get Margie my Sister some things a new dress and a few more things I do not want her to spend any of her money because I don't think Margie will ever be able to do any hard work on account of her ear so I hope you will let me have my money because I can earn more and save up where Margie cant. I was going to ask you Mr Gray if Margie could have a holiday when she comes out of the Hospital I will pay her fare out of my money . . .[11]

One girl asked for

£3 0 0 of my Bank money as I have a poor sister who has had a lot of illness and has been in the Hospital so long that she is short of money and clothes and I feel it is my duty to look after her until she is able to look after herself.[12]

Letters from state girls applying for their savings in the years after they left the Department give glimpses of hard and perilous lives. To some extent this is a distorted impression since most girls only applied for their money when they were in need. There were different varieties of need and it is true some state girls applied for their money so that they could buy a present for a sister, clothing for themselves, or furniture for their parents.[13] Some simply wrote that they were 'doing very well' and wanted their savings.[14] It was not necessary to give a reason when applying for money, which was in all respects a girl's own.

Despite all, some girls were grateful to the Department and made this quite clear on their release:

I have thought at times I wish I had never been there but when I see what some girls have come to with parents I can't but be grateful to God I have had the protection of the State . . . [15]

Country life, as we have seen, was for many state wards a trial, something they had to endure. Other girls in the country and city alike, were subject to physical abuse, or to illness of a worrying or debilitating sort. But one omnipresent peril confronted all state girls – moral danger.

CHAPTER 4

Sex and Marriage
1887–1940

1887–1914

I have tried so hard for the past 12 months' and both Mr & Mrs South think there is no reason why I should not be free. I know that you have taken the past and not judged me by that but Sir have not everybody had a past; some of our Leading Gentlemen of today have had A Past and perhaps if they were judged by it they would not hold the place's they do but I do hope you will look over mine I was very foolish ...[1]

The greatest difference between the lives of male and female state wards lay in the area of sexual morality. In all areas girls were treated with a protectiveness and concern that boys never experienced.[2] In providing this protectiveness the Department reflected and enforced the social mores of the time. It attempted to impose social control on working-class girls. Boys might be larrikins; in the parlance of the time girls were 'uncontrollable'.

The State Children's Council began in 1887 with the belief that it was essential for girls to grow up in a state of innocence and modesty, well-protected not only from acquaintances who might lead them astray, but also from unseemly books or talk. It is worth remembering how strict morality was in the last two decades of the nineteenth century. Only the worldly would attend the theatre even when the best programmes were being presented. In the 1890s respectable women, as was expected of them, would leave the dress circle of Adelaide's Theatre Royal at a hint of 'suggestiveness' in a performance.[3]

Respectable women of the middle and upper class were not only preserving their own reputation, they were also supposed to be setting an example. If they followed the advice of D.E. McConnell, whose book *Australian Etiquette* was published in 1886, they would know that a lady

walks the street wrapped in a mantle of proper reserve, so impenetrable that insult and coarse familiarity shrink from her, while she, at the same time carries with her

75

a congenial atmosphere which attracts all, and puts all at their ease.

A lady walks quietly through the streets, seeing and hearing nothing that she ought not to see and hear, recognising acquaintances with a courteous bow, and friends with words of greeting. She is always unobtrusive, never talks loudly, or laughs boisterously, or does anything to attract the attention of the passers-by. She walks along in her own quiet lady-like way, and by her preoccupation is secure from any annoyance to which a person of less perfect breeding might be subjected.[4]

This was the attitude the State Children's Department thought should be instilled into state girls. Girls found that gaiety and boisterousness would be interpreted as immodesty. Again and again the rudiments of respectable behaviour were drilled into their doubting heads.

be more careful in making acquaintances with lads until you know something about them and their family. You may think perhaps this debars you from knowing anyone – that is not so – anyone worth knowing should become acquainted with you in the ordinary way by a proper introduction, when you will have an opportunity of knowing something of their family, and their antecedents.[5]

This sort of concern was also felt in the community. A girl might need the care and control of the Department because 'All her thoughts, and money is spent on dress and young men. . . . I cannot bear the thought of a young life drifting away from all that is pure'.[6] She might be 'too young to be at large . . . for she is so easily lead to wrong'.[7] Guiding a girl through the years between puberty and marriage was so difficult a task that a few parents even asked the state to take over the management of their daughters:

I am a labourer but not physically fit for very heavy work, a widower, and have four children three girls and a boy, and cannot afford to employ any one to look after the children, indeed my being able to go far away to work it is with great difficulty that I can earn enough for food for them and we have only a one roomed hut to live in. If your Board would receive the three girls - ages about 8, 11 and 12 I should be very grateful and would do what is possible towards their maintenance – the boy is older (14) and can go to work with me.[8]

The daughters of this man became state wards. Another solitary man who feared for his daughters' morals wrote to have the girls placed where they would be 'looked after'.[9] More rarely, a mother felt that her absence at work all day put her daughters at risk. In a few instances widows wrote in about their daughters.[10] In very rare cases a girl herself would appeal to the Department if she felt in moral danger.[11] But usually it was the police, Departmental inspectors, or anonymous letter-writers who discovered the girl 'on the brink of ruin'.

Foster-parents and employers were expected to protect young girls. They frequently wrote to the Department seeking guidance on the 'fine print' of their mandate.

I find for the past 3 months she has been very disobedient, neglects her work and several times a week makes a practice of going out at night and remaining out till 10 and 11 o'clock with a young man John North who is now working with Mr West a chaff cutter at Freeling. I find he is a worthless fellow and in indigent circumstances, I have forbidden Maud either to see or speak to him.[12]

I have asked her to go to Sunday School, where she could meet with girls of the Friendly Aid Society and she does not care to that is too much restriction in her estimation ... I certainly cannot spare her to go out in the afternoon to walk about the Semaphore with girls she may casually meet. I have tried to get Florrie girls for companions that are respectable and older than she, not girls who giggle if they see a boy in the street, and am quite willing that she should go out with them but they work in the day and Florrie is at liberty to go to their homes if they write ... I think it would be a revelation to even you who has had so much to do with children if you could hear her conversation when she is speaking with any one she is familiar with ... If she goes out it takes her 15 minutes to dress but if she simply tidys herself in the afternoons it needs 30 minutes, all these things speak for themselves.[13]

Some employers took considerable trouble to protect and control the young domestic in their charge and judged their success partly by the impression the girl created in the district. The following letter was written from a town in the mid north in 1912:

Ella has made a good impression among the residents here so far as to be spoken of by the elder people as that nice mannered little girl from Mrs David's. I will also say that during Mr David's absence she has done all she possibly can and freely done it to assist me ... It is for Ella's sake we guard her well as if in the future she intends to settle in this neighbourhood it would be a great pity if she lost the good social standing she as a newcomer has gained as the daughters of the most respected homes are at present quite friendly with her. It is for the same reason, namely undesirable escorts joining her that we are afraid to let her ride out alone, as it is long and lonely roads in these parts. She has plenty of social enjoyment and company in the home as several young men and maidens visit here and treat Ella on terms of perfect equality. We allow them the free use of the home and the organ.[14]

One of the Department's chief aims was to prevent girls falling into 'bad company'. This might involve the help of employers who were expected to inform the Department of any dubious friendships a girl might make; in other cases it meant cautioning the parents of girls released on probation. Employers would write about a girl stopping to talk 'to swagmen under the bridge' whenever she was sent on a message.[15] If a girl went on unchaperoned outings it was agreed she might become the prey of 'very undesirable young men' who would flirt with her but have 'no intentions of an honourable kind in the future'.[16]

Improper company was not always as strictly defined as this. Very often it was as much a particular locality as a type of person. Girls had to be kept away from 'bad associates' in Port Adelaide or the 'temptation' of Glanville, both poor, working-class areas.[17] Close examination would be made of any relatives who tried to have a girl released from the control of the State Children's Council. A girl was not likely to be released to a married sister who was

in the habit of having frequent very noisy parties both in their own home and elsewhere. They entertain large numbers of young fellows and girls who seem of a low type. These parties usually take place on a Saturday and continue until 3 or 4 on a Sunday. By the time they disperse the 'party' appears to get very 'gay' with drink.[18]

Some families were completely 'beyond redemption'. If the girls in such families were young, there might be some point in removing them but if they were over eighteen or nineteen there seemed to be little point, especially if they had already succumbed to 'temptation'.[19]

Employers and inspectors for the Department were also expected to report any tendency towards improper behaviour on the part of girls. This might be a small thing like calling out 'very bold things' to men passing the house, talking to the children of the house in a way thought 'evil', or it might be something much more serious.[20] If there was the slightest doubt about proper behaviour the Department had to be consulted. Sometimes an employer would persuade a girl to write so that a potential source of conflict might be eliminated:

I am just writing a few lines to ask your advice on a certain matter. A young man residing in this neighbourhood wishes to pay his attention to me. I told him he may and then he asked me to go for a drive occasionally with him on a Sunday afternoon. Do you think it would be improper for me to do so provided my mistress allows me. Of course I should always ask her. I think he is a nice young man. My mistress speaks well of him and she also allows him to visit at her house.

In this instance the matter was referred to the Council and the secretary had to write informing the girl of their refusal.

The Council, however did not think it well for you to do this, and would prefer you to attend Sunday school as you have been doing in the past, and for the

Girls were expected to grow up to be innocent and modest, well protected not only from acquaintances who might lead them astray, but also from unseemly books or talk. A state girl, circa 1912.

young man to visit at your home in the way that Mrs Tombs has been kind enough to allow.[21]

Employers were also expected to protect state girls against the attraction of the workmen on the property. This was particularly a problem in the country at harvest time when workmen were likely to be living near the house. A respectable state girl would ideally reserve her company for a man of means who would approach her with an honourable lack of haste. For the state girl the company of her fellow workers was supposed to be avoided. She was urged to behave with decorum and reserve however lonely or in need of friendship she felt.

Time and time again, employers wrote querulously about 'dangers' that wards seemed not to see.

Mr Lennox thinks it best for me to mention also that Eva is not fit to be where there are so many working men kept. I don't mean that Eva has done anything worse than make quarrels among the men, and as this is such a busy time for Farmers it makes it hard to lose them and there are two of them will leave us if Eva does not go back.[22]

Feeling that she is in our care while with us, I have always impressed upon her that she is to have nothing to do with the men and workboys and she gives me a good deal of trouble in that respect for she flatly disobeys me. Today she has been three times at least over to our cheese business room (where there are two men working) expressly against my orders . . . I like her she is so willing and unselfish and good-hearted . . .[23]

Some girls were considered so weak that they were not responsible.

At certain periods she cannot restrain herself from temptations of Sexuality and if Alex is about the stable or anywhere in sight she makes a special effort to get to him. Mrs Willis and my mother keep her under guard by day but the risk is at night she could easily leave her room without being heard . . .[24]

Some state girls, however, found no trouble in 'being good'. Girls might write to the Department stating their good intentions, especially if they were bored by men who were interested in them.

Mr Houlgrave seemed to have some misdoubts as to whether I would go and live [with] him if he asked me. Dear Sir, I have a soul to save as well as the rest of the world and I think more of myself than to sink so low as to listen to the complimentary remarks passed. I do not wish to praise or dispraise myself . . . but I can assure you you need not think I would have anything to do with that man at any time.[25]

Even girls who appeared 'bold looking' by contemporary standards were sometimes found by their mistresses to be 'quite the reverse – is very timid and is very quiet and well-behaved when she has to go to the village which is about a furlong from our house'.[26] On occasion a girl would be pursued to such an extent that her decorum would be strongly tested. One mistress wrote about a chance meeting:

She used to 'walk' with him at Kadina. After she left there she never heard anything of him, until the day she was with the children in Martin's waiting for the performance of 'Robinson Crusoe'. She was in the crowd and asked a young fellow in front of her what time the affair would start – when he turned to answer her she recognised him and asked him if he remembered her etc. Then came his letter which she did not answer. He tried to get her by 'phone but got me instead![27]

Later developments in this friendship illustrate one of the major grievances of domestic servants, commented on by Jessie Ackermann[28] among others – the problem of where they could meet their young man without incurring the wrath of their mistress.

I am giving Nell a good many privileges but am not prepared to give up my sitting room or provide a piano for the entertainment of her visitors. Neither does she strike me as being the sort who would expect it. The young man may think differently – Is he not prepared to give up an occasional Saturday afternoon for Nell.[29]

State girls were often assumed to have 'wayward tendencies' by both their guardians and the Department so that merely innocent or silly activities might be treated as first steps on 'a downward path'.

The historian Gertrude Himmelfarb has argued that 'the image of uninhibited sexuality was part of the contemporary image of poverty' in Victorian England.[30] State wards themselves often recognized that they were regarded this way. One girl wrote to her boyfriend in 1913:

I have quite enough boys now hanging around. Everyone I meet are all the same bold as they can be. I dont think boys love me alone but they know I am slightly warm so they hang around. It doesn't matter where I go its all the same . . . If ever you see me talking to other boys don't think for one moment I would not have anything to do with you again.

> I remain yours for ever
> Sure as grapes grow on the Vine
> I'll be yours if you'll be mine.[31]

State girls could not afford to be mischievous or fun-loving in regard to young men for to do so would sully their reputation. The Department took very seriously the illicit letters it intercepted whether the author lived in the country or the city.

Dear Rose,

I thought I would just write you a few lines and let you know how I am getting on I . . . have the best fun out you ask me was there any nice boys up here there is any mount of them such nice boys I have got a real beauty up here I could have a fresh one every Sunday if I like but one is enough for he takes me to church every Sunday horseback but you must not go telling father or any of them tell Vi what fun I am having . . . my bloke is waiting to take me to church that is twenty miles so we have a good long ride together I will tell you all when I come home.[32]

I am just going to send a short note over by Johnny this morning to ask you how you got home Saturday night with those two darling boys especially the driver. I hope Mrs Sims was not cross with you as I am sure it was after ten o'clock when you got home What are you going to do Sunday if you are going into the Bay in the Evening plan to meet me about eight o'clock somewhere . . . Mrs Summers is going away for a week after next week. Then we reckon on having some fun now dear Betty I think this is enough . . . it is also Josie's day out tomorrow so I will be all on my own Mrs Summers has been asked out to spend the day in town.[33]

A letter intercepted by the Department was one way that 'foolishness' in relation to young men could be stopped. Having one's mistress report one to the Department was another:

Leah is still acting very foolishly. A young fellow under 19, has seen her home for the 1st time, last Sunday and this evening she has him in the kitchen unbeknown to us playing Ludo. True we know him very well and believed him to be a decent fellow, but not suited to look after her for he is not able to look after himself.[34]

She tells me there are too many young lads who come to see this girl and as she is rather fast and they have to employ men about the place they feel that it would be wise to get rid of her as they have to be constantly on the watch. What shall I do with her, I don't think she is really bad but a silly girl . . . [35]

Other, more reckless girls were judged to be not merely silly but 'bad'. This did not mean that they had had a sexual relationship with a man at all. To 'lose one's reputation' meant only to defy the standards of the time, to engage in what, in an age of tight lacing and straight backs, was called 'loose behaviour'. It meant putting oneself in a situation where intimacies could possibly occur. A girl might begin by being 'fast and familiar with every boy and man about the place' or be seen by a sharp-eyed mistress 'two or three times in the town streets with different young men each time'.[36] More serious was the girl who did not come home till

10 o'clock when she came in the company of a 'gentleman'. She stayed out under the trees opposite my house. I sent out my other servant for her and she refused to come in and stayed there for an hour longer. My son says the man had his arms around her and she says that she has only met him once before. I cannot be burdened with the responsibility of a girl who is simply determined to go wrong and about whose future I regret to say . . . I know will be a very sad and hopeless one.[37]

Acting on one's own initiative without first seeking the advice or sanction of one's mistress was another way of bringing condemnation down on oneself. What had actually happened was not particularly important – any secret activity with men was disreputable. Many girls covertly attempted to relieve the monotony of existence without the vulnerability that acting alone would have brought. This mixture of responsibility and casualness is shown in an inspector's account of Emma Connell who went for a walk at another girl's suggestion when

all the family were out except Mrs Ellis's mother who is an invalid . . . when her work was finished they both went out. They met this man and all three went to the wharf. She returned and gave the invalid her tea and in the evening Jenny Hyde and Emma Connell walked up and down outside and after they remained in the back verandah together waiting for Mrs Ellis's return . . .[38]

The letter below, written from Port Elliot in 1910, shows the same mixture of bravado and commonsense.

Dear old Ada

I suppose I will get a good grumbling at next time I get a letter from you for keeping you waiting so long for an answer, well Kiddy not my fault (as usual) . . . how is the Cook getting on with her bloke my dear if it was me he had to deal with he would not play the fool I can tell him if he wanted to put it off he would put it off for ever or not at all dam it all. I show them they cannot play with me they just think they can do what they like now a days go with you one day somebody else the next but show them that you don't care a dam for them if they turn that bisness on you and they will turn and chase you then you mark my words for it Ada.

I tried it on so I know their was a few young fellows staying down here Christmas time from Town of course because they were Townes they thought they would show off a bit and have a bit of fun with the Port Elliot girls because they evidently thought we were a lot of country mugs and would think it grand to be seen walking around with the Town boys well to tell the truth so some of them did but not this chicken, two or three of my pals and I had been watching these boys for a few nights so we went out one night with our minds made up to tell them what we thought of them if they asked us to go down the rocks we said to each other we would go but all go together not one one way and one the other because I wouldn't trust the young Devils enough to go on my pat well there were

83

3 of these boys used to go out together so this night 3 of us girls goes out they did not know the boys neither did I but I had been introduced to them and they had asked me to go out to or 3 times with them but I refused every time because I was on my owne but that night we were all out together so we thought we would give them what they wanted ... up comes the three of them all raised their hats good evening Miss Wright so of course I introduced the other two then they said come for a walk so we all said we would rather go down on the rocks as it was rather hot so off we went well look her Ada we gave them nothing we told them what we thought of them and a little more and would you believe me when we said good night to them they said we hope to have the pleasure of your company another night if you will allow us so I turned around to the one that said it and I said I thought perhaps you would have had enough of our company tonight so they all said now look here I mean if you are the 3 most sensible girls we have met since we came down here we like to see a girl that can hold her own ground ... the girls we have met since we came we could say and do just what we liked and they never said boo, well Ada we went out several times after that with those boys and a more sensible lot you would not wish to meet and we write to them now, ... a boy is what you make him let any boy see he can take a mean advantage and he will take it, but don't give him a chance and he won't expect it.[39]

The girl to whom the long, affectionate, worldly letter was addressed was having a boring time.

My Dear Florence
   What struck you old girl you sent me a bonzer letter the longest you have sent for many a long day I was needless to say jolly glad to get it I am dash lonely up here we have not got cook yet, you asked me about Rose she has taken another place up at Strath a cook getting 25/– a week at Lady Wyatts. I bet there is plenty to do and she do it for the money she is an old terror for money ... Now about yourself you are a dash little flirt ... you make yourself so darn attractive you must be getting jolly Handsome. Wait till you come down to town I won't allow it then I am just longing to see you again but I suppose I will have to muster up patenc [sic.] till you come down here. I am going to town on Wednesday for the day wish it was for good I am sick of the sight of Mt Lofty and all its inhabitants there is not a dash place where I can enjoy myself there is a dance up here every Saturday night but we are not allowed to go out that night ... I did not go to the fortune teller I had not got the pluck to go alone so I went to the theatre instead you know I have a hobby for it every chanc I get I am off there I do think its grand. I went to hear a lecture (Tues) the night I got you[r] letter by the way I got one from my old fostermother the same night so between them I did not know what the lecture was like ...[40]

Other girls seem to have rushed into deep water more quickly. A girl might leave her room one evening 'after 9 o'clock' and be 'seen about Glenelg with lads' or it might be even more serious.[41]

Last evening after the girl had gone to bed Miss Rudd finding the house draughty went into the girl's bedroom & saw the window wide open. She asked the girl why she had it open, when looking behind the door she discovered a boy Tom Young in the room dressed only in his shirt – When discovered he jumped out of the window Lucy Kay was dressed only in her night dress . . . Y. sleeps in a cottage some way from the house . . . the same age as Lucy but very much younger in appearance and knowledge. [She] professes to regard it as quite an innocent thing to allow the boy to sleep in her room.[42]

But the Department took it very seriously and Lucy, who was over thirteen years of age, was sent to the Girls' Reformatory. Any possibility of sexual intercourse having occurred was usually enough to ensure that girls were sent to the Reformatory. The secretary wrote of one girl who had absconded from her place of service in 1907

in company with a young man. She went to the same home as he shared as an employee. She was arrested there on Tuesday and has acknowledged some very questionable conduct with young men and there is strong reason to suspect more than that. In view of this and her past very sad experiences I have transferred her to the Reformatory at Redruth where I hope she may be brought to see the folly of her past conduct.[43]

An illicit letter sometimes put a girl under the same cloud.[44] The Department tried to keep some girls away from men completely. The matron of the Industrial School wrote of one girl: 'I cannot trust her anywhere about where the boys are and feel sure she would be better in a home where there are only females'.[45] There was also an assumption that girls were far more likely to be led astray in early adolescence, and that they would be more 'sensible' by the time of their release at eighteen to twenty-one. Ultimately it was hoped girls would be able to resist temptation after their release, like the girl who wrote:

I am just writing to you about the situation I went out to North Adelaide to see about, I found that it was not at all a suitable place for a young girl, as the man was living in the house alone, his wife is dead, and of course I could not live in the house alone with him.[46]

Throughout the period 1887 to 1913 there was a concern with the 'uncontrollable' girl, a notion and description which indicates a great deal about what a 'good' girl was supposed to be like. A girl would be called uncontrollable if she was left alone at home all day and the neighbours noticed her passing time in the streets or if she allowed men into the house in the absence of her parents. Very often such girls, the daughters of widows, were preoccupied with looking after younger children, but in some cases they were reported to be doing as they pleased.[47] In 1902, for example, the police reported that the daughter of a washerwoman

has larrikins in the house and several times the neighbours have complained of her conduct and nightly she walks the Streets till about 11 pm in Company with boys and girls of low repute.[48]

Alcohol and a dislike of work were part of the uncontrollable girl's vices.

Constable L.C. Booth reports that the girl Victoria is in the habit of loitering about the streets in the evening and on the Park Lands with larrikins ... She often stays out all night and gets under the influence of liquor. Her father is in constant employment and could pay something towards her support.[49]

He states that she is quite uncontrollable he has got several situations for her but she ran away from them. She often remains out until 3 in the morning and on several occasions all night with the boys. The family cannot do anything with her. The neighbours also state that she is a very bad Girl. The mother and father have been dead for several years. There are 6 in family ... the one in question is the youngest. She was 15 last September.[50]

Another girl was described as 'bold and impudent and evidently beyond the control of her grandmother'. A period as a domestic servant in a distant country town was recommended for her.[51]

One step worse than loitering about the streets was to be seen in the company of women of 'low repute'. There appears to have been a sophisticated grading system for such women. Sometimes they might be referred to as 'women of loose character' but on other occasions the description would be more forthright:

The constable has seen her speaking to prostitutes on several occasions and has cautioned her but she seems to take no notice ... her mother states that she is unable to control her and would like to send her to the reformatory school.[52]

Prostitution probably began as early as the infant colony of South Australia, and certainly it was so flamboyant a 'social evil' by 1867 that a special report was presented to the House of Assembly detailing ways in which the evils of prostitution could be lessened.[53] But despite the efforts of reformers, prostitution persisted. The police were eventually able to 'rank' the city's prostitutes, writing in 1909 that a woman was 'a courtesan and not of the higher class either'.[54]

Prostitution was very much part of city life when C.A. Chandler investigated the world of the pimp and prostitute in 1907. He found that the 'beastly bludger' was thriving in the city, especially in Hindley,

Flinders, and Franklin Streets, and in betting clubs and billiard rooms. Prostitutes were especially common in North Terrace and Elder Park, and there were dozens of child prostitutes aged eleven and twelve. He mentions, too, that clients of such places included the staff of Government House, ministers, leading politicians, lawyers, and other professional men. Indeed, there were 'such a lot of gentlemen cads about that it was unsafe for a respectable woman to stand in the streets to wait for a tram'.[55] Rosina Street was a well-known place for prostitutes to work.[56] Houses at 44 Wakefield Street and 2 Kent Street were also well-known brothels in 1907 according to one of the Department's inspectors.[57]

Prostitution may have appeared attractive to the uncontrollable girl who disliked domestic service but the reality was sordidly different. In 1902 a girl of thirteen was introduced to prostitution by an older married woman whom she knew slightly. The girl, Dora, was the daughter of a plumber and lived in Parkside, an inner suburb. The older woman, Mrs Hyde, encountered Dora who was returning from an employment agency and asked her to go to the bay at Glenelg.[58]

She paid the train fares for the two of us. We stopped at the Bay till 10 pm. We met a man on the beach near a merry go round which was there, she spoke to the man, and he asked us to have a ride on the merry go round, the three of us had a ride on it We then went to an Hotel at Glenelg and had drinks, I had a glass of Ginger Stout, all three of us then came to town in the train, went down King William Street and to the North Terrace Railway Station. The man went away in the Port train.

A few days later Mrs Hyde met a man on the western side of Victoria Square late on a Wednesday evening, still with Dora in tow.

She spoke to this man and he walked home with us to Mrs Cleese's house, it was then about 1 o'clock. The man went out and bought two bottles of ale, they drank the ale, Mrs Hyde made me up a bed in the front room and I went to bed. The man and Mrs Hyde went to bed in the front room also. They were not in the room when I went to bed. They were in the front verandah There was no light in the room, they went to bed in the dark, I don't know if they undressed they were whispering in bed and Mrs Hyde was laughing. In the morning when I woke up she was in bed undressed, but the man was gone.

Later that day Dora went with Mrs Hyde and they got a room at 217 King William Street. Dora, Mrs Hyde, and her two sons all slept in one room and when Mrs Hyde brought men home to the room, Dora slept in a single bed and the two boys on the floor.

She had been with Mrs Hyde about four weeks when one Saturday night two men came home with Mrs Hyde, having picked her up near the King's Head Hotel.

it was between 10 & 11 pm then, the children were asleep in the room, I was in the bedroom and had the candle alight, they had some drink I did not have any drink, one of the men blew out the candle, Mrs Hyde said to me the four of us can sleep in the bed, Sam can sleep with you I will sleep with Johnny, I did not want to do this, and would not go to bed for a long while afterwards. They all undressed and got into bed in the dark afterwards and then I undressed and got into bed, after we were in bed a little while the man called Johnny had connection with Mrs Hyde and after they had stopped Sam got on top of me and had connection with me, he hurt me a good deal (This was the first time I ever had connection with either man or boy) Sam had connection with me again about an hour afterwards, I went to sleep after that, and the two men went away early in the morning. I said to her next morning, I think I had better go from here, she said don't go home I wouldn't if I were you. I saw Sam give her 3/- on the Sunday morning and he said give that to Dora I said I dont want it and she kept the money.[59]

Sam and Johnny came back several nights later and also on the following Saturday night. After that Mrs Hyde moved again to a house in Little Mill Street where she rented a room and there, a week later, Dora's father ordered her to come home. She twice ran away from home to rejoin Mrs Hyde who shortly afterwards was charged by police with 'Being the occupier of a house (and allowing) a girl under 17 years to resort therein for immoral purposes'. Dora was sent to the Girls' Reformatory.[60]

Other wards were sexually exploited, drifting into traps set by the more worldly. In 1903 two young absconders from the Salvation Army Home walked around the streets late at night until they met two young men who

took us to pie stall and paid for food for us. They took us to a place and Mary and I slept there. They asked us to meet them at same place next morning. We met them next morning about 10 o'clock. We went down to Queen's Hall . . . One young man's name was Andrew the other was Davey. Davey played the piano and Andrew showed us some pictures which rolled up and down on platform. Davey then played piano. Andrew was dancing by himself. Andrew called Mary into the room said he wanted to show her some things. The door was just on the jar. I saw them go into the room. Did not shut the door. I heard Mary call out Oh don't and heard them struggling. Then Davey took me into a place from Gallery. It was a dark room. No windows in it. Could show anyone room. Patchwork carpet on floor. Davey was kissing me and putting his arms around me. He picked me up in his arms and put me on the floor. I said Don't do that. It wasn't what a respectable young fellow should do to a young girl. He disarranged my clothes. He undone my clothes and did something to me. He did something rude. He got on top of me. My clothes were disarranged when he got on top of me. He tried to do something. I tried to get up but he kept me down. I was singing out. I stayed like that on the floor for 10 minutes. He put something into me. I felt something. He then got up. He walked away from me but not out of the room. Then said 'would you like to get your hair tidy before you go out' I said yes. He took me where Mary and

Andrew were. Mary was doing her hair. Andrew was standing watching her. Andrew said to Mary What lovely hair you have. We went out into the room Davey gave Mary some money to get dinner with and Davey gave me 1/6. Left them about 1 o'clock. They told us to meet them again at 4 o'clock at Queen's Hall.[61]

When they met the young men again almost exactly the same events took place. The men continued to pay for meals and beds and took them to a lecture in the town hall and for walks around the city streets. After three days of this Davey and Andrew disappeared, probably because their picture show travelled to another town. Neither of the girls ever saw them again. The girls were arrested by the police and sent to the Reformatory. In the eyes of the Department they were already 'bad girls', as the medical examination they were subjected to after their arrest disclosed that neither girl had been a virgin when attacked.

This was not something about which there was any debate. If a girl could be shown, in any way, to be what the moralists of the day saw as 'bold' or 'loose' then it was highly unlikely that she would succeed in claiming that she had been raped. What happened to two girls who did dare to assert through the courts that they had been sexually assaulted illustrates the hypocrisy and cruelty of society's attitudes to sexual offences against working-class women.

Both girls were working in country towns. The first girl brought a charge of rape against a young man but the charge was dismissed 'on the ground that the girl according to the medical evidence had had intercourse with other men and had been unduly free with the prisoner prior to the alleged offence'.[62] The second girl, a servant, who charged a man with assault in 1891, had been asked by the son of the overseer of the station to get him some dinner. Before she could do so he seized her and took her down a passage and into a bedroom. A struggle ensued during which her clothing was stained and also slightly torn, but the assault stopped short of actual rape. The cook, finding her in tears in the kitchen half an hour later, took the state girl in charge and went to a neighbour's house and next day into the town to the police.

During her account at the trial the lawyer for the defence tried to snare the girl in her own words, contrasting what she had told to the police with what she was now saying. The magistrate too left no doubt where his sympathies lay:

Mr Daniel pressed her to swear definitely whether she did or did not tell the police that he carried her into the room and she hesitated as if trying to recollect. She again said she did not think she did. Counsel still pressed her and there was a long pause. The SM said she must answer the question, and must not keep the court so long. As she was the prosecutrix they had a right to hear all her statements. If she were a mere witness he would send her to gaol if she would not answer. The girl began crying and after further hesitation said, 'I will swear I did not tell the police he picked me up in the hall and carried me into the dressing room'. Mr Daniel then pressed her to say why she hesitated so long to answer . . .

The girl was·rather inadequately represented by a police inspector and the judge ordered that the case be dismissed, notwithstanding district opinion.[63]

Despite the efforts of the State Children's Department to protect state girls, most sexual assaults seem to have taken place not on the streets of the city but in the homes where wards worked.[64] Most girls were shocked when they were assaulted and reported the incident out of indignation.

On Thursday evening I was in my room about half past eight. I was undressing to go to bed. Mr Souter opened the door and came into my room. He said May have you finished in my bedroom, if so go and blow the light out. I had just taken my dress off. I went to Mr Souter's room to blow out the light. He followed me. As I blew out the light he caught me round the neck pulling his arm round it and said 'Kiss me dear'. I said let me go. He said no stay here and held me by my arms. I wrenched myself away and went back to my room and to bed locking the door.

The next morning the Friday the 16th February I was in the kitchen putting something in the safe. Mr Souter came into the kitchen and said Have you cleaned my boots May. I said Yes Sir. He came to me and felt my breasts. I said stop it please Sir and he went away to the front of the house.

This was about ¼ to nine and at about half past nine I told Mrs Souter She said I am sorry. I know my husband is a bad man. I said I want to leave. She said I don't want you to go.[65]

Most commonly it was the master of the house who sexually assaulted a state girl, using his authority to subdue her or, if that was not sufficient, physical force. There is no way of telling how many girls were raped by their employers. Certainly only a very small percentage (less than 1 per cent) of girls actually gave birth to an illegitimate child (see Appendix 4). Then as now, reporting a rape was not easy. State girls had to give signed testimony to a policeman who took the details down in longhand. They had to have a vaginal examination by a doctor, which was possibly made more unpleasant for a woman by the ignorance and mores of the age.

Rape would seem to have been more common in the country, possibly because farm life provided more opportunities for assaults.

The first time he had improper intimacy with me was in one of the paddocks over the hill out of sight of the house towards Bendley. I had taken his dinner out to him. The boy was at school. This was in harvest time. It must have been in November 1889. It occurred again about a week afterwards one morning when I took him his lunch. It occurred after that quite often. I said nothing about it to anyone . . . The first time he did it he promised me a side-saddle but he did not give it to me.[66]

Girls from the Redruth Girls' Reformatory on a picnic circa 1918. Redruth Reformatory was a former gaol near Burra which housed as many as thirty-five girls before being closed in 1922.

Farm life usually meant that a state girl would be far from the house, and alone at times.

I went down to the barn. It was between 8 or 9 o'clock. I do not know what day of the week. Mrs Braun sent me with a message. It was something about the wheat they were bagging up or picking. I saw Mr Braun there was noone else there. I told Mr Braun the message I do not know he said. It was raining hard and I waited. Whilst I was waiting Mr Braun got hold of me by the arms. He pushed me up against some bags of wheat. He held me there and I struggled to go get away. Mr Braun pulled my clothes and did something else. Something did happen. Mr Braun put his hands between my legs and he put something that was between his own legs into me. That was the first time such a thing ever happened to me . . .

Mrs Braun was out and he came into the separator room and it was quite dark. He asked me something about the Separator. I did not understand. He came in to see himself. I went to go out. Mr Braun shut the door and stood in front . . . I struggled and he threw me to the floor. He pulled my dress up and did the same as before . . . [67]

If a pattern of brutality and threats had already been established, rape became a cruel extension of that brutality.

Mr Hart used to thrash me with a whiplash. He whipped me for being late at school and for not learning to say grace at table. He told me that he would thrash me if I told any one what he did. About the end of the year that I was sent there I was in the garden picking up apples after dinner. I was alone and Mr Hart came to me. He gathered up some apples. He said lie down under the tree so that no one can see you Victoria. I did not lie down. He pushed me down on the grass under the tree he lifted up my clothes. I was lying on my back. He lifted up my skirt and turned them up over my face He then unfastened my drawers and pushed them down to my ankles. He undid the fly of his trousers. He was kneeling between my feet when he did this. He then got on top of me and put his person into mine . . . I said you are hurting me. He did not answer. I was crying all the time.[68]

Sometimes it was a workman who assaulted a state girl.

he is continually seeking for opportunities to speak with her alone, and often comes to the cowyard when she is milking. He has several times made improper overtures to her in veiled sentences accompanied by unmistakeable signs and once when she told him he ought to have more self respect than to go on like that he replied 'I am not going to do anything without your consent but if I can get your consent I won't answer for what I may do'.[69]

Other state girls were raped by farm workers in the kitchen of the house or by 'gentlemen' they met on city streets.[70] It was an age when working-class girls seem to have been regarded as easy prey for middle-class men, and rape was an aspect of class oppression, not random violence from male to female. Ignorance did not help; when girls reported rape they had no words to accurately describe the outrage.

One girl who fought for days against rape was Florence Wright. As we have seen, she was quite able to deal with 'town boys' when they descended on Port Elliot in the summer season. But her employer's nephew was far more menacing. What had begun as flirtation was rapidly developing into something much more dangerous.

The next time I was alone in the house he came again and sat in the kitchen talking. I gave him a cup of tea and was sitting on the table drinking mine. He drew his chair close to me pulled me off the table onto his lap. He began kissing me again. I said leave me alone. He said I wont make you kiss me. I said I wont kiss you. He said because you want me to keep you where you are. I won't let you go without you do. I said what do you think Mrs Jacka would say if she knew you came here while she was out. He said I have a right to come when I like. I said but you should leave me alone. He then began flattering me and kissing me – I said what would Mrs Jacka say. He said you would not tell her for your own sake. You have no proof my word is as good as yours. Are you going to tell her. I said no. I would not like her to know but if you come again I will. He said I wont let you go till you promise not to tell her. I then promised not to tell her for my own sake . . .
In February Mrs Jacka went to Strathalbyn to stay. She was away about 3 days.

She sent me to her mothers while she was away. I had to come back to get my own blanket and put the silver away this was one evening about 8 pm. Ed came to meet me on my return. He carried the basket. When we were nearly home he said where are they going to put you to sleep tonight . . . I said upstairs. He said what room. I said No 6. He said I might walk in my sleep tonight. I said Whatever do you mean. He said Come and have a look at you. I said you had better not do anything of the sort . . . He said you have not tasted any of the pleasure of life yet. I said I dont want to. He said say yes and I'll give you one now. I said you'll do nothing of the sort.

About a fortnight ago he came here. The family were at the Harbour I was upstairs ironing and was just leaving Mrs Jackas room. He came halfway up the stairs. He said hello Florence Old girl. I said what are you doing here. He said Come to have a look at you. He came right up stairs. He said I take a great interest in you and kissed me. I said I am going down goodness knows what baby will do . . . [the baby] went into the front bedroom. I went after him. Ed came and sat on the bed. He pulled me down on his knee. He kissed me . . . He said thats how you feel you are an off-handed little devil Florence. He said when was the flag up last. I said what do you mean. He said how nice it is to be innocent. I wish I was like you I'll tell you in plain English. He said when did you have your Courses last. I said you have no right to ask me such a question. He said there is no harm in telling me that. I said I am not going to tell you. He said has your boy never asked you. I said no. He said He's a fool. He said I know when it was. It was three days ago. What harm in having one now. I said indeed I won't I never did such a thing in my life and I am not going to now. He said you are going to want to if you are married. I said I am not going to get married. He said then why not take the chance while you have got it. That is all men marry you for. I said is it. I said there is time and moderation in all things. He said there is no time like the present. Take the chance while you have got it. He then pushed his hand under my clothes. He pushed me back on the bed . . . I said get out you Coward and began to cry.

What happened next was not, it seems, unusual around 1910. Some men told state girls that they would not become pregnant as long as they had intercourse standing up. Ed continued by showing Florence a box of contraceptives.

He said You are frightened. I said Yes. He said There's nothing to be frightened of. You need not be frightened of me: I would not get you in a 'fix' for the world. I don't blame you for not going with every Dick, Tom and Harry but they would not care a hang if they did – I do. He said I'll tell you what I'll do. Did you ever see any of these. (He showed me a sealed box containing three things like lumps of soap) He said they were 'soluable pessaries'. I said you ought not to carry them. Where did you get them. He said if you use one of these no harm can come to you. Half the married people use them. I said I don't care.

He caught hold of me and tried to push me back on the bed. I cried. He let me go. He said I'll let you go this time Flo. Thousands of boys would have jumped on top of you by now.[71]

Florence finally escaped minutes later by promising that she would let Ed 'give her one' (to use his phrase) when her employer went to town. The Department reacted immediately her letter arrived and removed her from the district.

Some girls were too frightened to mention they had been sexually assaulted. Very often it was only if they became pregnant that the nature of the assault came to light at all.

Pregnancy for an unmarried state girl was a disaster of overwhelming magnitude. To the stigma of being a state ward was added this most public confirmation that she really was a 'bad' girl. From an economic viewpoint, pregnancy meant it was usually impossible for the state girl to remain independent of charity. Her wages were mostly so low that she could not hope to support herself and her child. The child, usually born in the Lying-in Home – a refuge for destitute pregnant women – at a cost to the Department of about 7s a week for maintenance of mother and child, would often, when weaned, have to become a ward of the state and be placed with a foster-mother while its natural mother tried to support herself.

Some wards accepted cash settlements from the father of their child.[73] The Department and the police would try to ensure that maintenance was paid although this was often difficult. Girls often wrote to the Department for help in securing more generous maintenance payments from the father of the child.[74] While living at the Lying-in Home for the obligatory six months after the birth of their child[75] many girls, reflecting on the hardships ahead of them, tried to make everything they would need for the baby.

kindly send me £2 of my bank money as I want to buy things and make up for myself and my baby for when I go to service as we make everything with our hand and it takes some time to do . . .[76]

enough to buy stockings and flannel to make some flannel things for my baby because if you have plenty of things to start with for your baby its not so hard to keep things going . . .[77]

Most girls who became pregnant were working as domestic servants when their condition was discovered, and the reaction of employers was usually one of indignation and dismay.[78]

as far as we know she has had no companions. She has been allowed out on Sunday evenings for Church. She has left her box but has taken almost all her belongings. During the time she has been with us she has been a good honest and industrious girl.[79]

One service home reacted differently. The mother wrote that they intended to 'treat her in this matter as if she were my own', adding that they would like to adopt the girl's child and keep the girl on in their home. It was later discovered by the Department that the girl had not been raped by a stranger after church as she had claimed, but had been having an affair with the son of the house. Later that year they were to marry.[80]

Girls were sometimes offered marriage by the young men who had made them pregnant. If all was suitable the Department approved such an outcome, but girls were never forced into marriage. They could refuse and some did.[81]

How many desperate girls tried or succeeded in procuring abortions cannot be estimated. Advertisements for abortifacients were common in the early 1900s and, as has been noted by Neville Hicks,

women already knew that household commodities could be used as abortifacients and knew how to prepare their own quinine pessaries and vaginal sponges from materials readily available for other, innocuous purposes.[82]

But confidence in abortifacients was often exaggerated. As one girl reported:

he said sit down and don't be frightened you won't get into trouble and if you do there's more ways of killing a cat than one, he then overpowered me and had connection with me. After this I met him twice a week and each time we had intercourse . . . I saw him and said to him 'I believe I am in trouble' he said I was joking but if it was so he would get me out of it. He afterwards gave me two bottles of medicine which I took but they did me no good. He told me after the child was born to get a foster-mother for it and he would pay for it. Since my confinement he has given me 30/–.[83]

As many girls found it hard to support themselves let alone a dependent child, any hardship such as illness or loss of employment usually doubled the burdens the single mother had to bear.[84] Families might be able to help by sheltering a girl in the years when her child was most dependent. One girl wrote that her brother-in-law and sister had

said that the baby could stop with them so I am with Effie at the burra Dear Mr Whiting Effie wishes to be remembered to you and hopes that you quite well . . . the baby is looking fine since I came up to the Burra and I am feeling better myself as well . . . Effies boy is such a fine looking little fellow and he is fat, as well and in good health . . .[85]

Girls without family often tried desperately hard not to lose the child they loved to the state.

I am in need of a few things for my self as well as my baby Mr Gray. I am very fond of my baby and I intend to keep him. Dear Sir would you mind writing home to my Grandfather and asking him if he will let me bring my baby home with me in June 19 as I will be 21 and if not I will go to service with my baby but I am not going to part with him it would brake my heart to part with him he is such a lovely big boy . . . [86]

No girl probably ever knew that her devotion might move even 'the governor's lady'. As Audrey Tennyson, wife of the South Australian governor, recorded in 1900:

The immorality among the young girls is terrible & I am told very much on the increase. The other day there were 18 babies in the workhouse, all for the first offence & heaps more coming on – varying from 15, but generally about 16. It is too piteous, but most of them apparently quite callous. They keep them there for 6 months, the babies are taken by the state & boarded out & the poor young mothers are sent to the Reformatory until they are 18.

A charming Matron tells me as a rule they are really nice quiet well-behaved (of course many are not) & are not in the very least vicious. She told me of a poor thing the other day & that really if she had often to go thro' such scenes she could not bear it. It was a case of The Cenci [a verse play by Shelley about incest] & after the 6 months the girl was only 16½ & they came to fetch her away to the Reformatory for 18 months, & the poor girl clung to & fought for her baby & begged & entreated not to be separated from it. It was too heartrending for words & at last, instead of boarding it out with strangers – her own mother was allowed to take it, which somewhat consoled her.

There is a poor girl there now expecting in September whose mother shut her door on her & the police took her here & she was so miserable that one night the girls rushed for the Matron as she was tying a handkerchief round her neck saying she would do away with herself. She is only just over 17.

They like my going to see them, as they are locked into 4 walls, a bright sunny courtyard & extremely nice rooms & offices, so that except the mothers who just see their own girls, nobody need ever know they have been there & no girls can be there a 2nd time, they then go to the other part of the house which is public. Some of the babies are so sweet & pretty it makes me so envious when I see a nice one. [87]

Going to work with a baby usually proved just as hard as the girls had anticipated. The opportunities for conflict with the mistress were increased; she might be critical of the way the baby was being brought up or could claim that the child was interfering with the girl's work too much. For the girl herself the situation was usually one of hard choices – neglect her work or neglect the baby.

I haven't settled down to the place since I've been here . . . I've tried hard enough goodness knows I've done every thing that I've been told to by everyone in the house . . . Mrs Nelson seems to think I put too many clean Clothes on my baby she said it made to much washing used to much water. Ill till [sic.] you Mr Gray I am not going to let my baby go dirty to please Mrs Nelson or anyone. She doesn't have to wash my clothes or the babies.[88]

After a baby learnt to walk things became increasingly difficult. One mistress wrote:

The girl being gentle and tractable neat and respectable in appearance the baby exceedingly quiet and kept in a distant part of the house, it proved possible to continue with the services until the present time when it has grown too old to make it convenient to have it much longer in the family.[89]

Some girls had to relinquish their child after struggling for years.

I am writing to you to ask you if you'll take my child as I have no means off keeping him. I have tried my hardest to keep him but I cannot do it. I cant gett more then five shillings per week my self without the child and there is no licence foster Mothers up hear & my father says he cannot help me and I cannot get a place with him.[90]

I came home ill I had to give up my situation and so I have not a penny I can call my own. I fully intended to return to Adelaide a fortnight after I came home but I did not . . . Oh please do advise me what to do as I am still going further and further into Mrs Davey's debt, I feel real broken-hearted . . . my father and mother do not know that I have a child to keep and I could not tell them father would never for give me.[91]

Every convention imposed on state girls was intended to block such a tragic destiny. State girls were expected to follow a set procedure in every aspect of courtship from the moment they spoke to any young man until the moment they were married. Church was an acceptable place for a girl to meet boys, but only if friendships were not formed in a covert way. One mistress wrote in alarm that her state girl had begun to go out of church before the service ended, disappearing somewhere and reaching home hours later than her mistress.[92] Another wrote that her charge was 'much too familiar with the boys and men through being allowed to go to the Salvation Army before I got her'.[93] A relationship should begin with an introduction. Girls were rebuked for 'picking up' a man at an 8 hour day demonstration, or for behaving outrageously after taking 'a fancy' to a young man of the district.[94] The mistress of the house was expected to carefully check the character of any young man who wanted to 'keep company' with a state girl. Surveillance was expected to be thorough. A mistress might write a note to the Department if she thought a girl's frocks were crushed and dirty as if she had been sitting on the ground while out with her young man.[95]

Have you any objection to a young man Albert Sands by name walking home from Church with Dorcas Billings He is a steady good young man and is perfectly open in his attentions to Dorcas comes to this house and spent one evening last week with her in the kitchen. Also wishes her to have tea with his mother some Sunday.[96]

The Department approved of girls being courted by suitable men but it did not encourage a relationship if there was no affection on the girl's part. Permission to see a young man was quickly curtailed if he was found to be a drinker or to have a dubious background.[97] A suitable young man was one who wrote to the Department stating that his intentions were honourable.[98] It helped his case if the girl's employers reported that he had 'good honest intentions' and was in 'respectable circumstances'.[99] State girls knew what to write regarding young men.

I have got a very nice young man he resides at Unley Park and only told me the last time he was down hear on Thursday that he hoped to settle down very soon . . . possible he could get enough saved to get a nice little home together.[1]

I feel you ought to know I am going with a young man and he is waiting for my letter of freedom to come and then we are going to be engaged openly but he has waited for 6 months and we both thought it unwise to make it openly known that we were going to marry so we are waiting till I am free . . .[2]

While courting, only a very small range of activities were thought proper. A girl might walk home from church in a group with her young man; one girl was even allowed to walk home from church at night in a group, providing there was a moon.[3] Other girls, by 1911, were allowed to go to a play on New Year's Eve.[4] Although some girls did fall in love 'with all their heart',[5] they were careful when writing to the Department to emphasize that their young man was steady and not too insistent in his affections. A fiancé who called 'nearly every night' to see a girl at her place would be a cause of irritation.[6] The Department also discouraged a match when they thought a prospective husband too young.[7]

A state girl could not marry without being released from the Department (though sometimes elopements and clandestine marriages took place), but where a particularly suitable marriage was planned, a well-behaved girl was occasionally released so that she could marry.[8] Some girls found it hard to admit that they were wards of the state, and wrote asking when it would be best to do this,[9] others had discussed marriage right from the start as something that would take place after their release from the state.

Many girls were very happy about their approaching marriage:

as soon as I can I am going to marry Mr Sexton he is very kind to me and I think he will be a very good and kind husband and I am sure I will be good to him . . . I am staying with Mrs Sexton she is teaching me lots of little things and is very kind to me I am very fond of her and very fond of Mr Sexton.[10]

Others married men merely described as 'steady, industrious thrifty . . . a good workman thoroughly honest and straight-forward'.[11] Less fortunate girls married men the Department saw as 'insignificant'.[12] Girls might simply be tired of moving about from place to place.

I have been keeping company with a young man since I have been down here and when I told him I was going to Woodford he asked me to get married to him he offered me a comfortable little home I am very fond of him he has always been kind and straight-forward with me. I have told you what I intend doing because I know you will advise me rightly I want to know if you will let me have a few pounds to get my things ready or let me have my bank book . . . We are going to get married in August all being well I think I will be much better in a home of my own than roaming about . . .[13]

Marriages were sometimes hastily arranged if a state girl discovered she was pregnant to a man she had known for some time. One girl ruefully wrote to the Department that her mistress had wanted her to see a doctor,

but I am sorry to say that I know what is the matter with myself that is the reason I am writing to let you know that I wish to get married in a fortnights time to Mr Oscar White.[14]

Girls who were going to marry usually wrote to the Department for some of their savings for linen and a trousseau. Sometimes they had left the state's control several years before.

I am going to be married in November and I should be glad of the money So if you would let me know I should be greatly pleased and Obly [obliged]. I am still living with Mrs R.S. East as I have been hear 3 years in August and I like it very much they are very kind to me indeed I thank you very much for thy loving kindest to me I am sure I need thank God that he took me to shuch a place as the State God only know were I should of been to day if it was not for thy grate kindness to me so I will close with kind regids to you.[15]

I am going to be married and it will be very useful to me at present. I have been getting on well every sinse I came over and that is going on for four years now. I am going on for twenty years of age now. I can thank the State Childrens

Department for all I have learned and my Schooling too I dont know what would become of us if you had not taken us in.[16]

Some girls needed financial assistance to be able to marry at all:

I am to be married next week and being very short of money I thought I [would] write and ask if you would be so kind and allow me to have mine.

I have been out of a place for some time as there is not many places in the Port of girls just now.[17]

As I have been ill for nearly 4 months and unable to work ... I only have a little over £2 left and I cannot get sufficient clothes for my marriage and so I only hope you will let me have my money as I will not have enough to get clothes unless I can have it ... the young man is a fellow I have known since I was 9 years old ... you will not be able to disapprove of him he is steady neither smokes or drinks he is very nice in every way ...[18]

A few girls married the father of their child months after the birth, and others married happily despite having an illegitimate child.

In happy instances the Department would send the couple a small wedding present. And sometimes a state girl would send one or two of the officials a small piece of her wedding cake.[19]

Changes 1915–40

During the 1920s and 1930s life changed slowly for state girls. Any social changes that arrived following the maelstrom of World War I (and it is doubtful whether there were many changes in Australia), were slow to affect the lives of ordinary women. Flappers were few and insignificant. Any changes that came arrived even more slowly for state wards. It was still thought that girls needed control and protection until they married. Employers were still expected to firmly supervise the young girl in their employ, to keep her 'from the company of young men as much as possible, and certainly never allow her out after dark at night'.[20] Girls continued to be returned to the Department for being 'too familiar with the boys'.[21]

By 1929 the issues that preoccupied the Department and employers can be captured in the comments an employer wrote about a girl, Sandra, who wanted to visit her foster-parents in a country town. Her employers thought it would be

quite alright if they lived out of ____ I would not hesitate but being in the town there are others she can meet and whose influence would be detrimental to her as these girls are not very careful in their choice of companions.

Six months later, when Sandra had shown improvement, she was allowed to visit her former foster-mother. But soon there were problems, as the foster-mother reported:

I am sorry to say Sandra has got herself disliked she is such a wild little thing and mad after boys she keeps too late hours on Saturday night when she is in here so my brother and Wife will have no more to do with her ... There is always a home for Sandra at my place we don't mind her spending a day with us any time but we would rather not be responsible for her on Saturday nights.[22]

A state girl might still, by the late 1930s, have to explain the circumstances under which she came to be alone with a man, even if it was just a short trip to take some sheep to the station.[23] State girls were not supposed, either, to be left alone on the farm if there was a 'workman on the premises' while the family went out for a few hours.[24] A girl who showed any sign of being 'rather inclined to the Opposite sex' should have someone 'kind and firm' to control her it was noted in 1936.[25]

Evidence of real attachment was often revealed when a girl was separated from her young man. A few girls had their affections tested by World War I. One girl wrote in 1916

I do not know what I would do if anything happened to him. But I must pray to God to watch over him and protect him ... There are hardly any lads at all in Goolwa now There has been 68 already gone to the war, two of whom have been killed and one died in camp ... I suppose you have received Ralph's letter by now. I wrote to him this morning, it was too hot to work so I did some sewing ... would be leaving for the front about the middle of March. I dread the thought of him going so far away. He gave me his bicycle but I only ride it around the yard. The house is about a mile from the road, a sandy old track to go up.[26]

When state girls made respectable and happy marriages they were in fact taking on another protector: husband replaced the state as acting parent. Hence the importance attached to the character of any man mentioned by a state girl. Girls were expected to tell the Department of their every move in relation to young men. Some did so.

We still see each other though only for about an hour on Sunday when I go out to Sunday School. He comes to the meeting with me and takes me home ... He works for Mr Brown at ____ and his name is Oscar South His home is also at ____. I know sir what we are not allowed to have boy or men friends but I cant help it sir. I think there are some better friends among the men and boys than there are among the girls. But still Sir, you have your own ideas on that point.[27]

I will take my punish whatever it is for I know that I shouldn't of did it but when I am lead I can't help it, as I am easy led into mischief but I will promise faithfully that I will not do it any more not even talk to a stranger (a man).[28]

In any situation where a young man was paying attention to a girl, the girl's mistress was often the final arbiter of opinion – a situation which changed little in the fifty years covered by this study. This control operated in the late 1930s in much the same way as it had in the 1890s, as this Departmental account shows:

Laura has a young man Mr Colin Christophers – a Methodist Local Preacher – paying her marked attention. F/M says he comes to the house – she does not allow girl to run the streets – Man does not know Laura is under our jurisdiction. I suggested she should write to the Secretary re this matter.,[29]

A relationship might be entirely innocent, yet a girl's age would make it impossible. A seventeen-year-old girl might be thought too young for the following sort of involvement:

I have been about a bit with a boy at my last situation. He used to come from the pictures with me Saturday afternoons and I was never late home. I also went to his Sunday school picnic with his Mother and Father and him. He is a very respectable boy and his mother and father are very refined people. I have heard from my Sunday School teacher that he has been to my last place to make enquiries about me.[30]

The Department constantly received reports of state girls being 'foolish' or 'worse' with young men[31] and girls were sometimes considered too 'corrupt' to be placed out in homes where there were young children.[32]

Occasionally a more tolerant view of a girl's behaviour might appear. One foster-mother wrote to the secretary in 1927 about a former foster-child who had run away from a state institution to her home that: 'she is just at an age when girls seem to be unsettled and don't seem to know what is best for them'.[33]

Despite the Department's and employer's strict surveillance, girls still managed, not unexpectedly, to meet boys by different means:

whilst on the beach with a Nurse Attendant this afternoon [they] asked permission to return to the home for their coats, these girls instead went for a walk towards Glenelg and did not return with the rest of the inmates. They were found about 5 pm in a shelter shed between the Home and Glenelg in company with two young men.[34]

Of an eighteen-year-old, one employer wrote:

I thought perhaps the girl was lonely – but yesterday the full facts came before me.

She goes out to meet a young fellow who is in the habit of attending Sunday School a mile or so below our place.[35]

The Department was often appalled at the young men that some girls met. Miss Kentish reported of one in 1922:

I saw Mr Taylor at the hotel. I should judge him to be a 'gay man about town' He took the matter very airily and said Susan was a sweet little piece. He didn't know when he had been so pleased with a girl. He met her at dinner at the Hotel she having been brought there by another man some weeks ago . . . Susan dresses in the extremes of fashion.[36]

The worst fears of the Department were sometimes confirmed when they intercepted girls' letters. This one was written in 1926:

I am very good I go to church I have to because I have got with some relidous buggers. I swear when I get out of their sight. I have got a boy I went to the Flicks pictures I mean last night with him and the Saturday before he is a rough devil he belongs to the W.H.S. that is the Wandering Hand Society but still you easy give him a box in the ears and then it does them good.[37]

Sometimes letters from boyfriends were intercepted too, bringing fresh confirmation of all the Department's suspicions:

I will be very pleased to meet you next Tuesday and I am longing to see you again Mary, it seems so long since I saw you last, I suppose you thought I had forgotten all about you as you never had any letter . . . I will meet you in Town at the same place next time you have [an] afternoon off; I don't mind coming till the Town dear its quite a pleasure to come and meet you . . .[38]

Things are very slow in Town now so you are not missing a great deal. I saw an amazing thing today. There is a movie being advertised on the hoardings called 'Where is my wandering boy tonight'. There was a very decent lil dance at Henley last evening 8 til 1. The hall was beautifully decorated but Oh! so crowded.[39]

Some girls were repeatedly warned about

fast conduct with boys. We have had numerous complaints from reliable people on the Parade Norwood concerning her conduct there and her bad language . . . Mary admits misconduct on several occasions with Ledger and says he gave her 2/- each time as well as money on other occasions. On one occasion a misconduct took place between the girl and a man named Carter as well as Ledger, each man keeping 'nit' for the other. The girl also admits having taken wine from four strange young men on Osmond Terrace Norwood a few months ago.

I have been informed that Mary goes to a place in Hindley St. owned by some foreignor.[40]

Prostitution seems to have become far less visible during this era. Few explanations have been advanced for this, although perhaps the decline in class distinction based on clothing – the possibility of judging a woman's character and social position by the way she dressed – may have contributed to it.[41] Some state wards worked as prostitutes in the 1920s, each time earning a few shillings from clients.[42] Other state girls managed sexual liaisons by choice but were subsequently discovered and investigated by the Department.

She says she spent the night at the Grosvenor with a man named Tom Boyd. They shared the same room. He she understands was a policeman from Port Adelaide. The porter at the Grosvenor said a girl and a man answering the description arrived there about 2:30 am and took a room. They had no baggage whatever. The man was said to be big and hefty and looked as if he lived an outdoor life. I think it is sure to be Anne and her friend.

They were in a motorcycle and side car.[43]

Some girls managed to resist rape, others did not.[44] One employer in a country town took his state girl to the circus and left her there unchaperoned after having

distinctly told her, that when the show was over to go straight to his trap which was in Turner's yard, but when he went to the trap he found she was not there . . . they [the girl and a friend] hung about the Circus tent talking to the two men employed at the Circus.

This state girl was locked in a van and repeatedly raped.[45]

At least one desperate ward managed to obtain an abortion in the 1920s.[46] As in earlier decades, only a very small number of wards became pregnant and had a child. At any one time throughout the 1920s and 1930s there were likely to be only two to four wards in the McBride Home or the House of Mercy, both refuges for unmarried mothers. If a state girl was too young to be released when she had her child it continued to be the practice to send her out to service with her child. The Department would inform a prospective employer that

there is now a good girl of 19¾ years who, however has a male child of 1 yr and 7 months whom she must take with her. Her wages would be 12/6 per week and you would receive 8/- per week as maintenance of the baby. He would have a good outfit sent with him and this would have to be maintained by you. The girl clothes herself.[47]

Some employers, while preferring girls without the encumbrance of a child, seem to have taken a tolerant attitude to the matter:

104

This home is well known to the Inspectors who have frequently visited it . . . Mrs Piper does not mind having a girl with a child she thinks it is company for the mother, makes her more contented as the home is about 2 miles from Smithfield and rather lonely. She would prefer one without a child . . . [48]

But for girls with a child, life continued to be as hard as it had been in earlier decades. One state girl wrote in desperation in 1917:

Just a few lines asking you would you please remove me from my place as I cannot manage to look after my baby and do the work to it is to much for me, my child is so cross as he is getting his double teeth and he is just walking and it takes me all my time running after him I will soon be run off my feet and dear Sir I can't stand him crying it worrys me it is not like as if it was my own home, I like it here the people are very nice but I can't expect them to pay me for doing nothing and I love my baby and I am going to look after him whatever comes or goes . . .

Her letter was answered by the Department:

My dear girl,
    Your letter of the 15th complaining that you do not like your place of work although the people are kind to you is duly to hand. I have written to your employer to ask if any better arrangement can be made.
    Something I assure you shall be done for your comfort as soon as possible, just have a little patience.

In this case the girl's situation was adjusted satisfactorily.[49] But another girl was told she could return to a situation (after illness) only if she came without her child.[50] Impossible to know with accuracy how many state girls managed to keep their children, but one who desperately wanted to wrote in 1919:

Mr Houlgrave if it is in your power do not separate Thelma and myself from each other as if it is in my power I am going to try and bring Thelma up to be a much different girl than I have been. I am going to bring her up to right and not wrong if I can so you see Mr Houlgrave why I do not want to foster Thelma out as I would like her to be in my care altogether to let the Council see that there is some good in me after all . . . what a fine child she is growing she will be two next month she is such a good little soul . . .

This was written in July. By September the situation was still precarious and Thelma's mother was writing:

My one desire ever since I was up at the Burra was that I should stick to my child that I would do my best wherever I went and I have tried . . . I pray every night that we may not be parted, if you let me know it will set my mind at ease . . . [51]

As long as the future for any girl who went 'wrong' was so unutterably bleak the Department felt it must err on the cautious side when dealing with girls in love. Love was a subject about which state girls were eloquent:

I've been almost mad worrey in how you got on I hope that you will forgive me if I have troubled you in any way I am going back to Adelaide shortly don't suppose I will ever see you again I shall not forget you, I hope when your lonely you will think of me sometimes and not always as one of the worst. My girl friends came to meet me, they at once asked why I was so quiet, they don't know what it is to be lonely, but I think you understand. You said that you were a bit of a devil yourself but I trust and respect you as I do my father. It is nearly twelve o'clock so I must close hoping I have not offended you I remain your

ever sincere friend
Barbara[52]

They could also rage against the restrictions placed on them, as this girl did in 1922:

Mr Houlgrave why must we write through you, if you were in our place now truly in love you would sooner private correspondence than others to read it first I feel I would sooner not write. It is very hard on us state girls Mr Houlgrave all these laws we are sent out anywhere we get half the wages others get we are not allowed out in the evenings and so on. I have kept to your rules I never ask to go out after dark its very hard to other girls who are free they go out to anything thats on the next day our part is just to hear what a good time they had & how nice it was & so on, while we are kept from all those things just because we are state girls & those are your rules. You don't seem to try and make us happy you seem to make everything hard as possible . . . Now when [her fiancé] was up here I still kept your rules we are never out after dark we behaved ourselves we loved each other & now he's gone I can't be happy. Mr Houlgrave won't you please give me a place closer to Robert if ever you have loved you must feel for us miles away then besides we have no parents we know of which makes us love ever more dearly we must live for one another. I have not been very well this last month my nerves are awful I want a rest but can't have one others get a holiday every twelve months but we work till we break down then, would not be allowed to have a holiday Mr Houlgrave why are you against Robert you seem as though you are against [what] every one does & says up here. I have not been as bad as some girls under the state I was whicked at my place before this but I couldnt help it I was taken from a place I liked and placed where I didn't like it but I didn't care what I did . . . I hope you will answer this letter & would you please place me nearer to my dear boy the boy I love not keep us away from each other.[53]

The following letters were written by state girls in 1914 and 1936 and they illustrate how little change there had been about what made a good husband.

the question is a young man wishes to correspond with me and I thought it best to get your permission first as I no it is right . . . he is a decent respectable young fellow and well known and lived in the district of Julia . . . as you have said you like us to have a young man as long as his respectable . . . [54]

whether you will grant my wish in being friends with Mr B. Kelly I was introduced to this gentleman at church in the quire and he wishes to be my friend he is a very quiet and refined man but I take no interest in him until I write to you, I did not tell him where I came from I just told him I would write to my guardian and he said alright, I was told he never has had a girl before and he works on his fathers farm he does not drink for I would not have a man who does, & I write to you as you are my helper. [55]

Some girls, aware of their position in the world, could write in quite pragmatic terms of the advantages of marriage to a man with property. One girl, doubtless aware of the great loss of life on the Western Front, wrote in 1918:

he has told me he loves me and I love him, and I would like your permission to write to him he lives at Rockleigh and his name is Oliver West I have known him since I went to school although, we have not written to each other. I saw him at Mount Pleasant when I was there and I thought I would ask you if we may write to each other . . . I know that it is going to be serious for young girls now and I think it is only our duty to marry if we gett a good chance because when we are out of the department we have no good guardians to guide and protect us from the evils of this world so you will quite understand why I am asking your permission. [56]

Many girls seem to have seen marriage quite accurately as a form of security both emotional and financial, and as especially valuable for those without family or fortune. The men they intended to marry often saw their role as one of protector too, one man writing:

I will fix up with them once your mine dear you are not the State schools and they will have to see me then. We are going to look after each other and they wont have anything to do with you then dearie. [57]

Girls realized that once married their future might be secure.

The young man's parents have been very good to me and wish me to live with them as soon as I am free. I should love to be with friends and settle down as my own home is all broken up and I never wish to enter it again.

People all say Ruth if you let him go or tell him the word no you should never get

Marriage and children were the secure happiness that many state wards, alone in the world, hoped for. A former state ward and her adopted son in 1912.

another one. I haven't written to him and let him know that he should write to you . . . as there was another boy wanted me and came to our place but I chased him home straight off, as I knew what he was like . . . This young Joseph gets the whole farm and everything whats on the place house and everything whats in it.[58]

But the stigma that many state girls had to bear sometimes affected their chances of making a good marriage, as it affected every area of their lives. One inspector reported in 1924:

I understand the young man who is keeping company with Pauline says openly in the district that he would never think of marrying her, he says 'fancy marrying a girl like her with a father like she's got'.[59]

And in the same year a girl's employer wrote of her fiancé:

Mr Wright is a very nice gentleman he is always kind to his girl and me and his parents too everybody likes him. Ruth could not wish for any better as she is a state child.[60]

One man wrote rather condescendingly:

In the first place she never told me she was in the state which made things uneasy . . . I intend to keep company with her as I think there are many worse than she is.[61]

Girls often seemed aware of class division when contemplating marriage. As one girl wrote in 1923,

people around his way rich people said to him he shouldn't marry a poor state girl, but he told them he wouldn't just like to marry a rich girl as he says its right for a rich man to marry a poor girl because to help their lives through worry.[62]

For some girls the secretary became a sort of 'daddy long-legs', a confidant to whom one could write about those moments in life that most people never talk about.

I do not know what my parents will say, as I know they wanted me to stay home for ever, but I think I will be happy . . . at the time of his proposal, many things ran through my mind and I sincerely hope I have given the right answer & everything will turn out well.[63]

Whatever girls wrote or thought, the only young men the Department found acceptable were those who were respectable and hard-working. As in the earlier period, the Department continued to investigate the circumstances of any young man advanced as a fiancé. The following letter is from 1918:

My dear girl,
   I have your letter asking that you might be allowed to become engaged to a young man. Before anything can be done in the matter it will be necessary for you to forward me further particulars ie the man's name, his religion, his earnings and the names of his parents. It might be well for the young man to write to me himself and he might at the same time forward any recommendation possible from the Police, or the Clergyman of the Church he attends.[64]

If a marriage was not ideal, the Department might still consider the match the best a girl might expect. As A.M. Kentish wrote in 1918, 'I am of the opinion that it might be the best thing to allow them to marry. Gwenda is not a good girl and I fear we will never do anything with her'.[65] In some cases it seems to have been thought better for a girl to 'marry rather than burn':

Wendy is not happy in her home and only a month or so ago reported to this Dep. that both her parents were again drinking.
   Are you aware that Wendy had a moral lapse when she was only 15½. On that account I would be inclined to recommend the marriage if suitable.[66]

Once engaged, decorum was still important; a girl should not be exposed to temptation. Visits by the fiancé, if he lived nearby, were to be at the discretion of her employer, and a monthly visit was considered reasonable in 1923.[67] A girl whose fiancé visited every time her mistress went out might find herself rebuked.[68] One young man was told in January 1917 that

It has been arranged that you may go to see Susan at Mr Smith's house one evening a month, the special time to be arranged between you and Mr Smith.
   During these long light evening hours you will be allowed to take Susan for a walk as long as you are back at the house before dark. There will be no objection to you taking her out one evening in 3 months. This is a very special concession made to you because I have a good deal of confidence in your rectitude and I have every confidence in Susan's good conduct and right wishes.[69]

Evenings could be occupied by making clothes and linen. Some state girls had a glory box prepared long before they became engaged, but others had to begin it when it appeared they would marry. The following two letters were written in 1936, the first from a state girl, the second from a mistress:

Will you send me some fancy-work please a supper clothe and if you cant get that get some Doyles please I am getting my hope box ready do you agree to me getting married ask dad will you please give my love to him please and my sister please I have got two pillow slams and one table centre and a sandwich doyle and two round ones and I am going to crotchet some so that will be quite OK . . .[70]

I have been giving her six pence extra for the last ten months. Which I told the two Lady visitors. With this 6 pence I have been buying her for her trousseau box 6 pillow slips 7 tea towels 3 white towels 3 table cloths.[71]

Not all girls made 'sensible' engagements, and some managed to marry without informing the Department. Sometimes, but not always, they were then released.[72]

In 1920 a girl wrote from her position in the country arguing that since she *was* married she should go out to service as a married woman bearing her husband's name:

if I went as a single girl it would be found out there is always some one who knows everything. . . . i·am married and no one on this earth can ever make me single again . . . i love my husband Mr Houlgrave and why should i be ashamed to carry his name . . .

The secretary wrote explaining that nobody would be told about her marriage 'or anything else concerning you', adding that he hoped when reunited, her husband would realize how 'very loyal' she had been.[73]

Marriages were still occasionally allowed because of a girl's pregnancy.[74] The Department was not always pleased about such marriages but usually consented.

Marriage, even happy marriages, still meant expense. In many cases this was where a girl's savings went – on setting up a home or providing for the next generation.

Mr Lewis I need this money Sir as I have only been married a few months and we have brought our furniture straight out are not in need of money for ourselves but I am to be a mother in a few months & I would like the money to get the clothes for baby . . .[75]

Adolescence, as we have seen, was regarded as a time of peril for state girls. All aspects of life between the ages of thirteen and twenty-one were controlled and restricted as a result. The belief that state wards should grow up to be innocent and modest changed little in the years from 1887 to 1940, and the penalties for breaking strict moral codes were not to diminish for several more decades.

CHAPTER 5

Growing up a State Ward 1915–40

A picture emerges from the foster-homes of these two and a half decades and to some degree it is a picture of the flavour and measures of ordinary family life. For very few in the 1920s and 1930s was childhood luxurious. For many it was kept from being merely mean by love alone. Houses were shabby, parents strict, pleasures rare. A state girl's words in 1928 chart the fault-line between what was acceptable to the community and what was not.

I have lived with Mrs Carr ever since I was five years old, I call her mother and Mr Carr 'father'. I often wash up the dishes in the afternoon after school I mind the new baby. I like minding the baby better than playing. On Saturdays I sometimes wash over the kitchen floor and tidy up and wash the dinner things. In the afternoon I play or go to the pictures when mother has money enough. I do not do any hard work . . . On Sunday nights mother takes us down to the beach to hear the band play . . . Mother gets very cross with me sometimes for coming home late from school or being naughty. When I am naughty she often slaps me with her hand and when I am very naughty she gives me three or four cuts with the cane on my back or legs. It makes me cry but I have never seen any marks on my legs or anywhere else. Once I saw mother slap the new baby with her hand because it would not leave off crying.

Father sometimes slaps me with his hand but he never gives me the cane. He is only cross when he gets drunk . . . We hear him coming down the street singing and Mother says to us 'There's your father coming home drunk again'. Sometimes he comes home singing when he isn't drunk and then he has the laugh on us. When he is drunk he rouses at Mother something dreadful and goes to hit her he calls her a b__ bitch and other dreadful names. He has called us b__ bastards. Once he fell down coming in the door. One night Mother said he walked about all night with a razor and threw it at her and cut her over the eye. She showed me the cut in the morning . . .

Father has not had any work since last November so he has not had any money to get drunk but sometimes Mother gives him 6d to get a drink and then his friends they buy some more.

I should not like to leave mother and father.

The inspector then 'went to Mrs Carr's home which is a small four-roomed cottage with an enclosed back verandah and small yard'. Noting that the foster-home was in a poor and rough locality, the inspector talked to Mrs Carr, who stated:

My husband has been out of work since last November, he was for 9 years temporary porter in the railways and was put off when so many other men were dismissed. He tramps all day long looking for work and once a week goes fishing. He has never kept me short of money for the house and we are now partly living on what I have saved.[1]

The Department tried to remove the children but neighbours produced testimonials in favour of the parents and the children were allowed to stay.[2]

World War I caused some degree of disruption to the South Australian community[3] and the shock waves were felt in the State Children's Department. Many women found it difficult to control their children with father absent and a few appealed to the Department to help. Mrs Best brought her twelve and a half year-old daughter to the Department in January 1915, claiming that she was

quite out of hand. She wanders away from home all day and plays with other naughty girls. The child slips away unbeknown to her. She is very anxious about the matter and asks if we will assist her. The father is at the war. I warned the little girl and she wept bitterly and promised to be better. The mother asks if we may call . . .[4]

Even when the war was over, problems just began for many families. Wives and children had to live with men changed by the experience of the trenches. One of the inspectors, Miss O'Connor, arriving to investigate a father who, so neighbours complained, was maltreating his son, found a rather more complicated situation. The wife explained over a cup of tea that

her husband is a difficult man to live with since he returned from the war . . . The man gets into violent rages and appears to lose his reason at times. [The neighbours] are all very respectable they have great sympathy for Mrs South and are much concerned as to her treatment by her husband. It is evident all these neighbours feel distressed at having a rough quarrelsome man such as South living near them they in consequence magnify ordinary paternal chastisement with absolute cruelty.[5]

The depression arrived early in South Australia and by the end of 1928 its effects were everywhere. One of its consequences was that more girls were released on petition to parents or relatives. The 1929 annual report mentions that difficulty in finding suitable service homes will continue until 'a return of prosperity'.[6] Everywhere there was evidence of hardship.

Child's guardians are having a very bad time now. Mr West is unable to earn much and has been compelled to ask for relief. I am writing a special report re subsidy for Ruth.[7]

This child is much loved. Clean comfortable home. Jo has improved in health since she started to play basket ball. Mrs Riley has 3 sons at home who are out of work.[8]

In 1930 Evelyn Penny noted:

I think that in these times when so many are applying for children because they are in financial distress searching inquiry should be made into the means possessed by all applicants.[9]

Her thoughts had been turned in this direction by the poverty of a foster-parent, a spinster who had two children placed with her and who wanted to receive payments from the Department once a fortnight instead of every three months. The woman revealed to Miss Penny that

for several weeks last winter she only had 2/6p a week for food and managed on this with the help of some vegetables she grew and a few eggs. She did not apply for rations or any other assistance.
In the end two friends learnt of the privation she was suffering and sent her articles of food in a very considerate way so she got through alright tho' she became very thin.[10]

While the depression undoubtedly lowered the standard of living in many established foster-homes, high standards were still maintained when inspecting new foster-homes.

In regard to accommodation within the foster-home it seems that it would be rare for a state girl to have a bedroom to herself but it seems to have been mandatory for her to have had a separate bed.[11] Girls were treated with greater consideration than boys in this respect because they were believed to be more delicate. A room with a cement floor might be acceptable for a boy, but for it to be used by a girl it would have to have a 'good thick warm covering'.[12] State girls were still not allowed to sleep in sleep-outs or rooms with unlocked french windows. Prospective foster-parents would be asked whether the bedroom they could provide had 'any outside exit beyond the usual window'.[13] In contrast, a boy's room might be satisfactory if 'bags of wheat now in it were removed'.[14]

Foster-home standards rose in the early 1920s and rose again once the depression had passed. In 1924 Miss Penny could write of a foster home:

Not a first class subsidy home. The cottage is built so close to the next house that the bedroom is a gloomy room and the whole house has a grubby appearance and lacks freshness. Mrs Chambers impressed me as a kind woman of good principles but I should not have recommended it as a satisfactory home for a state child.[15]

A better subsidy home went beyond the essentials. In 1920 one girl was placed with a family in

one of the Abbetoirs cottages of 5 rooms and all conveniences, comfortably furnished and well kept. The room prepared for the child is bright and fresh with comfortable large bed, this room she will have to herself and will attend the public school nearby and the C of E Sunday School.[16]

But the best foster-homes imparted something special. Miss Lapidge noted of one in 1925:

I have always considered this a first-rate home but was impressed with the improvements shown about twelve months ago. This has continued and while it may be lacking in material advantages the moral and spiritual teaching is manifest in the children when of service age; they are good living, industrious respectful and are permitted to consider her house as their home and return on their day off.[17]

As in earlier decades, there were some girls who were very lucky in their foster-parents. Sometimes circumstances might lead to this affection being revealed.

This child came to us when my Daughter and I were in great trouble and Her priceless love for us both has helped us through some very dark days. now we find we cannot give her up willingly ... [when] my Daughter's Husband returns home from the War He will then I think sign the adoption papers.

... a certain soldier who is leaving for the front within the next fortnight intends to leave his will in favour of the above child.[18]

More often there would be ordinary words and down to earth demonstrations of love.

We put a little aside for her in Mr Miller's name as she is not to know until 21 years ... and then she can do what she like with it either buy a house or something for her as she is all we have and could not be more than our real own could be.[19]

Other state girls were given valuable Christmas presents. Some were taken on holidays to the beach or on camping trips.[20] Attachment might be influenced as much by what the state child did as by the temperament of the foster-mother.

Laura has been in this home many years and is treated as one of the family – is known as Laura Henry – She has been extremely delicate and F/M has lavished care and attention upon her ...[21]

Good home and F/ps who treat this girl as a daughter – and say if she remains as good a girl as she is now – She may look on their home as her own and stay with them until she marries – Eve is extremely fond of her fosterparents – she gave F/M a little set of clothes for the coming babe. F/M is extremely touched.[22]

Some foster-mothers took their role very seriously, surrounding a state girl with

Working-class childhood: Trenerry Court, Adelaide. In 1919 an inspector from the State Children's Department wrote of a family in this street: 'The house contains only two rooms and kitchen very poor but tidy. The only sleeping accommodation I saw was a single bed ... The other two sleep on the floor on a mattress'.

every essential to a good upbringing and making a serious study of how to train her character in the best way to counteract any undesirable tendencies that she may have inherited from her parents.[23]

In the 1920s state girls were expected to be helpful around the house. They were supposed not to dawdle before school but busy themselves making their beds, tidying rooms, and possibly, 'one or two other simple duties'.[24] Tardiness was not approved; one foster-mother complaining in 1939 that

I have tried for over two years to impress upon her the need to be quicker but she is naturally very slow.

My other little charges do their duties willingly and much more quickly than Anne, and get away to school in plenty of time.[25]

The writer Hal Porter remembered that each child had a 'Saturday task', and that 'our being made to do something [had] its moral and disciplinary value, and [was], moreover, a custom of that class in that era'.[26]

The long walk home from school each day provided an opportunity for escapades for some girls, much to the disapproval of the inspectors.

I spoke to her re playing on the way home with boys – and she said she walks home with her small cousin who lives with Mrs North – some boys were fighting with him and she joined in to help him – she promised it would not occur again.[27]

One new interest that state wards were allowed, undoubtedly because of its 'character-building' reputation, was the Girl Guides' Association. It might 'bring-out' a girl who was 'very backward'.[28] Younger girls joined the Brownies. Other hobbies became more common. A few girls were taught the piano by their foster-mothers, one telling the inspector proudly that her ward also had 'a sweet singing voice'.[29]

Some children were undoubtedly easy to love. They might be the toddler who 'hardly ever gets her clothes soiled' or a 'very nicely spoken little girl'.[30] This might have dangers too, as one inspector reported in 1934.

I gave Sara a little lecture re talking in school: she promised to be a better girl – When I asked her if she had Influenza she said 'No But I had a second issue of the Flu' – she is a very attractive child and consequently rather spoilt.[31]

Applications for children which only stressed the duties of a foster-child were carefully scrutinized. Many letters of application were explicit about what the foster-parents would want the child to do, but had hardly a word about what the child might expect in return.[33] In such cases

Girls were expected to provide their own clothes after the age of sixteen. They spent most of their day in apron and work-dress but were also allowed to have a church dress and hat and were always to look neat.

decisions would have to depend a great deal on the inspector's feelings about the home. The sorts of deliberations that might be made by the late 1930s are shown in this report:

I don't think there is much wrong with this home. I believe Nancy has improved in health and mentally since placed – F/M could not possibly spend much time away from home and have the home and outfits etc as she keeps them and Lizzie Jones is always wishing herself back there – As far as I can gather F/Ms and [her brother's] lives are spent in good service for others – If child was not well F/M I am sure did not know it.[33]

And yet the Department could not afford to be too particular, as it was sometimes very difficult to find enough homes for state children. In 1921 advertisements were placed in the *Advertiser* in order to find more homes for state children of school age.

It is obvious that some foster-parents applied for state children for company. They might be recently widowed,[34] or be young married women unable to have children of their own. The letters young women wrote often conveyed a special sort of longing.

I am so very lonely it seems to me I am never going to get one when I waited so long I went to the fostermothers office to see if I could adopt one but they are nearly all infants or too old . . . it is awful to be so lonely a little child does comfort you and make home bright.[35]

Poignancy, however, sometimes concealed motives a great deal more pragmatic, and it was the part of the inspectors to disentangle calculation and despair, not an easy task.[36]

One group of foster-mothers who were always viewed in a favourable light (though still subject to a visit and a report) were the 'professional' foster-mothers who had had, or still had in their charge a state child growing up in a satisfactory manner. Very often such women gave no reason why they wanted another state child; they merely explained that they had the space available.[37] Their mothering abilities needed no paper testimony. If a foster-mother was well regarded, her home became 'an approved home for state children'.[38] They took a 'professional' stance, not becoming too involved but providing temporary care. As one woman put it:

I don't mind what age the baby is the younger they are the better I like them. I hope not to wait too long as if it is a baby likely to be recalled well perhaps it may not be till I am in a better position, if it is well I will have to put up with it. I gave Hilda a good start and I hope she is doing well.[39]

Some state children continued to be overworked by their foster-parents. No accurate measure could ever be made of the number who were so exploited, but descriptions of the work some children had to do can be quite revealing. In 1936 a girl who was 'small for her age and rather backward with her schooling', told the inspector that she

was getting up between quarter and half past six – she had to milk 4 cows before breakfast – then afterwards wash the milk buckets – wash-up before going to school, generally milked 3 cows . . .

The inspector

told Mrs Edwards that I thought she was asking too much of Elise she is small for her age and rather backward with her schooling – and if she was tired before she got to school naturally she could not give her best – Mrs Edwards said she was not asking Elise to do more than she asked of her own girl but if we wished it she would not ask her to milk the cows – I said one must remember Elise is still a school girl and not placed out on service terms – I recommend special mention be made of what work Elise is doing when the home is again visited.[40]

Another girl had her foster-home investigated when the Department received an anonymous letter in 1916 alleging that she was ill-treated. In defending herself, the foster-mother asserted that she

only punishes Ruby when she is naughty. She assures me that Ruby is a very difficult girl to bring up and has done some things which made her feel she must punish her severely. These things are what she calls 'inherited tendencies' – of a sexual nature. The next door neighbours told me that Mrs Clark's chief fault was extreme impatience and bad language.
    Returning to Mrs C's I overtook Ruby wheeling a bag of wheat in a handcart. She had wheeled it from Port Adelaide a distance of 1½ or 2 miles. I got her to leave the wheat at the nearest house and she returned home at the same time as I did . . . I told Mrs C. it was outrageous to send Ruby to Pt Adelaide for a bag of wheat. It was as much as I could push.[41]

In the wider community there can be no doubt that many children began contributing to the family income long before they left school by collecting bottles, minding babies, or running errands. One child of nine and a half years-old was described by her guardians as 'very gentle, respectful and is very smart at learning the ways of the household and is also very obliging'.[42] It was not considered anything out of the ordinary in 1925 for a girl of eight to make two beds and empty potties every morning before school. Working life began very early. Dorothy Roysland remembered beginning work in the 1920s.

I left school when I was thirteen: that was the leaving age in those days. We only went as far as the sixth class. My first job was minding babies for two-and-sixpence a week. The next was a lot harder: it was in a laundry. I had to get up at five-thirty in the morning to get the copper going and then have breakfast while the water was heating up.[43]

But there were limits. A girl not quite twelve years old, sent to Renmark by her mother in 1921 to work as a maid (her employers having been told she was fourteen), was removed by the Department. They found a suburban foster-home for her, and more suitable duties: 'she is to be kept in clothes given 1/- per week pocket money and attend the M__ Public School . . . is to give light service for a home out of school hours'.[44]

To be a foster-parent was a difficult task. It entailed the problems of parenthood and fewer of the joys. It cannot be wondered that, as shown in Table 7, many children were returned to the Department as 'unsuitable'. Some were bed-wetters, many more had what was referred to a 'bad habits'.[45]

By the early 1930s it was against the rules of the Department for foster-parents to use physical punishment on their state children. Nevertheless cases where a girl could only be controlled by slapping were reported. Charlotte Hunt, for example, was described as a 'fascinating child: though rather pert' in 1935. Two years later her foster-mother admitted that

she slaps this child on her legs sometimes – says she can't manage her if she doesn't although it is against the rules. Child very well cared for – and does not wish to leave this home.[46]

Table 7 Principal reasons for children being returned 1912–22

Reason for return	No.	%
Child unsuitable	782	13.2
Misconduct of child	720	12.1
Ill-health of child	368	6.2
Home unsuitable	472	7.9
Guardian unable to keep	857	14.5
Absconders returned	1 004	17.0
From hospitals	593	10.0
For dental attention	483	8.1
Ill-health or death of guardian	118	1.9
Mutual dissatisfaction	112	1.8
Other	396	6.7
Total	5 905	100

Table 8 Percentage of children returned 1912–22

Total number placed out   14 361
Total number returned   5 905
41%   of all children placed out were returned in any one year
10.4% of all children placed out returned due to guardian's dissatisfaction (child unsuitable, misconduct of child)
10.2% of all children placed out returned due to child's dissatisfaction (home unsuitable, absconders returned)
7.4%   of all children placed out were returned for dental or hospital attention
5.9%   of all children placed out returned due to guardian unable to keep

Source: State Children's Council, *Annual Reports*.

NB These tables refer to *all* children returned, that is, children at service as well as children boarded out.

It will be seen that the difference between the percentage of children returned due to guardian's dissatisfaction and those returned due to child's dissatisfaction is very different from what it was in the 1890s, probably as a result of greater care over placement.

Sex-play was another offence in children that was expected to be severely punished. Bernadette Daniels, then between nine and twelve years old, was described in 1929 as 'very forward with men'. A year later she was under investigation by the Department. A boy about nine, who came to the house to get milk, followed her into the cowshed:

She was going out of the shed and the boy said 'Come back'. She said 'No'. He then said 'Yes come back'. She then went back into the shed. Boy told her to sit down, the boy said to her 'Take down your pants'. She then pulled her pants down, but had her dress down. Boy then went out of shed, and got the milk, and went home.

Apparently the boy accused the girl of pulling up her dress and inviting him to have 'connection' with her.[47] Such episodes were taken very seriously in these decades by the officers of the State Children's Department and the Children's Welfare and Public Relief Department which replaced it in 1926.[48] Other girls were reported for 'practising self-abuse' or for hiding with companions in the school lavatories 'long after the school had closed for the day'.[49] Of more seriousness was the unacceptable dirtiness of one of these girls: after she used her bedroom fireplace for defecation, her foster-mother returned her to the Department, feeling 'very disappointed as she is such a nice looking child she is also very untruthful but she cannot keep her as she has young boys of her own'.[50]

State wards were often reported for theft. Again and again on the records of girls' lives would be an entry reporting very minor thefts (a penny even) or small items such as pencils or other children's lunches.[51] If a state girl began stealing more significant amounts of money there was a tone of fatalistic severity in the reports, a sense that little could have been done to stop the escalation of the girl's activities.[52] Ellen Black, the illegitimate child of a state girl, was reported in 1927 to be

manifesting very bad qualities. She is a bright child and until lately we thought well of her. Yesterday it came to light that for some time she has been very dishonest and a serious climax has just come.[53]

Girls were still made to write letters of repentance, such as this letter written in 1933:

Dear Sir,
    I am very sorry for what I have done I have stole told lies and have been rude to uncle, but I have said I was very sorry to him. I am going to be a better girl in the future and I am very sorry for you because I know now that you want us girls to grow up truthful and honest. But I did not quite understand what trouble it was going to bring me for telling such lies and stealing. I ask you Mr Burns one thing if you think you can ever forgive me for what I have done.[54]

Shaming and guilt were used to try to stop state children from stealing. It should be reiterated that state children were issued with regulation outfits and might be allowed to keep in their box small personal treasures that they acquired at Christmas. But until 1939 birthdays were not celebrated in state institutions and it was quite possible for children not to have any personal property at all.[55] Most theft, not surprisingly, involved 'lots of little things. Such as handkerchiefs and also sums of money from 20/- downwards'.[56] Small sums of money, but as one foster-mother put it, it was not the amount but 'the continual worry'.[57] Only in the case of a child stealing lunches would an investigation be made into why a child stole; spiritual hunger met with the secretary's severe disapproval.

It appears that you are developing into such a little thief everything has to be kept under lock and key; that you add to this wickedness, untruths. Just stop and think what a character you are gaining for yourself – the brand of a liar and a thief.[58]

Children would be warned that unless they ceased their disobedience, they would compel the secretary to punish them by recalling them or extending their sentence. Thus they would be the cause of their own punishment: they would 'compel' the secretary to punish them. Then their wickedness would be transformed to part of the cosmological world, the secretary becoming merely the agent of some immutable order of things. The prospect of punishment usually meant that children would write to the secretary in tones so contrite and formal that one is led to suspect that foster-mothers may occasionally have helped compose such letters.

The methods used to discourage theft were rarely successful. One foster-mother wrote of her charge who had, it should be noted, been given, not stolen, money:

she get the laundry work for me to do and the visitors gave her eightpence for her self and she spent it and ate all she bought before she came home I do not like her loitering about the streets you do not know what mischief she might get into she got 7 pence again last evening but she spent it again in lollies . . . I want to learn her to be saving . . . I think if you sent a letter to her it will do her more good than me talking to her she was very frightened when she got your last letter if I tell her she will have to go back she nearly breaks her heart.[59]

However, a greater acceptance of the principles behind child psychology meant that during the 1930s theft by state wards was sometimes treated with more understanding. For example, a child who spent her Sunday school money, instead of being 'condemned',[60] might merely be told that she should be more trustworthy and set a good example to the younger children in the home. It might be calmly noted that a girl was 'not always truthful'.[61]

In many cases the difficulties faced by foster-parents continued to be so great that it was impossible for affection for the child to balance the obstacles. Where there were already children in the home the difference in regard for natural children and foster-children might be marked. Evelyn Penny thought foster-children were happiest where there were no other children in the home.[62]

Foster-parents faced with the care of a girl who continued to be incontinent for example, despite their having done everything to help her, eventually would return her to an institution, feeling bitterness that she had been so 'ungrateful'.[63] A foster-mother might become quite worried over a child who had a mania for 'doing destructive things at school and at home' and yet not complain because of pity for the child.[64] Others felt that their charge had been given 'every chance' and that not having responded they could not 'have the worry any longer I have tried everything to do my best she as a wonderful home but she wants somebody much Harder to controll her'.[65]

Being a foster-parent also required immense energy. One elderly spinster had provided

an excellent home – but she has had Influenza and does not look very well – and she is getting on in years – all the same – as soon as she feels unable to Mother our children properly – I'm sure she will return them voluntarily – she is an excellent F/M.[66]

Standards of foster-care seem to have gone up in the later 1930s. Inspectors might report fine distinctions, one noting that a child was treated 'Not unkindly but indifferently'.[67] In other cases it might be reported that a

child's teacher was concerned as to whether she was really getting a fair deal in the home . . . she had given the girl a ticket for the Football Match and [fostermother] would not let her go and returned the ticket. Ellen says she didn't do her work properly that was why she was not allowed to go. Thirdly one of the children gave Ellen a piece of yellow hair ribbon and her F/M would not let her wear it . . .[68]

A month later, in August 1933, Inspector Lee reported again that

Miss Cleggat of the Education Department spoke to me about this child whom she had particularly noticed when she was at the school recently. The child seems to be very unhappy and repressed and says she is not allowed to play with other girls. Miss Cleggat wondered if the girl had a good home. I notice in Miss Copley's last report that she recommends that this home be watched.[69]

An inspector might comment that

Mrs Smith does not appear to have a friendly manner in speaking to the children. I was at the home when the children came home from school and she ordered the eldest girl to go out and help her husband milk, she is milking two cows at present. Mrs Smith stated that this child is very trying and at first she thought she would have to return her but there has been slight improvement during the past week. She will try to persevere with her.[70]

By 1939 quite specific maternal qualities were looked for in foster-mothers. One inspector doubted whether he would recommend the following home in the future:

F.M. does not appear to have any soft motherly instincts. When I asked if girl capable of doing the little routine duties etc. F/M threw her head back and said, 'Oh Yes, that is what I had her for'. I spoke to Elfrida with regard to her behaviour and she has promised to try and do better.[71]

The ledgers of children boarded out show that most state girls had a succession of foster-homes in the 1920s and 1930s.[72] Some girls adjusted to this, one confiding to Inspector Copley in 1930 that her present home was 'the best home she has had'.[73] But what was the effect on others?

Dorothy Jones was placed in 1930. Her first foster-mother decided to return her, asking for

a better class child, with refined nature, so that she can be brought up as her own.

Mrs White would like her to have dark hair and eyes, so as to resemble the family.

She will also take her without an outfit.[74]

Three years later, in 1935, Dorothy was again returned because another foster-mother had injured her leg.[75] Three months later yet another foster-mother returned the child, saying she was 'a good little girl but is not the type of child she wanted'.[76] Other foster-mothers reported that after caring for a child for nine years they had 'grown fond of the child but now she has got quite beyond me and does not seem to care for anybody or anything'.[77]

Larger than the numbers of girls who were returned must have been those who were threatened with being returned. The following two letters were written in 1919 and 1926 respectively:

She seemed to think that having had her so long we would not send her away but me posting that letter has let her see that she can go a step too far . . . We would not like to part with her there is only just Mr Duncan and her in the family and she has got just like one of us.[78]

I have always found Marie hard to manage and my only power over her was to threaten to send her back, then after a cry she would be a good girl for quite a long time but I have threatened so many times that it has lost effect.[79]

What did this do to the sense of self that these girls possessed? Often girls would beg forgiveness when they were threatened with return from foster-parents they loved:

I spoke to Judy whom I saw riding home from school, she expressed great pleasure at being in such a good home and promised to try and overcome her dirty ways and other failings.[80]

Just a few lines to let you know I am very sorry for the wicked deeds I've done. I like living with Mr and Mrs Bruce very much and I did not wish to leave them. If Mrs Bruce will give me another chance will you still let me stay hear and I will promis you to be a better girl . . .[81]

One little girl tried particularly hard:

Dear Sir,

I am writing to tell you that Mummy has written and told you how I behaved. I am not so naughty after all. When I go out the girls say I pull faces and dear Sir I never at all. Dear Sir I would die to think I had to leave dear mother.

When Mummy is washing I get up and help her with all my might. Dear Sir Friday we had an exam and I was top of the grade VI class. I have just got into the

way of the grade VI work. Mr Coglan said I am good and I think it would be a pity
to go away. Dear Sir will you let me stop. Mummy said we are not happy and we
are all very happy ... Mummy thinks I say things behind her back and I never
even mention anything.[82]

But despite the advice of the Department she was returned by her foster-
mother.

All these letters show that most girls realized who the arbiter of their
destinies was, and what they should write to placate him. In reply to their
letters, what sort of advice did they get? From Celestine Houlgrave, the
secretary from 1918–27, they received letters which reiterated that love
and approval were to be earned if one were a state child.

I know Mrs Bruce is very, very kind to you and in every way you are a lucky little
girl to have such a good home and I should be sorry to have to take you away from
such a home, but unless you obey Mrs Bruce this is what I shall be compelled to
do ... [83]

I am very sorry indeed to learn that you are naughty and rude to Miss Wran, who
is so kind and good to you. I wonder how you would like to be treated as you treat
others for it is really what you deserve. If you are so naughty you cannot expect to
be loved, or even liked by those with whom you come into contact.[84]

Rewards for 'being good' were discussed too:

I want you to make up your mind that you will be a good girl. Be straight forward
and nice in your actions and you will find that if you overcome these naughty
tricks, of yours you will be a happy girl and loved by all those in the home as well
as outside people and you will have many friends ... started to climb the ladder of
success.[85]

State wards were sometimes deliberately kept in ignorance about their
destinies. In response to distraught letters from a young girl who had
been sent from her aunt's home to service in the country in 1916, the
secretary initially replied that her naughtiness had forced her aunt 'to ask
me to take you away, and for a little while at any rate let you feel what it
is to be alone'. Several months later, when the aunt wrote asking for the
girl to be returned, the secretary replied that the girl was

coming to the office on the 1st (today) and I intend to keep her here for a week or
so without telling her how long she is to remain here. It will, I think, do her good
to have a week under the care of our Matron.[86]

The letters written by F.G. Byrne, the secretary of the Children's

Welfare and Public Relief Department, were never quite as severe, but they could be stern enough.

Dear Pat,

Miss Jackson, who recently visited you has reported that you did not pass your examination last year and I am very much annoyed with you. She further reports that this is because you did not put your mind to your work, and if I do not hear better reports on you from the School Teacher this year, I shall be compelled to consider some way of punishment for you.

You are over twelve years of age and only in the fourth grade, and there are lots of little girls who are only nine years and who are in the fifth grade.

Please remember you must work harder this year.

Yours obediently,
F.G. Byrne,
Secretary.[87]

Dear Tamara,

My inspector has reported that you have been very impudent to your school teacher and that you have a pert little manner.

Now these are two things that no little girl should be either impudent or pert, and I want you to try and overcome these bad habits . . .

No one likes little girls who are impudent, and I feel sure you do not want to grow up with no one loving you.[88]

Physical assault of state children seems to have occurred slightly less in the years between the wars. Assault fell into two categories: excessive punishment and straight-out cruelty. In the 1920s and 1930s many parents punished their children with a strap, and although such punishment for state children was forbidden, it does seem to have occurred.

When the Department received a warning about the ill-treatment of two sisters in a foster-home in the Adelaide hills in 1929, they sent an inspector out to investigate. Miss Lee, in accordance with instructions which stated that state children must be questioned apart from their foster-parents, closely queried what had happened and reported that

These two little girls did not make any serious complaint about being ill-treated when I questioned them at home yesterday. They also denied that they had ever been molested by boys on the way home from school or that they had heard any boy use bad language. I questioned the parents . . . denied that they had ever been cruel to the children but admitted that they did occasionally beat the children with a strap. They evidently believe in bringing up the children strictly.[89]

No further action was taken.

Other girls did suffer physical violence. In one instance a girl was beaten by a foster-mother who was suffering from delusions, and the girl was eventually removed from the home.[90] But it was something else again if a subnormal girl of eight years was being beaten with a cane by both foster-parents for misdemeanours as trivial as taking peaches or accidentally breaking a cup. Evelyn Penny reported that

We examined her body which was clean and well-nourished and free from bruises or marks with the exception of one long straight mark across her back on the right side about 4 inches in length of a pale yellow green colour. It appeared to be the kind of mark which would have been caused by a blow with a narrow cane and it was fading. In answer to questions Marjorie said she had been given the stick and strap by Mr and Mrs Maguire when she was naughty. She had been hit on the back leg and arms and sometimes she had seen marks on her afterwards . . . I consider she [Mrs Maguire] is much too free in her use of corporal punishment even for trivial offences as is her husband who according to Mrs Maguire had given Marjorie the strap for breaking a tumbler.

I consider that this form of punishment would have a specially prejudicial effect on a subnormal child.[91]

This girl was removed immediately.

The description of Marjorie as 'subnormal' highlights a change in the Department's practices which can be attributed to the Department's liaison with Dr Constance Davey, a psychologist employed by the Education Department from 1924–42. This remarkable woman began the first 'opportunity class' for problem cases and slow learners in South Australia in 1925 and in 1931 began a course to train teachers to work with retarded children.[92] As a result of Dr Davey's liaison with the State Children's Department, intelligence tests began to be used in determining the abilities of state wards and assessing what sort of work they could do. With the gradual spreading in the 1930s of the notion of clinical testing for mental retardation, it slowly became apparent that a sizable minority of wards suffered differing degrees of mental handicap. A girl might be described as 'below the average ability of her grade' despite being years above the 'average age'. It would be noted that

2 She is a good 'house-girl type' and would probably benefit by a Central School Course.
3 She will probably do poorly in Gr VII if she is promoted, whereas in a house-wifery Course would do well.[93]

Other age-related criteria came to be used in the 1920s and 1930s. A girl who refused to play with children her own age and preferred the company of younger children was commented on.[94] A few state girls were violently or oddly. mad.[95] Some undoubtedly inherited their sub-normality, the Departmental notes stating briefly that the mother was 'an ex-state girl', 'decidedly simple mentally'.[96] But it is not possible to assess how many girls were afflicted in this way. A number of girls were merely described as 'mentally and physically a poor lot'.[97] In many cases this would seem to have resulted from their impoverished environment, though few were as badly treated as the nine year old who had been hidden in a shed for years.[98] There were other children who through an itinerant upbringing were still at thirteen considered to be 'quite ignorant'.[99] State girls were often many years behind other children at school, so they would be the biggest girl in the class – at puberty certain to make a girl self-conscious.[1]

A girl might be noted to be 'timid and rather fearful' by the inspector. Dr Davey would find her to be 'a subnormal child with a mental age of about six years. She is nervous and shows definite signs of fear'. An Opportunity Class would be recommended and sympathetic considera-tion given to 'a change of environment' for the girl.[2] Other alternatives Dr Davey might recommend were the Montessori Class at the Industrial School or, for severely impaired wards, Minda Home.

A member and one-time president of the State Children's Council, Walter Hutley, advocated the employment of a full-time psychologist who could examine all children, so impressed was he by Dr Davey's expertise. Recalling the visit of a psychological expert from Sydney, he advocated the setting up in South Australia of a graded institution along the lines of the Mittagong Farm Home in New South Wales. He urged changes in order to 'bring the system up to date', to make it at least equal to other states and perhaps even be 'a model for the world' again.[3] But others expressed some opposition to Dr Davey's expertise. Mr W. Hall, a magistrate of the children's court, mentioned that he had found her 'elaborate theoretical' reports of no practical value to him.[4]

The problem of protection for retarded female wards was addressed by a Royal Commission on Law Reform which resulted in the introduc-tion of a provision for the indefinite supervision and/or detention in an institution of any female person 'certified by two legally qualified medical practitioners' to be mentally defective. This was contained in Section 126, subsection 5 of the Maintenance Act, 1926.[5]

In regard to physical health, many state girls came under Departmental care in poor condition, and some improvement when they were first boarded-out was often commented on. Attention to hearing and eyesight often brought results too: in 1935 one girl was reported by Miss Jackson to have 'brightened up very much since having her eyes attended to'.[6] Babies who suffered from ill-health were often more easily placed in foster-homes than older girls with more intractable health problems.[7]

With increased medical knowledge, century-old scourges such as diphtheria might not prove fatal in 1936, but ear infections still troubled many children.[8] Some children were hospitalized, a lonely experience in a big institution in the days when parents were only allowed to visit twice a week. One girl who stayed for six weeks in 1934 was visited several times by her foster-mother, the inspector noted approvingly.[9]

Schoolwork was an area where any slowness revealed itself but it was also an area where, especially in the later 1930s, some state girls managed to succeed. They seem to have been girls who had been in one foster-home for long periods, girls with close relationships, girls with 'plenty of clothes'.[10] Ellen Partridge was one such bright state girl. She hoped to do well in her 'QC' (Qualifying Certificate) and to do some commercial work after that. In fact she later went to Intermediate Standard at Muirden College during the 1940s.[11] She was not the only state girl to get her QC in that decade.[12]

It should be pointed out here that the Department was probably only reflecting wider community values in its attitude to secondary education. In the 1920s in South Australia only about 5 per cent of all children received secondary education of any sort.[13] For a girl to have extra funds spent on her by the Department in the inter-war years for schooling or training of any sort meant that a great deal of justifying had to be done. Proof that the funds would not be wasted had to be supplied at every stage. Certificates had to come from the girl's teacher, the headmaster, and her local minister. The girl herself would be reminded that she was very fortunate. The secretary of the Board of the Children's Welfare and Public Relief Department in 1934 told Ethel Wright that

It has been decided by the Children's Welfare and Public Relief Board to allow you to remain at school until the end of the year, at which time a report from your teacher will be called for. I hope this will be very good, so that the Board will not feel disappointed in allowing you this extra time.

As you know when children reach 14 years of age they are supposed to leave school, which in your case was last November. I am afraid you have not worked quite as hard as you might have, but I understand you are much better in health now, and there is no excuse for you not working the next months.

I should like you to bear in mind that this extra schooling is a special favour, and is not granted to every boy and girl under the care of the Department.

Your sincere friend,
F.G. BYRNE,
Secretary.[14]

References from the clergy and teachers were of a set form, inviting the referee to 'Strike out any portion of the above you cannot honestly declare to be true and initial the alterations'. The ward herself would also have to sign an undertaking to repay any monies lent.

Sometimes a girl would receive exceptionally good reports from her teachers, stressing not her achievements but how much she had improved. Sally Black's teacher wrote in 1915 that:

She is a very nice girl in all respects and has made what her teachers call 'wonderful progress'. All her sewing (and book work) is very neatly and carefully done. The improvement in sewing as indeed in all her work is very considerable. She was very backward when she came here, so that for our sake she had to be classified low. She is however associated in the class with others who are not much smaller than herself.[15]

The problems some girls might have to overcome were recognized by Departmental staff. Miss A.M. Kentish wrote in 1923 of a child who had not in the past been allowed to attend school: 'She had been to school for 3 days and the school teacher said that for a child who had lived in seclusion as she has, and who knows nothing, she did very well'.[16] Other girls were described as having books that were a credit to them or receiving 'an honour ribbon' for good work at school.[17]

If money for extra years of schooling was not forthcoming from the Department, a foster-family might occasionally keep a girl without subsidy after she turned fourteen in order that she might have extra schooling. But in the early 1930s, with the depression at its height, some foster-families found they could not afford this, one writing sadly:

we would have liked her to had [sic.] another year at school but things being so bad we are unable to do so at our own expense.
PS. We do not want to part with Sarah.[18]

In 1923 a careful housewife and mother of six, Rosabelle Farmer, described how after her daughters had 'showed promise',

I went to see the headmaster (Mr Gates) of the Unley State School. He was very much affected that I was taking them away. He said it was a great pity, and he almost begged me to allow them to stay. He said, 'Can you not possibly manage to let them have another year?' I said, 'No; circumstances make it necessary for me to take them away, and I cannot help myself'. He said that if he had had the girls he would have made something of them if they could have gone through his school. Q. 66583. However, your income would not run it, and you had to take them away?
A. Yes.

Her twin daughters of fifteen went to work as live-in domestics receiving sixteen shillings a week each, and giving ten shillings of that to their mother. Life as a domestic was considered hard though, even by contemporary standards.

our children are homesick. The girls are only 15 years of age, and they have been very good girls, and have denied themselves so much that we felt the least we could do was to give them a little home life before they went out to work permanently. We promised them that if they stopped at work until our debts were paid then they could come home for 12 months. Three months ago I went over to see their employer, and she was very pleased with them, and wanted me to allow them to stay there permanently, and I promised they would remain there for six months. That six months will expire in September and then they will come home.[19]

But for state wards, the years between the ages of fourteen and twenty-one were spent almost entirely at work and away from family. This life is described in the next chapter.

CHAPTER 6

Going to Work
1915-40

Should there be a great number of guests, the maid helps her mistress in this. Sandwiches, thin bread and butter, fancy biscuits, and dainty cakes should form the eatables. As fresh guests arrive, the maid brings in fresh tea and hot water and removes the previous things. It is not customary for the maid to remain in the room, but she should be ready in case any fresh cups or saucers or plates are necessary, which should be brought in on a tray.[1]

Just how unpopular was domestic service between the wars? Was it second choice, or was it despised and avoided at all costs? It has been shown that the percentage of the total female workforce in domestic service declined from 30.61 per cent in 1901 to 21.42 per cent in 1921. Between 1921 and 1933 the percentage hardly declined at all (from 21.42 per cent to 21.39 per cent), but by 1947 it had fallen to 5.84 per cent.[2] This decline was matched by a rise in the percentage of women working in health, education, commerce, and finance. As early as 1913, visitors to Australia noticed how girls disliked domestic service and why:

Most girls positively refuse to take up domestic service as a calling, although it offers more than double the money to be earned in factories ... There is a growing contempt for housework. The reasons for this have been so frequently discussed that it is sufficient merely to state the fact and mention that the chief objections are the length of hours, confinement to the house in the evening, and the universal custom that all domestics who wish to spend any time with a young man must go into the street in order to have the pleasure of his company.[3]

Most state girls, however, continued to work as domestic servants in the years between the wars. Despite shorter working hours and great advances in domestic technology, domestic service was disliked as a form of employment more than ever before. It seemed even more humiliating to be a servant when other girls worked in factories, offices, or shops with fixed hours and companions their own age. However, the Department continued to see domestic service as a safe occupation and also, importantly, one which fitted a girl for her life's work.

134

I suppose like all girls you hope some day to have a home of your own, a husband to look after, and possibly children to bring up. How do you hope to do it, making no effort now to learn, making no effort to do what you should. You are instead of learning to do well, learning to shirk work and to be a slattern. If you think this is the way to be happy you are greatly mistaken.[4]

This clear statement of one of the advantages of service was written in 1914 by the secretary of the State Children's Department.

By 1932, even though it was the Department's unofficial policy to give state children the opportunity of working for their foster-parents as domestics,[5] most still went to work for strangers. They went to middle and upper-class homes in good suburbs.[6] Letters of application to the Department for a girl often stressed the chief advantage of state girls, namely that they could not change their situation at will.[7]

In the war years there were wide fluctuations in the opportunities open to servants and a general shortage of servants in the years 1917 and 1918. In the latter year, applicants had to wait at least three months, and by 1919 the Department had a waiting list of ninety-six names from Methodist applicants alone. Some applicants even stated that they would 'not be particular' about a girl's religion in the hope of getting a servant more quickly.[8]

After the letter came the inspection of the service home. Moral qualities continued to matter after certain minimum standards in regard to accommodation had been met.[9] The opinion of the local police might still be sought.[10] The inspector would report her impressions of the mistress of the house.[11] A little more attention began to be paid to whether a mistress appeared to be kind and intelligent. It was a point in her favour if she announced her intention of treating her state girl as 'one

The twentieth century saw other job opportunities slowly open up for women, and domestic service became increasingly disliked. One of the new jobs was the telephone exchange, Adelaide, shown here in 1907.

of the family'.[12] A wife might be quite young, in some cases without children, but as long as she was considered to be 'a nice sensible girl' all was well.[13] A mistress who announced her intention of 'training' a girl was always highly regarded: domestic work might then still be a skilled occupation.

'Better training' was advocated as the solution to the servant shortage in the United Kingdom at this time. Training schools were set up, but of course did little to arrest the decline. In Tasmania in 1926, a two-year training course had been started for state wards intending to work as domestic servants, but nothing as thorough as this was done in South Australia.[14] Girls were very often used as unskilled labour in different institutions such as the Central Depot, the Industrial School, and Seaforth Convalescent Home. Although they might pick up some skills there, there was no formal training.[15] Cows were kept at Seaforth Convalescent Home until 1940 and many a girl learnt to milk, but skills learnt in a large institution may not have been very applicable to a suburban home. One inspector commented on this to the secretary in 1922:

girls who are placed out, in nearly every case they are not sufficiently trained in plain cooking and housework there is rather too much outdoor work expected of them, such as milking, feeding of calves scrubbing and such like, housework ought to be made more interesting to them.[16]

State girls were expected to adopt the spirit of an apprentice when first sent out to service.[17] They often commented on their own lack of skills. Diana Winterbourne confided in 1936 that

I am very slow and rather nervy. I have had no proper training and am not experienced enough in washing and cooking to satisfy Mrs Grant I am very forgetful but I hope soon under Mrs Grants instructions to get into Mrs Grants ways. Perhaps then my wages could be increased to the 8/-. This would please me much more than receiving 8/- per week when I know that I am not worth it and I would like to keep my place.[18]

The State Children's Department in South Australia thought that small homes and young girls were the ideal combination, older girls being sometimes, 'hard to teach' according to many mistresses.[19] A girl who was not getting on well was sometimes thought to need 'a smaller home where she could be taught and not have so much to do'.[20]

As well as acquiring skills, state girls also were expected to acquire the right attitude to their mistress. They might have to learn this too. Increasingly throughout the decades between the wars, it did not come naturally. One girl had disgusted her employers by her 'ridiculous pretensions'. She was a girl who often displayed insolence in her speech and particularly in her manner towards them.

I have myself been present when she has looked at her mistress with a sense of contempt. Shirley had a great wish to be better educated so that she might fill some position in life other than that of a domestic servant and she was accordingly given special facilities for study so that she might enter the Telephone Dept, but after two attempts to pass the entrance examination in Spelling Arith and composition and failing both times she abandoned the idea.[21]

Inspector Shaw commented on another girl in 1934:

Girl answers back – and is inclined to be pert. Simple home – I admonished Ruth re her pertness – it is a pity if she does not overcome the habit as she is good at cooking and sewing and works well.[22]

Girls were expected to keep their place for as long as possible. Failure to do so might result in a girl's sentence being extended with an explanation such as the following, given in 1929:

In another year your name will again be placed before my Board and I hope by that time I will be able to give an excellent report of your conduct. I have your record before me and I see that since you were 14 you have had four different service placings. Miss White returned you because you refused to do what you were told; Mrs Alp because you could not get on with her; you came back from Mrs Connell because you were too slow and now Mr Black returns you for impudence. This is not a very nice record for a girl of 18 years to have and the sooner you make up your mind to do your work properly the better it will be for yourself.[23]

By 1928 the secretary of the Department's Board could add that because 'times are very bad now' girls needed the protection of the Department to prevent them becoming like 'hundreds of others around Adelaide out of work', instead of enjoying 'a nice home and plenty to eat'.[24] By 1929 the secretary could write that he found it 'very hard to procure situations', for girls in their late teens, and by 1933 there was a 'considerable delay' in finding situations for girls.[25] The annual reports for these years mention difficulty in finding situations for both sexes.

The depression also affected girls who were able to remain with their own families on probation, since many of these families were out of work. One girl whose mother complained in 1933 that her daughter could not get work, was reduced to having only

a couple of old dresses besides the clothes she has on, she has no singlets, stockings or overcoat.

A dirty grubby looking house and they haven't much heart I think for anything, they are all out of work and have scarcely any clothes any of them.[26]

137

The family was described as having 'not much push' although it had been conceded that the father was 'a sober hardworking man when work can be found'.[27] The struggle to find work that many girls had is repeatedly detailed.

Girl still out of work 3/7/30.
Still out of work. Mary is trying to get work in a factory – Rozella.
Girl still out of work 23/7/30.
Mary is still out of work but has the promise of the first vacancy at the Rozella factory.[28]

The depression also meant that more state wards had to move away from their foster-homes once they reached the age of fourteen (the South Australian school-leaving age after 1915), because there was no work for them in the neighbourhood.[29]

For those who did have jobs in domestic service there was as much pettiness as ever. As one girl alleged:

I got on with Mrs Brown splendidly for the first few weeks and I thought for always. But Mrs Brown has a very hasty temper, and of course takes things in a very different way to what I really meant it . . . If it was not for the perpetual little rows things would run smoothly. You see I have to tell Mrs Brown every time I wash a pair of gloves or anything.[30]

Another girl complained that her mistress

finds fault with every trifling thing and then snaps my head of just about so you can quite guess how I can't help cheeking her I am always sorry afterwards about it but can't help it she gets me so worked up that I feel like crying and running away.[31]

As seems to have been common in the middle classes, girls still had to bear with their mistress commenting on the clothes they wore on their afternoon off.[32] What was disparaged as an 'elaborate frock' might be found by an inspector to be merely 'a plain little voile suitable for her position'.[33] Another burden domestics hated was the absolute lack of privacy available to the girl who lived-in:

the eldest girl came up into my room which is used as a lumber and sewing room and went through my things and read a letter that I had written to Nurse Walker, I mentioned that I had to take orders from a girl of fifteen and eleven she told her mother that she heard me say so . . . I should think that I could have something private if I have not got a nice room . . .[34]

Many women wrote of having to endure 'nothing but cheek and insult from morning til night'.[35] To an observer writing of Australia in 1920 it seemed, however, that

There is no better domestic worker anywhere. She can do anything, unlike the English girl who always wants her work to be defined, and she will do it with a smile, if you treat her well, and refrain from displaying your superiority. But she must be allowed her freedom and she must be well paid and have ample consideration.[36]

State girls were alleged to be slow to get up in the morning, others 'disobeyed or questioned' orders, one even questioned religious belief.[37] Above all, they were said to be inefficient, one irate housewife stating that her girl was 'little better than no one at all'.[38] A few mistresses prided themselves on knowing how to manage a moody girl; far more complained of 'back answers' or of a girl 'as stubborn as a mule'[39]

Many women tried to be fair. One wrote in 1915:

now as I write she is in her room simply on strike. She is a fine girl with many good points in fact I like her and admire many things in her character but I will not put up with impudence from any of my maids . . . I know it is mostly temper because she likes and respects her home here, of course she is an excellent worker and so clean, besides looking such a fine girl and the making of a handsome woman.

The next day this girl had regretted her 'strike' and wrote:

I must admit I was very rude to Mrs King also that I promised you that I would try to do well in my new home But all people are not alike Matron was always kind and good to me. She never complained unless she really had to. I have tried very hard but Mrs King is very hard to please. I don't think Mrs King told you, that she is never at rest unless finding fault. Anyway Sir I will have another good hard try to do well . . . [40]

Another woman wrote in 1937:

I have had Ann here for over 6 months. The first few weeks she was here I could not wish for a better girl. When the Inspector called in February, I told her Ann was very moody, but that I did not want her reported for anything, but since then, I have done everything in my power to make her happy, and keep her in a good mood. I have asked her several times, if she is happy, or would she rather go back to the home, and she assures me she wants to stay here and is happy. But it seems as if she is getting worse. She seems to have such a horrible little temper, the least thing puts her out, and she gets in to these tempers, and slams the things about, and bangs the doors, and it seems to knock about and scratch everything we possess . . . We cannot correct her about anything now, or alter the run of her work at all, or this is what happens.[41]

139

Doubtless some girls were exasperating, but many found constant correction very discouraging. Betty Adams wrote in 1934 asking whether

I could come back to Seaforth because I don't like it up here any more. I get treated alright, but when a person does all he can and then gets nothing but growled at all the time one feels like going somewhere else.[42]

And Clare Hill complained from the country:

Mrs Trumpington is like a bear with a sore head. Well I don't think I'll be hear very long I'm sick to death of place they think themselves God almighty because there got a motorcar and Tracter.[43]

In *Memories of a Country Childhood*, Judith Wallace remembered that 'The kitchen was a wonderful place to be in. It was roomy, warm and full of activity . . .'. She and her sister were sometimes allowed in the servants' sitting room.[44] But in a smaller house children might cause tension whether they were younger than the ward or the same age. One girl caught a child

placing her fingers in the custard. I corrected her and took the custard away. She flew into a rage and picking a piedish from the table threw it at me and hit me in the back I smacked her on the hand and she went screaming to her mother. Her mother said I was not to hit her . . .[45]

Children could make a girl very tired:

I am writing to you to ask your advice I am not very happy about my present place everything is always wrong no matter how hard I try to do good there are five children here and there most rude they spit at me and pinch me tell tales and what so ever, but I will try hard and stop three months if you wish . . .[46]

Sometimes a girl felt that children 'love to tease me and say all they can to make me unhappy', but another girl might optimistically conclude that 'the children are the only bother but I will soon be able to manage them'.[47] Even if children had irritated a state girl, she was not supposed to inflict physical punishment. One girl was returned in 1914 for slapping a two-year-old's face.[48] The inspectors seemed to have been aware that children could annoy, one writing:

I think perhaps the girl has got tired of the children they are all small and during the time they have been living in North Adelaide Mrs W has only had part of a house . . . they certainly annoyed one another as I observed for myself during my visit . . .[49]

Physical abuse of a petty sort continued to be a hazard. Clare Hill wrote in 1923 that her mistress was always:

calling me a lazzie dog cow and pig she also kicks me and hits me about the head and about my back with bits of broom handle, she tell me I've got no brains Well I know this is no game to be bruised about . . . I now I never came from a good home I had to learn the best I could and it make it hard for me know I think to myself and ask myself have I got a friend or not it seem to me that no one care a bit when I get knocked about like this.[50]

Clare was sent back five months later by her mistress.

The following two assaults took place in the 1930s. In the first, an inspector reported that:

Mrs Koln confessed to me during one altercation with Barbara, she gave her a couple of hits with a strap over girl's arm – Barbara said they did not hurt – however I advised F/M not to do so again – Barbara has promised to behave better in future.[51]

The second account concerns a girl who had complained in 1937 that her master

had pulled her hair on many occasions and once recently had pulled her to the floor and banged her head on the asphalt floor. He had also come into her bedroom when she was late getting up and pulled her out by the hair.
   I asked Mr Bach if these statements were true. He admitted pulling the girls hair at times saying there was no other way of making the girl do as she was told and Mrs Bach was too lenient. He said he had banged her head on the floor but on one occasion when he pulled her hair she slid to the floor. He stated he had never pulled her out of bed but certainly had often thrown water over her in an effort to get her up.[52]

Mrs Bach stated that she would have returned the girl before 'but hoped she would improve, also it was hard to get a local girl to go out on a farm'. The girl was removed.
   However easy it would be to sympathize entirely with state girls, some did seem to dislike a slap less than continual nagging. One girl recalled in 1924 that 'I had all my own way at Smiths and other places by cheeking them. Mrs Durer gave me a couple of cracks so I did not cheek her. I liked her'.[53] The reasons for liking a mistress were multitudinous. Some were liked because they were understanding and prepared to forgive, others because they appreciated the affection a girl gave to the children.[54] One woman wrote after her state girl had been with her for five years,

I can truthfully assure you that Sue is a very good girl (morally) and a very willing girl. To most people she appears dull – her appearance is against her. When she leaves here I hope she gets a country place as she is so fond of horses and cattle. My loss <u>will</u> be somebody's gain if they can only understand and appreciate the girl.[55]

This seems to have been a common appraisal. Other women wrote that a girl was as 'honest as the day' or 'kind and willing and always so happy'.[56]

The ways in which a kind mistress could help a girl remained the same. In 1934 Mary Jeferson was said to be pleased and satisfied with her situation, her mistress having made her some house frocks. Two years later she was still contented and her mistress was now giving her sixpence extra to help with her glory box.[57]

But kind mistress or not, housework was still hard work. Clarice Hoffman complained in 1917:

I have got all the housework to do all the washing and ironing all the cooking and baking. Mrs Smith engages a lot of Visitors here every week from 8 to 25 Visitors a week so you can see Mr Gray for yourself I have plenty to do. If I worked like this in some places I would get in wages as much as 20/– a week as I know girls who do get good wages and do not work anly [sic.] more than me. I get tired of too much. I have to dress in uniform and cuffs and collar and cap [with] Visitors at least and always wear unaform when no visitors, but not cuffs collar and cap as I can't manage it with all the work. These people have not been in Australia very long, I am the second maid they have had since they have been out here, the first maid they had only stayed 2 months and they couldn't get another very easy so they went to our department for a girl . . . Mrs Smith expected me to do sewing for them on my own sewing machine. I told her no I never do this for any body altho' Mr Gray I did do a little for her for kindness as she cant Dressmake herself and she has no machine.

When Mrs Smith got a dressmaker in for a week I lent her my sewing machine and when I got it back it had the spring broken. I felt very cross about it and said I would never lend it again I said to Mrs Smith when Ladies can afford to dress in beautiful silks and satins and keep maids I think they could afford to get a sewing machine . . .

The inspector found that Mrs Smith was a kind woman and that Clarice had a pleasant room but added that

I couldn't help feeling that all the work is left entirely to Clarice, she assured me that it was she does the cooking washing and ironing . . . Clarice struck me as being good and truthful, but she is of small physique and says she gets so very tired and cannot keep up with the work.[58]

A delicate girl was too much of a burden for most households, as many a mistress complained.[59] Despite advances in domestic technology in the

1920s and 1930s – such as gas stoves, laundry tubs with hot and cold running water, vacuum cleaners, and kitchen appliances – domestic service still required physical strength. And the hours were long. Any number of events could dramatically alter a girl's workload for the worse. The mistress might go to hospital for a confinement or the washerwoman might leave.[60] Dramatic changes in workload would bring Departmental intervention in most cases, but in others girls had to complain:

I have been working since I was fourteen years old and I have not had a holiday yet. I have been working very hard in that time and in this place, I think I have worked too hard for I am quite run down. Mrs Jones says herself I am very much in need of a holiday and it would do me the world of good. I am working from 6 am until 8 pm without a break. I think that is far too long, because a working man only has 8 hours a day. Every working man and woman has a holiday every year, and I think I could have one too.[61]

The sort of place considered just too hard was described by Inspector Perkins in 1919:

The house is two-storied and contains 11 rooms in all two of which are let. No other help is employed except May and there are five children in the family these are alleged to be troublesome . . . May attends no church as she is not able to get through her work in time to walk there in the morning . . . would like to sing in the choir but is not allowed to attend the practices.[62]

There is some evidence that a hard place ruled by an unkindly mistress was less and less tolerated in the 1930s. Marlene Brown was removed from her situation by the Department in 1935. As the inspector reported, an argument precipitated her removal from what was undoubtedly a very hard place

Mrs Schwartz said last Saturday week Marlene threw a wet chamois leather used for cleaning at her.

I questioned Marlene who admitted this but said Mrs Schwartz had just before caught hold of her dress to make a complaint and tore her dress right up the back. She showed me the frock which was torn but Mrs Schwartz said Marlene had pulled away from her. Later in the day Mrs S threw a dish of water over her.

Marlene said she rises at 5.30 am and gave me a list of her duties until 9 am which would keep her very busy. She said if everything is not finished up to time Mrs S becomes very annoyed.[63]

This girl was removed.

But many things had *not* changed by the late 1930s. In 1939 girls still had to clean grates too heavy to lift and carry heavy baskets of wet washing (which they were not allowed to begin on Sunday afternoon).[64]

They continued to do heavy work under constant direction and correction.

There seem to have been many ways in which girls sought to resist the lowly status that being a domestic servant inevitably conveyed. Refusal to act in a deferential manner was one way. It not only irritated employers but also implied the domestic servant's steady dislike of her position. Many girls aspired to being able to board away from their 'situation'. That, at least, led to their having some independence and privacy.[65]

Many girls refused to act in the manner of an inferior. They made it clear that service was galling to them and ensured that their lack of deference was noticed, as the following two incidents from the late 1930s show:

Mrs White states Jo at times was very cheeky on one occasion told her to shut up – resents correction.

In course of conversation with Jo I reprimanded her for her behaviour and warned her if she did not do better she would have to be transferred to the G.P.S. [Girls Probationary School] – she pertly replied she didn't care – no one believes the girls – the mistresses word is always taken – I again gave Jo a very straight talking to – she has promised to try and mend her ways.[66]

Mrs Smith stated she gave Wendy some good second-hand clothes for morning use – she stated she would not wear them . . . I reprimanded Wendy for her behaviour.[67]

All this was intimately connected to knowing one's place. What that meant in 1914 is shown in the following letter written by a state girl to her sister who was working in the same big house where she had previously worked.

when I am down in town I'll ring you up that is if you are allowed to use the phone (I was) I bet you were disappointed when Ma came and spoiled your plans and guess it made you feel a bit small to show you up like that . . . I often stood out at the gate or over one of the fences talking to mine. The boss and Mrs used to go seem [see him] sometimes but I didn't care Well old sport you say you wouldn't like to be tied down just yet, but Married life is all right . . . I suppose you are dreading the time for day at homes, but the[y] dont start till April do they I used to have to take tea out on the verandah I didn't like it much either . . .

I used to get a bit nervous sometimes but Mike and I would sit and talk then when I got tired I'd go to bed. It isn't nice being le[f]t in a big house on your pat is it. You being used to a farm makes the difference to there isn't much work to fill the day in sometimes, Do you like the Boss? . . . the baker isn't a bad sort does he ever ask where I am Fancy the Benzine man asking about me. I was out with him one night when Mrs Shaw caught me . . .

Miss Penny wrote to the secretary that she thought this house a very lonely home for one of our girls, as they are in no sense treated as members of the family and the evenings especially are very dull for them.

Dorothy is very anxious to go to a Country place where it would be less lonely and more homely.[68]

Over the next twenty-five years the views of the Department did not change greatly. In 1917 Mary Porter was described as difficult to employ because she 'hardly understood her position in the house and until she learns it will hardly be a success'.[69] In 1922 Miss Kentish reported that a girl was

a very large order and tries to make herself out as very important to the other maids. She declines to wear the uniforms provided by Mrs McDonald and sails about dressed in finery. Instead of attending to her duties she is found reading a book. Mrs McDonald says she has not seen one sign of humility or desire to make good and she is not the type of girl she could be happy to have about her children.[70]

In contrast to conditions which remained unchanged, such as lack of privacy and the possibility of assault, hobbies and amusements became more common in the 1920s. To some extent this was a response to a situation of scarcity: to keep one's servants one had to offer greater freedom and better conditions. One girl wrote in 1921 of being tired, then went on to the more pleasant aspects of her place: 'I have a lovely garden coming on to I have quite a number of pansies all round in and they are so pretty I pressed two or three the other day'.[71] Throughout the 1920s state girls complained about the hours they had to keep, especially when they had an evening off.

The girls who come to see her all tell her they stay out till after nine at night, and it is a very sore point with Dot that I insist upon her being in at regulation hours I feel sure a few words of admonition from you would do her good. She really can be a smart little girl if she likes.[72]

Another girl explained in 1923:

I think half past eight a bit too early for a girl of 19. I know we are told that it is for our own good but it is certainly not much encouragement to a working girl. As every girl likes to have some enjoyment to look forward to. Very often I could have an evening off when it would not be convenient to have an afternoon. And besides if I go out to tea, my whole evening is spoilt . . . you either have to explain why or make some excuse.

As a result of this letter the girl was allowed to remain out until 10 p.m. on her night off.[73]

By the 1930s other pleasures and recreations seem to have been relatively commonplace. A girl might write of going to the beach or of swimming – with the family of course – but even so, a pleasure unknown to earlier generations of state girls. One mistress had:

no complaints to make about Sara – she has been very willing and been very good the time she has been with her – they have moved residences – also had the youngest boy down with Scarlet Fever during this time Sara has been very good. She gave her an extra Spiff (10/-) Mrs Wood has gone to __ Bay for 2 weeks holiday taking Sara with her ... Sara is buying a bicycle on time payment.[74]

By the late 1930s it seems to have been customary for girls to have at least an afternoon off every week, from about 1.30 p.m. to 6.30 p.m., and some girls had, as well as this, 'time between dinner and tea'.[75]

Holidays were another liberalization that appeared increasingly throughout the late 1920s and 1930s. Some state wards had managed to get holidays from the earliest days but they seem to have assumed more the nature of a 'right' as the 1930s advanced. There were girls who were taken on holidays with the family they worked for, but a real holiday meant time away from the family, time away from one's employer.[76]

State wards were only allowed to stay with the most respectable families for holidays. Employers were sometimes able to assess the friends of their state girl, and this was considered more satisfactory than having just the girl's word that a family were respectable.[77] By 1938 girls might write of feeling 'entitled' to a holiday:

I am writing to let you know that I am contented in my situation and still on at the above address I hope to spend a week at Victor Harbour and would like to have your permission. I want to go next Wednesday if all is well From the time I started working until now I have not had a holiday. I have saved the money I need and feel entitled to have a week off from work For some time now I have been feeling a bit run down ...[78]

A girl might allege that some 'Welfare girls ... are allowed holidays, so if it is right for one why not others'.[79]

Girls were expected to behave with decorum on holidays, and the dangers that a holiday might mean if a girl were to stay with her natural family are well outlined in a letter written by the Department's secretary in 1937 to a country employer about a girl's wish to have a holiday:

I have delayed answering the letter in order that it might receive proper consideration, so that I might be fortified in my decision by one of the lady members of the Board who has always taken a keen interest in this particular girl ...

As you yourself have mentioned the girl going about Easter time, it is suggested that she should go up on Thursday, the day before Good Friday, be with her people, and return to you on the Tuesday after Easter Monday.

It is felt that, whilst the Easter tide festivities are in progress, the girl will perhaps be a little more settled and will avoid any opportunity of being out and wandering the streets and perhaps getting into some difficulty, which might upset the good work done over the last twelve months.

I suggest that you can tell Anne the decision, and, so long as she continues to be a good girl and satisfies you, she can write this Department for a rail ticket a week or ten days before the suggested holiday.

Yours obediently,
F.G. Byrne,
Secretary.[80]

It is difficult to properly assess whether state girls were paid good wages. They were certainly paid regularly, and the amount entered into a special book. The Department was strict about that. But other factors constantly impinged. An important minority of state wards were mentally subnormal and therefore unable to earn regulation wages. Girls who were subnormal but able to work were very often returned 'time after time' according to the president of the State Children's Council, Harriet Stirling.[81] In the 1930s subnormality began to be more accurately and clinically assessed:

Marjorie North, a pleasant looking girl of 17 years of age was again examined by me today. She has the mental ability of an eight year old child, and can be taught to do routine laundry and housework. In my opinion she needs constant care and supervision as her defect which is of an inheritable type is not noticeable to the casual observer.[82]

If a girl was a slow worker and careless in her personal habits she was very often paid little at service. If she were lucky she found a service home where she was treated kindly and valued for herself and for trying 'to be good'.[83] Some girls were eventually found to be too severely retarded and were sent to Minda Home. Other mildly retarded girls were able to work but even so their employers might report that a girl was

not worth more than her clothing and keep. She is weakminded and has no idea of the value of money for anything and does not remember anything for 10 minutes at a time. Her only saving grace is her innocence and is consequently good with the children. Mrs Palmer would be willing to keep her for 2 years on the above terms and will give her 1/- per week pocket money. [She] has to employ a woman to mend and make her clothing even to mending her stockings and she is unteachable.[84]

During the depression it is apparent that there was a downturn in the number of households that could afford to pay a general servant, and this affected state wards, one employer in 1934 offering to give only 'clothes and pocket money' because she could not pay 'the present rate'.[85] At times girls were given a few extra shillings if a member of the family had been ill or the state girl was put in charge of the house while the mistress was away. As Miss Shaw reported in 1938 of one employer, 'She is very fair to Freda – if guests stay in the home on holiday etc she always pays girl 2/– pwk extra – besides what the guests give her'.[86]

Only in very rare cases did the relationship between a girl and her mistress remain purely financial, and this further complicates the question of earnings. It was precisely the reason why girls were sent to service. The service home was to provide a refuge from the temptations of the working-class girls' world; its support was 'supposed to help compensate for the admittedly low wage'.[87] The state girl to some extent earned her living not only by the work she did, but also through the deference she displayed: 'A girl that has a bad temper, that is idle and refuses to do her work, never expects and ought not to get the regulation wages'.[88]

The number of girls who were paid less than the minimum cannot be calculated but what is apparent is the vast range of wages. By 1939 a girl who came in daily to clean might earn only 7s 6d a week, whereas a girl who lived in and had to be available to babysit at night earned £1 a week.[89] One girl in 1937 'spent an afternoon with her sister Elizabeth and came home very dissatisfied as Elizabeth told her she could be getting 10/– per week and there were plenty of places near her'.[90]

However, higher wages did mean accepting more responsibility. In 1940, to a girl who complained that her mistress did not give her enough direction, the Department wrote:

You must remember that when you secure a position at £1 per week plus your board you must work. Mrs Wright is not going to pay you good wages and expect to have to tell you every little thing you have to do.[91]

And girls were often reminded that to accept 'wages and keep' and then not do their work efficiently was equivalent to 'stealing'.[92]

Evelyn Penny, who more than any other inspector seemed to have a sympathetic ear for state girls' complaints, believed that the girls were underpaid by 1922.

I consider that it would be a good thing for boys and girls over 16 years of age who are capable of earning higher wages to be given the opportunity of doing so.

It would be an incentive for them to do good work, would satisfy their sense of justice and make them much more contented. At present they often feel a grievance against the department when they realise that outside boys and girls are earning so much more than they do even when they are quite as efficient.[93]

Wages were raised in 1925 but in 1926 Miss Penny still thought that

The greatest discrepancy is in the case of girls of 16 and 17 and 18 years of age. I do think they are much underpaid in comparison with outside domestic servants.

Domestic service is a well paid branch of employment and even young girls who are inexperienced can command a good wage.[94]

At the time of the 1926 Royal Commission on Law Reform the wages of state wards were again under revision but were not raised.

The wages of state wards were set and were always limited by a ceiling determined by age. Therefore any help with clothing that a mistress gave her domestic could add to that wage. Before a ward reached the age of sixteen years she was not expected to make her own clothes; her mistress had to clothe her, providing 'a good and complete outfit' at sixteen.[95] An employer would train a girl to sew and, if they lived in the country, help her choose patterns and material from a catalogue. Occasionally a girl might prefer to receive help with clothing rather than earn the regulation wage. One such girl was described in 1936 as 'well-clothed', her winter outfit having cost over £4. She was treated 'as a daughter' and quite content to stay on at 4s a week, a wage the Department considered 'exceedingly low'.[96]

Many girls wrote complaining how hard it was to acquire enough clothes once they turned sixteen. Sometimes they asked to be able to dip into their savings to provide things they needed. Shirley Jones wrote in 1934, asking:

may I have that money which was sent to you from Matron Till I need the money to buy clothes.

It is no fun going about in my working dress all day, I cannot put my best dress on in the afternoons because I wouldn't have anything to wear to Church on Sunday.

Mrs White is going to help me to make my dresses, as soon as I am able to buy some material, so I will be very much obliged if you will let me have my money which consists of £1-9-0 as soon as possible.[97]

Another expense could be a set of false teeth or glasses. Girls had to pay for these out of their savings in most cases.[98] If ever it appeared to the Department that girls were being extravagant about purchases their requests were refused.[99]

A good mistress was one who 'set to work' to put a girl's outfit in order the moment she arrived.[1] Scrimping by an unscrupulous employer was sometimes revealed when another more honest mistress went through the girl's outfit.

the goods returned were 2 pairs of combinations badly made with old body.

Chemise and drawers instead of the other pair of combinations. The ulster returned was in fairly good condition – but not new. The same remark applied to the bloomers. The petticoat was new, but inferior with an old body on a new skirt. The pinafores were much worn, one night dress was new but very inferior in quality, the other was much worn. There were no stockings in the box.[2]

It was rare for a state girl to have anything other than home-made dresses before 1940. One girl wrote in 1936:

Please will you let me have £1-1-0 of my bank money, as I want to get a Tailormade costume costing 29/11.

You see Mr Byrne I am only allowed 5/– a week to clothe myself buy stamps and other odds and ends that are needed and I am badly in need of a winter dress for best but I can't afford it. I have to get a pair of winter shoes for best and by the time I have saved enough money for them winter will be nearly over and I must have a decent dress for best and a costume would last me 3 or 4 winters.

I do like being dressed nicely when I go out I don't waste my money on things that I shouldn't . . .[3]

Any girl who protested about clothing was not regarded in a favourable light, as this report written by Miss Penny in 1921 shows:

I spoke to Sally who took the matter quite philosophically she said she could not possibly dress on her wages and must get what she wanted somehow, that she is a Socialist and intends to get whatever she can.

She seems a most impossible girl and to have no sense of shame or regret for her dishonesty or untruthfulness. She is very disrespectful in speech and manner . . .[4]

Not many girls had such a political approach to theft. It is impossible to draw hard and fast conclusions between the number of thefts and any sense of injustice felt by state wards but for a comment on contemporary standards Miss Penny is illuminating. Writing in 1926, she said

All children are given so much to spend in these days even while at school so that 1/– or 1/6p. wk for boys and girls of 14 or 15 respectively at work seems a very small amount . . .[5]

Occupational destinations are not given in the annual reports of the State Children's Council after 1930 so it is impossible to assess exactly how many state girls worked in other occupations. The 1939 annual report mentioned proudly that two girls had 'lately' taken up music as a career and one had taken up accountancy. The report added that

Many have entered the nursing profession, whilst other girls have secured employment in offices, shops, and factories; others have learnt dressmaking and tailoring.

A small trend away from service is apparent in the 1920s but whether this continued throughout the depression is hard to assess.

Girls on probation with their families were more likely *not* to be working as domestics, reflecting the freedom they sometimes had to choose their own occupation. They were to be found working in milk-bars, in Coles variety stores, or assisting on a fruit stall at the central market.[6] One girl bought a hawker's license and went from house to house selling cottons, needles, and tape, but this, according to one probation officer, was definitely not 'suitable work for a girl'.[7]

In the 1930s many more wards seem to have been employed in boarding-houses or as 'dailies' in private homes. By the end of the 1930s some were even employed as domestics in hospitals, a job quite as arduous as working in a home.[8] Wendy Rogers wrote in 1939:

I am still on trays now, because my feet will not stand the running up and down with the trays I am doing kitchen work now and it contains of washing up the dishes, wash half the kitchen floor, the nursery and the nursery office, the stairs bathroom and also half the main passage, And on Thursdays and Saturdays the silver has to be cleaned and Wednesday the cupboards have to be scrubbed so I am on my feet all day long and one thing I forgot to mention was I set our table and the Sisters table for every meal and wait on them.

I am not very happy at the Hospital because none of the girls want me because I have come from the home so when anythings on either have to go by myself or stay home by myself.

An inspector from the Department was able to ensure that the girls at this hospital had slightly more time off duty.[9]

The desire to learn a trade, to do anything as long as it was not service, grew stronger and stronger as the twentieth century advanced. As early as 1914 one girl already in service described her passionate desire to learn a trade almost as though it were something subversive:

I was telling the boy I was wanting to learn a trade and Mrs Martin had crept down to room below us to listen to what we were saying which she very often does and I am certain she is telling you these things to keep me from learning a trade.

The secretary advised her to 'save as much money as you possibly can out of your wages' to make certain she had a good stock of clothes, and ended by saying:

I feel sure that if you could show the Council that you have been careful, and that you have saved money, that you are doing the things that are necessary and that are possible towards helping yourself, that the Council would be prepared to help you in the pecuniary aspect of your apprenticeship . . . they have helped others and I am quite sure that they could be willing to help you.[10]

Being employed as a 'lady help' was one way of avoiding some of the stigma attached to being a domestic[11] but what most girls wanted was a job in a shop, office, or factory. Girls continued to hanker after an office job even if they had found 'light duties' in a friendly home. As one girl wrote in 1923:

this is the lightest [place] as there is only three in family. Mr and Mrs Smith and little child and I will often go out in the car with them . . . I could have got into the post office some time ago where I could have worked my self up higher but I did not think I would like it at the time and I have been sorry since . . .[12]

But despite this desire the State Children's Department and its successor, the Children's Welfare and Public Relief Department, still maintained a fairly strong distrust of other types of work. The inspectors continually reported that a girl in other than domestic work did not keep 'good hours' or was

suffering from an exaggerated sense of her own importance due, doubtless to her rise in wages and status in her work. She now acts as saleswoman in a wholesale firm instead of being a hand in a factory.[13]

Ambitious girls might work as domestics to support themselves and at the same time train as dressmakers, secretaries, or hairdressers. But even industrious girls would be advised to be cautious, as these two were in 1939:

Girl very anxious to learn hairdressing and is to ascertain what, if any money she can earn at the training school while learning. She quite appreciates her position, in that she must live while learning. She also has dressmaking lessons, and has made herself some nice frocks.

I really think if she could earn more money, Mary would be content with domestic work, but Mrs Casey says she cannot pay her a higher wage. Girl has got the ambitious urge just now.[14]

she likes and is good at sewing. I saw a frock she had made for herself, and unaided, and which was originally a cross over apron, and she certainly made it remarkably well. Mrs Trembath says she can get girl work with a dressmaker at Brighton, but I respectfully suggest expert advice be sought before sanction be given for this. It is a far cry from sewing for a hobby, and daily for a living.[15]

Girls could learn dressmaking through the Housewives Association or

152

from the School of Mines on North Terrace, but however they did it, it was a struggle requiring careful management. A girl's enthusiasm, however, could make her think nothing of managing 'with what clothes I have' and walking 'two sections a day' to save bus fares.[16]

Some girls found work as waitresses, as child minders, or as shop assistants. Life was still hard; work was still arduous. One girl wrote of her work in a shop in 1939:

I have just got a nice position in a cafe as a waitress and I have to buy all my uniforms and I also have to have shoes, and I am badly in need of other clothing and unless I have these things it means that I will lose my position and I could not get more work if I have not got the clothes. I have been out of work for some time owing to measles and other sickness.[17]

Clothes were an expense, but having to scrimp and save to afford them seems to have been preferred to being in service and receiving cast-offs, as one girl angrily wrote in 1932:

At present my life is a jolly misery ... I have not been happy since I have been here, I suppose you already know that Mrs White is supposed to buy my cloths she has only bought me three pairs of stockings and all the other things I have to pay for that is 2 pairs of shoes under clothes bather and surf shoes and of course I never have any money left to buy myself any odd things, I have not had one new dress or hat since I have been with her and [that] is six months and I only have her left offs and I dont like it.

Sir I have got another job and it is shop girl and the woman is quite nice she has not told me how much I will get a week yet but Sir I hope you will let me go to it ... I am seventeen and I think a girl should be able to choose her own cloths not have other peoples left offs.[18]

The comradeship of factory girls in the 1930s is vividly described by Alan Marshall in *How Beautiful are Thy Feet*. The factory girl's life was hard but it had compensations: regular hours, time off, companionship. No wonder girls preferred it. By 1935 an inspector could calmly attribute the desire of so many state girls to 'try factory work', to their 'detesting' housework.[19] State girls were able to get work in the later 1930s at Keens Pickle Factory in Pirie Street, Thompson & Walton's Biscuit Factory, Kent Town, and Rossiters Boot Factory.[20] A few even rode to work on bicycles: mobile, independent, unsupervised, very different from their counterparts of the 1890s.

Learning a trade was one step better than being a factory girl. The State Children's Advancement Fund helped some girls. In 1926, £10 was paid as 'part board of state girl learning trade' and the following year this amount had increased to twenty-five pounds. However some expenses debited to this fund appear inappropriate. In the 1920s the tuning of pianos at the Industrial School and the salary of the kindergarten teacher at the Convalescent Home both came from the State Children's Advancement Fund.[21]

A successful girl often had a family behind her. As the Department commented in the annual report for 1940:

It is interesting to note that children who secure other than domestic and farming work are generally those who have been placed in the same homes for long periods, and are considered to be members of the families with whom the department has placed them.[22]

This occurs repeatedly when one looks at the success stories among state wards. One girl who was successful in the late 1930s was Lois Kelly. She was described as being in 'an excellent home' in 1937 and she had by then been in the same home for twelve years, living with a spinster. She was:

interested in Basketball in the winter and tennis in the summer She is doing exceedingly well at her dressmaking lessons. At present she is making herself a costume. Lois is a teacher in the Methodist Sunday School and attends that Church. Lois has completed a frock at the School of Mines. This frock is really excellently made. She is now on a skirt and is knitting a jumper for herself. Most of the materials have been supplied to her by her guardian. Lois begins a fresh term at School of Mines next week. She is keenly interested in all needlework and shows promise of excelling in this work.

She has a wonderful opportunity and I am glad she appreciates same.[23]

A few ambitious, intelligent girls were able by their own efforts to become teachers, but they had had to struggle mightily to achieve their ambition. The way was marked by obstacles that only the determined could overcome.

The regulations published in 1917 governing the higher education of state children were dauntingly bureaucratic. State children desiring further education after the age of fourteen years had to apply to the secretary on form A and accompany this by certificate B from the head teacher of their school, certificate C from a minister of religion, and certificate D from a medical practitioner. If the Council decided to assist a child then an agreement was signed whereby the child agreed to repay in instalments the money advanced by the Council.[24] This was form E. The references which had to be signed by the minister, teacher, and doctor were so fulsome that the slightest doubt would have made a scrupulous conscience unable to sign. A girl had to be a practising and devout Christian before she would be considered, and her behaviour, once accepted, had to be above reproach.[25]

There were different ways into the teaching profession in South Australia. One girl wrote in 1916 when she was twenty, asking for money for private coaching because she was now 20 years of age and allowed to choose my own situation I am desirous of becoming a school teacher.

There will be an exam in June for the entrance The examination will be equal to a fifth class standard I am studying all the subjects in my spare time, and hope to be able to pass the exam

There is also a medical examination to be passed After passing the entrance and medical examinations there is a six months course of training at the Observation School Currie St.

During the training time I should like to Board with Mrs Black at Parkside.[26]

This girl did not become a teacher. Another girl who wanted to be a teacher was Veronica Halstead. In January 1917 her mistress wrote to the Department to see if Veronica

could make an application to the School for the position of monitor. There is a vacancy and she would very much like to take it with your consent. She has been a good girl and we would like to see her get on well. The head teacher is at present having his holiday but the other monitor was in the fifth class at the same time as Veronica and he thinks she is quite capable of taking the position as she was a good scholar. We will do all we can to help her. I will help her with her sewing.

Veronica herself added:

I have as you know lived at Y__ in the employ of Mrs West for 6 years and have liked her so well that this seems like my home. I feel as though I would do anything rather than leave here as I have many friends around. There is an opening for a monitor in the Y__ School and I have a friend an old school fellow a monitor ...

I have longed for this kind of work since sometime before leaving school so will be exceedingly glad if I may do this.

Two weeks later the head teacher wrote explaining that Veronica had now taken

the position of paid monitor in my school and has commenced work in that capacity. She is suitable for the position in style and appearance and apparently has grit and ambition.

She is applying for entrance into the Service by means of the Short Course of Training and the following table will explain.

It has been suggested to me that the Council will help this child and if so Mrs West will require the assistance this year, while a little help from the State will be necessary next year.

In return for her assistance this year she receives daily instruction from me before school in addition to £15 mentioned below.

1917 To Pass Inspector's Test at his visit	To pass Entrance to Short Course Examination. In Nov.
Jan.–June 1918 Six months at Observation School (Training)	July–Dec. Appointment as Teacher if proficient

Remuneration
1917 £15	1918 15s per week while at Observation School
1919 To June £84 per year	
After June £100 per year	£84 per year while teaching

Veronica's energy and determination must have been immense. Her mistress reported that she needed many books and that her salary as a monitor 'will only keep her in clothes and books'. She went on to say:

We regret not being in a position to help her more. She has to leave home at 8 o'clock in the morning and does not get home till 5 in the evening and then has homework which takes about 2 hours, so that she has very little time to help me, therefore I would be glad if the Council could contribute a little more than 5/– weekly and if her board is paid for a year etc.

When the time came for Veronica to board in the city, fresh difficulty arose in the Department's refusal or inability to find a home where Veronica could board. One wonders how hard they tried, if the indifferent tone of their letter is any guide:

Concerning your letter of the 14th instant to hand this morning I regret that I have no home at present in which Veronica could be placed in or near Adelaide in order that she may attend the Observation School. If however you know of any respectable person who would be willing to take the girl at a cheap rate, and will let me know immediately I will see what can be done in the matter, otherwise I fear the girl will have to relinquish her idea of becoming a teacher as the Government will not pay more than 8/– per week for the girl's maintenance.

But Veronica's employers wrote back, arguing vigorously that it would be regrettable if anything should

mar her progress now she has gone so far. We understood from Mr Gray when she asked for his consent and help when she started to teach that the Council would help her through with it, and as she only needs help for another six months, it seems hard luck to give in now.[27]

Somehow things were arranged, and Veronica received an appointment as a teacher in July 1918, the Department sending her a cordial letter of congratulations.

Hers was a success story but also a story of determination. She was perhaps the only state girl who achieved a successful teaching career during the period.

CHAPTER 7

On Bearing a Stigma 1887–1940

Definition of a Stigma

The original impetus of boarding-out was that children would be 'absorbed amongst other children and go to ordinary schools and take a share in ordinary work'.[1] Yet there is overwhelming evidence that throughout the whole period covered in this book state wards suffered a stigma in varying degrees, and one illustration of this is the story of Rebecca Turner.

In 1925 the Department received a letter from a teacher reporting that his wife heard everywhere in the town: 'who is that big lump of a cheeky girl who gets out [of the bus] at your school'. The girl was a state ward and the teacher had written to the Department, invoking the intolerance of the district to support his own.

He wrote in reply to an enquiry from the secretary of the State Children's Council who had received a letter from the girl's foster-mother stating that an attempt had been made to have Rebecca removed from the school. The teacher considered that Rebecca brought trouble on herself by her 'untruthfulness, cheekiness and domineering character'. More incidents followed and eventually the Council sent Miss Lapidge out to investigate. In answer to questioning, the teacher admitted he had written his letter in a moment of irritation and that he was now sorry he had done so. Miss Lapidge thought him a young, inexperienced teacher who had heard 'grossly exaggerated and mis-stated' gossip.

One may well ask why this child, the star of the school play, by all accounts a delightful and intelligent personality, was treated in this way?

Miss Lapidge thought she was advanced beyond her age, but Rebecca's foster-mother defended the girl far more fully:

I am writing this in the hope of protecting Rebecca from an unfair attack on the part of some of the residents of __. They have formed a new school Committee and I have heard that Rebecca was one of the subjects of the meeting and they said that she swears dreadfully and if they hear of her swearing again, they are going to write to the State Department and get her removed, they seem to have a set on the child and are like a pack of hounds, always hounding her down ... If she belonged to a rich person one would say Rebecca was high spirited and quick with her tongue, as she is a state child we will say she is Cheeky but not any cheekier than any other normal, healthy child and a good deal better than most ...

The little boy who goes to school with her I have often heard him swear in the course of a conversation, tho he is a nice and well behaved little chap in every other way, but of course that does not matter he is not a state child. As for the __ children for over 2 years before Rebecca came here, I had been hearing about their swearing and dirty tongue ... yet they will say that Becky brought all the swearing etc here.[2]

Rebecca's forceful nature and the love of her foster-mother enabled her to resist the prejudice of the district. Her success in doing so was unusual. Most wards of the state seemed to have suffered to different degrees from insults or innuendo.

This stigma was exacerbated, particularly in the early years, by the extent to which working as a servant meant accepting a position as an inferior.

As a matter of fact Clara resents being a domestic servant at all and feels very bitter because she is made to address her mistress as 'Yes Ma'am' speak of Mr Smith as 'The Master' and call the sons 'Master Edward' etc.[3]

And the stigma of being not only a servant but also a ward of the state seemed to have been present from the beginning of the system. One girl wrote in 1897:

I have always been kind to his children and treated them with great respect and I do not think that because I am a State Girl I should be trampled on as I am by him.

The language he uses to me is most unfit for any man's ears much less a girls ... I suppose you have heard all about our squabble well after that I feel as if rather than stay here when my time is out I would go around gathering up 'Bottles Bones & Rags' I will do my very best to keep this until I am 18 but when a man calls a girl a dam dirtie slut & a Bloody William it is quite time to part I like Mrs Connolly and the children very much but I cannot stand Mr Connolly ... Well he should remember that I am flesh and Blood the same as himself and have got feelings as well as him but people think that we State kids as they call us are made of iron or Logs I felt it very much and cried nearly all night.[4]

Doubt over a girl's ability to remain 'good' might also cut:

I have tried to do my best to please her and keep in my place. I am not going to allow her to say and do as she pleases with me because I am a reformatory girl . . . I cannot have her say things about me that isn't true I know I used to be bad once but I have learnt a lesson and can take care of myself now.[5]

And speculation about *why* she was under the state's care could haunt a girl:

you will think I am a funny girl but I just want to know whether it was my own fault or who's fault it was that I was put under the State control. I was asked why I was put in the State yesterday and it made me feel very nervous and ashamed I just said I did not exactly know the reason.[6]

In many cases it wasn't the mistress in particular who made life hard to bear but the other members of the household:

They praise me up in front of my face but I turn my back and it is just the other way I went there I had my hair down but Mrs Martin did not like it so she said I had to put it up so I did so and now it is up it does not please her she says she as more to do now I am hear than she had to do when the other girl was hear . . . the other girl was 25 and I am not 18 yet but I do more than I have done before I get up at 6 oclock get her cocoa and take it to her room . . . and another thing there daughter is so cheaky and she dose all sorts of things to make you cross and I am not let to say anything to her for it her mother said I was to tell her but she does not care . . .[7]

In particular, daughters were often hard to get on with:

Mrs Darnell's two girls used to treat me as if I was no one, they used to snap me up and would only speak to me every two or three days, Once as I was cleaning out the kitchen they said 'try to be clean for once' and I told Mrs Darnell and she spoke to them about it, and they all laughed about it. Mrs Darnell had never complained that I was not clean.[8]

But what seems to have rankled most with state girls was being accused of things they had not done, of stealing or lying. Others' expectations – that being bad girls they would do bad things – cut most girls to the quick. Jasmine Smith, who later became a nurse, wrote:

Not one little thing am I able to do right. There is something to find fault with everything I do. Not only that I am often accused of doing things I would never dream of . . . today she told me that I was always too smart with my ears when it was anything I had no business to hear. When I asked her what she meant she told me that Miss Fox had found me two or three times lately standing at the kitchen door listening to what was going on in the next room. For a moment I was too surprised to say anything. The next moment I fairly boiled over. Before I knew what I was doing I had stamped my foot and called her a 'liar'. Mr Gray I could not help it. It _was_ a wicked lie . . . What is the use of trying to be good when things like that are said of you.[9]

There were dozens of ways a girl could be made to feel stigmatized.[10] A few managed calmly and forcefully to resist the community's prejudice:

I have often had people say that only the scum are cared for in the Department, so that refers to others and myself, who are innocent of any offence or crime what ever. But looking at it the right way I myself think it is only the common class who talk so.[11]

Many more remained

very sensitive of being a ward of the state, as many people look down on them and no matter how friendly a visit is paid she is always upset particularly as she is afraid it may affect her position.[12]

Visits from inspectors either to the service home or foster-home were one of the reasons why girls rarely succeeded in keeping their status hidden. Foster-children would often, in any case, be visited at school, which meant that they would be revealed to their peers as being state wards.

Some girls internalized the stigma of being a servant. One wrote, admittedly trying to gain her release, but nonetheless candidly:

I like it so much because it is so quiet and that is what I like. I have now been here 5 months and I am glad to say I have not made friends with any of the other maids around here.[13]

One of the ways that girls felt 'different' most was in regard to clothing. Until 1939 it was rare for a girl to have any clothes not made in the needle-room of the Department, by the girl herself, or by her mistress – home-made clothing of the plainest sort and not very much of that. By 1926 the effect this had on girls was becoming apparent:

A state girl of 16 years only receives 10/- per week (9/- to herself and 1/- to her bank account) It is impossible for her to keep her outfit up to Standard let alone dress like other girls of her age in the same position, unless she is given presents of clothes from her mistress or her daughters or they make her clothes for her and this cannot always be done.[14]

The difficulty of remaining 'decent' in one's clothes when there were items such as new false teeth to be bought, is shown in this letter from Kate Edwards in 1920:

I do not like the clothes they give me from the needleroom. I would be very pleased if you could place me out very soon, as I have to get my teeth also, and I have not yet enough money to pay for them unless I do go ...[15]

If a girl had a kindly mistress who dressed her well she was still not allowed to keep any dresses above the regulation number when transferred to another service home. One mistress reported in 1926 that she had:

gone to considerable trouble to keep her nicely clad so that when taking her out she may not appear different to other girls of her age and as a result when I fixed up her box to be in compliance with your regulations she was very annoyed.[16]

The Department's attitude – even when a girl was spending her own earnings – was that clothes should be sensible.

With regard to your application for £2/-/- or £3/-/- to help buy a watch, I feel I ought to point out that it would not seem as if you were really in a position in life to afford paying a lot of money for the outside appearance of such an article. After all what is very important is that the works in the watch should be of good material and properly adjusted ...

I should think that you could obtain a chromium plated wristlet watch at approximately, say, 32/6d, which could be quite good enough for any work for which you are likely to require the article.[17]

Another girl, who in 1938 had just turned sixteen, was chided for the carelessness with which she treated her clothes:

I would suggest that you put your money away every week, so that you will have something to draw on when you need new clothes ...

I am very disappointed to find you are so careless with your clothes. There is an old proverb which says 'A stitch in time saves nine', and you will have to be very careful of all these stitches, otherwise you will find your 6/- per week will not be enough to keep you decently clothed.[18]

Even when a child was adequately clad, adequacy was not always normality. In one family in 1922, the foster-children's clothing was so 'meagre' that it had 'given rise to a report from an outsider which is not pleasant to receive about our wards'.[19] Mary Denny was described in 1925 as being

dull, timid and unresponsive. She keeps aloof from other children and does not join in their play. In appearance she lacks care in details, her bloomers being too long and made like a boy's knickers.

She also wears the same frock every day and her hair is not arranged nicely.[20]

The difference a kindly teacher could make to a state ward was immense:

When first she went to the Flinders St School she was for 12 months in grade III and was taught by Miss —. She was very happy and made good progress.

Since her promotion to the 4th grade she has been very miserable under Miss —. It is alleged that the latter frequently slaps her on her bare legs, and makes fun of her before the classes and is most impatient with her dulness.

Recently Fay came home to lunch and lay on the sofa and cried and refused to eat anything, she seems to dread going to school and worries about her lessons.[21]

There were girls who were 'very popular at school . . . in the Basket Ball team', girls who were described as 'bright nicely spoken . . . [and] very well behaved'.[22] But that these girls were probably exceptions, seems to be indicated in the letter that the headmaster of a country school wrote in 1923:

she is a bright and intelligent girl very well cared for in her present home . . . she seems rather above the usual run of State Children it has been my lot to encounter . . . she is a promising student and is not singled out by the other scholars for unkind treatment in any way whatever, quite the reverse is the case, as the girls rather sympathise with her.[23]

Another way in which girls suffered from the stigma of being wards of the state lay in the fact that the family for whom they worked could, if they chose, reveal to all the world that a girl was under the state's care. And 'state child' was a pejorative term. As the superintendent of the Boys' Reformatory told the Royal Commission on Law Reform in 1926,

State child and reformatory or industrial child is not the proper way to refer to children whose worst fault is that they have not had a decent chance from the very start of their lives. More suitable names are desirable.[24]

State girls often had to endure others indulging in speculation about their ancestry: 'I am quite willing to leave here at anytime because they till everybody I am under your care'.[25]

my mistress and I had a falling out and I told her I was not going to stop with her she is unbearable sometimes to stop with her and she can get another for I am tired of her and it isn't nice for her to tell everyone where I came from. Dear Sir I am not ashamed of myself if I am a state girl for that isn't any reason for her to tell everybody.[26]

So strong was the stigma attached to being a state ward that occasionally a girl who had grown up barely aware of being a ward would refuse to associate with a sibling who had suddenly 'appeared' in her life.[27]

163

Whether somebody who had been reared as a state ward was sufficiently 'refined' to take her place in a respectable household was a question that occasionally had to be faced if a 'long lost' relative made an appearance. Thus in 1919 the Department was asked about Ronda Smith, who it was hoped could be re-united with a sister now married and living in Sydney:

As Mrs White is married to a reputable and rising Solicitor of this City, I should like to learn something of the educational qualification, and disposition of Ronda Smith and whether in your opinion she is sufficiently refined to enable her to take a place as a member of Mr White's household.[28]

History records that Ronda Smith *was* sufficiently refined, and she travelled to Sydney on a first-class fare.

Younger girls might be protected from the full burden of being known as a ward by the love of a foster-mother. One wrote in 1926 of her dislike of having her charge known to be a ward, and added:

she feels very conscious also of every body having to know that she is in the S.C. Dept, as a growing girl she is very quickly hurt which is quite natural at any likelihood of being shunned as often seems the case when girls learn particulars of her.[29]

Another girl complained in 1937 of the prejudice of a country town:

People at __ say that if Wards of the State are not released at 18 years, then there *must* be a reason, and she feels it a serious reflection on her character.

She wants her freedom so that when asked to functions etc. (approved by Mrs Ryan) and which she has to decline if they are not attending, she can avoid the necessity of having to answer awkward questions, viz. 'Why are you so controlled by Mrs Ryan' 'What mystery is there about you?' etc (No one in the district knows she is a Ward of the State.)[30]

Others raged against the discouragement they felt:

I am not a saint the best of times, but I have done my best for them and I am now so discouraged I feel as if I could give it all up ... They hate me I know they cannot stand me, and they take every opportunity to find fault. I am just full up of it all. If I were a private girl instead of a State girl I would not stay here. They consider me dirt under their feet. Until now I have been used to being treated as a fellow human being. I would rather be hurt bodily than to be hurt with the tongue like I am here.[31]

There were no vast changes in community attitudes in the fifty years from 1887 to 1940, as these two letters from the late 1930s show:

Mrs Jones stated that they are looking for another home – they have such horrid neighbours they have found out Wendy is a Ward of the State they say unkind things to hurt her feelings – the words are not actually said to her but so they can be overheard.[32]

Mrs McVittie does not know that Anna does not belong to Mrs Walker – who has a prejudice against Welfare Children and she has gone into the place as Mrs Walker's own child. Both Anna and F/M are worried re this – I recommend them to tell Mrs McVittie the truth – it is bad for the girl to live a lie – and also have to tell them to keep her job – she had to say she was coming in to get a tooth fixed – to get off to report in Office – Even if she loses her job this should be rectified.[33]

But small changes in the Department's attitudes can be detected in the late 1930s. Writing in 1939, an inspector noted of a girl who was working in a hospital:

the only objection I have to this kind of placing is lack of privacy during an inspection – this no doubt will be better, when the new quarters for the Staff has been completed – Sister apologised for the present muddle . . .[34]

The Department also began to consider how a girl might feel regarding decisions made about her life. This sort of thinking is apparent in a thoughtful letter written by F.G. Byrne in 1937 in reply to a request for a holiday:

The decision is that, much as we would prefer Anne to remain away from her home forever, it does not seem likely that that can be brought about. Consequently it would seem better for the Department to fall in with the girl's wishes and grant a privilege, rather than create a defiant ward who would endeavour to deceive us.[35]

By contrast, previous secretaries seem to have excelled at scolding:

Perhaps you are not aware that when you are corrected or told to do things properly Mrs White is only carrying out the instructions of the Council, and it is up to you to do your part too.[36]

I was more than astonished to learn you were a girl of 19 years, as on reading the report I imagined you were quite a little girl who had not sense enough to know right from wrong.
    No man would come to marry a woman who had no idea of cleanliness . . . you sulk. This is very babyish, as no sensible girl would ever lower herself to sulking.[37]

Little joy illuminated the letters sent even to good girls. To a girl who had received permission to join a gymnasium class, Celestine Houlgrave, secretary from 1918–26, wrote: 'I hope you will find great benefit from this, and that you will give me no cause to regret having given you this permission'.[38]

Francis Gordon Byrne, who was secretary from 1932–37, could be severe but he was never as condemnatory as Houlgrave and seems to have absorbed some of the psychological expertise of the innovative Dr Constance Davey. The softening of attitude to children's misdeeds is well illustrated in a report from Miss Lapidge, where she stated of one child that, 'It is not wickedness but rather naughty tricks of that age'.[39] To a girl who in 1937 wrote confessing that she had told a lie, Mr Byrne replied:

I am glad you felt it a matter for your conscience to write and admit your mistake in telling Miss Salmon untruths. I cannot compliment you on your conduct, but I do feel that there is a deal of hope for one who owns up to their own wrong doing.[40]

One thing which ensured that state wards continued to feel 'a sense of difference' was the Department's tardy acceptance of social change, of anything new. Two things the Department opposed resolutely were hire-purchase and the buying of bicycles. Hire-purchase was opposed because the Department thought it might lead girls into debt (as it sometimes did). Occasionally girls were allowed to buy clothes on 'terms'. One girl wrote in 1916 that she was

in need of a rain coat and as there are some on sale at Smeyed's I thought you might not mind if I asked you to allow me to have a small portion of my wage that you keep in the bank I am quite willing Dear Sir to sign a paper that I should in return pay 1/– a week until the amount is payed back to you. The coats are now 21/– but on account of other clothing being so dear I have not the slightest idea of getting a coat unless you consent to my wishes. I have not a coat of any description and it would only take 21 weeks to pay the sum back but of course you will have to consent to that.[41]

Her wish was granted, although the Department wrote in sensible terms warning her against the practice.

Bicycles first became common in Australia in the 1890s, and clubs for both sexes flourished around the turn of the century.[42] The bicycle gave women mobility and independence but could be seen by the old-fashioned as offering too much freedom to young girls. The sorts of issues that possession of a bicycle raised are conveyed in this letter from a kindly mistress who considered there was 'bicycle mania' among the young men and women of Edwardstown in 1914. Her ward had

within the New Year bought a bicycle on time payment £14 on pretence of practising I have allowed her out before dusk and twice only to my knowledge she has broken her promise and has returned after dark.

Having always grown up with the idea that servants are human beings I may have been a little more lenient with these girls than I should have but it is not necessary to say that any tendency I have in that direction will certainly be checked.[43]

The Department reminded her sternly that it was a regulation

that all girls in the care of the Council are to be in the care of their employer before dark, and they are not allowed to be out after dusk unless in the company of their employer (being a woman) or some trustworthy person (a middle-aged female) known to you.[44]

Two years later, in 1916, the secretary wrote to a ward in the country:

I have your letter of April 20th with regard to a bicycle. I do not like young girls having bicycles to ride about at all, and still less do I like them to be bought in the fashion that you propose to buy this, that is a second-hand bicycle from an advertisement. Again I cannot consent to your taking the money out of your Savings Bank account. If you want to buy a bicycle you must save the money out of your wages, and buy a good one as soon as possible which for cash you will be able to get cheaply.[45]

By the end of the 1930s there *had* been a change and many state girls owned bicycles and rode them to work with the Department's approval.[46] Throughout the 1930s there was a gradual acceptance of a great many other things that would have led to a girl being sent to the Reformatory in the nineteenth century. One girl in 1937 was reported to have

been going out w. boys unknown to Matron – on two occasions. Refuses food sometimes – slimming. F/M . . . won't allow girl to pluck her eyebrows nor use a lot of make-up. I had a serious talk with Kim re her foolishness and she promised to make amends.[47]

By the mid 1930s a girl in service was allowed to make herself an evening dress, finery that would have been unthinkable in the 1890s. Sensible girls were allowed to go to neighbourhood dances provided they went 'with a suitable guardian'.[48] Girls were allowed more freedom but they were still expected to behave with decorum and return straight home after the dance or pictures. This is apparent in the letters the Department wrote back to girls about going to the pictures. One girl was told in 1937 that 'the Department will have no objection to this so long as Mrs Coombe is quite satisfied you are in good company, and that you return home immediately you leave the pictures'.[49] Going to the pictures with a

The bicycle gave women mobility and independence. Three young women from a country town pose with bicycles - and hats - in 1907.

female friend seems to have become quite common but going with a male friend at night was something completely different: something a girl might have to 'own up' to later.[50]

In the 1930s the radio brought changes to the lives of some state wards. An employer might allow a state girl to listen to the radio so that she could join radio clubs or listen to birthdays broadcast by station 5DN Adelaide.[51] Other minor changes were legion in the late 1930s. A responsible state girl might drive her employer's children to and from school, she might travel on a train unaccompanied, and weekly church attendance does not seem to have been so rigidly enforced. A girl might also belong to a hockey team.[52]

There were two rather important changes. Domestic service in the country was no longer seen as an ideal but was increasingly regarded as a punishment, something which could be used to threaten girls. As an inspector, Ellen B. Pile, reported in 1938:

I gave her a good talking to and told her the next time there was even a small complaint, we would have to seriously consider sending her to a farm in the country, and if there were any repetition of recent happenings, the Board would have to decide, whether, in her own interests she be left under their care, after she had attained 18 years . . .

I told her to, that if we had any more complaints, she would be sent on a farm to work where in spite of 'foot ache' she would have to work hard all day, and no opportunity for pictures or dances . . .[53]

The Department also began to place girls 'on trust' in areas which a decade before they would have simply forbidden. This led to letters such as the one below in response to a girl who sought her release from the Department in 1937:

I am going to make what will appear to be rather an astonishing suggestion but one which I feel may have the effect of showing you that, after all, if we trust you, you may do better than if we attempt to lead you always.

If you feel that your conduct entitles you to do it, I suggest you should make an application to this office either to be returned to Barton Vale, or to be entirely released from the control of the Board. One thing or the other would seem to me to be wise, perhaps your freedom would spur you to better effort, and though I can make no promise with regard to the matter I will undertake to bring any request you make, before the Board for consideration.[54]

Other necessary changes only arrived after the recommendations of the 1938 Committee of Inquiry into Delinquent and Other Children in the Care of the State, which is discussed in Chapter 8.

'All alone in this wide world'

One of the most painful aspects of being a state ward was the sense of not having a family of one's own. The Department's policy regarding natural parents only changed at the end of the 1930s.

In 1929 the policy was clearly stated in a letter to a mother who was thinking of marriage and of reclaiming her daughter whom she had not seen for five or six years:

It is of course, not the policy of this Department to indulge to you, or indeed to any parent, who has the keeping of a particular child, but you seem to know that the girlie is with a Mrs Middleton and that she is in good hands. I feel confident that my Board is not likely to give the child back to you unless you can offer her a better home than the one she is in at present.[55]

This is, virtually unchanged, the policy that was first stated in the 1887 Regulations:

Relatives shall not have access to children placed out, except in the case of a child becoming seriously ill, or under special circumstances, with the sanction of the Council; but, on application to the Secretary, they may be informed as to the health and general wellbeing of their children.[56]

Any contact that a ward sought to have with her natural parents was of course complicated by the Department's distrust of them. That there might be excellent reasons for the Department's disapproval is not the issue.

In the years 1887 to 1940, just as now, there were many families who were neglectful or cruel to their children, but today more is done to help keep the natural family together and to support it through crises. Where children cannot eventually be returned, the natural family is not maligned and contact is sometimes permitted.[57]

Most state wards in the period 1887 to 1940 were not boarded-out as infants and they therefore grew up with some memory of their natural family. That this memory became an embroidered thread, a romanticized dream, did not prevent it from also becoming a memory that could haunt:

I am far from happy I have not known a days happyness since I was parted from my brothers and sisters and I never shall untill I am with them again . . . it is a very lonely place where I am you cannot see a house within a mile it comes very hard on me, one who has been allowed to do just as one likes.[58]

Mr Byrne seeing that I have to stay for another year and I'm almost 18 I would like you to let me visit my mother, I don't see why I shouldn't . . .
I miss my mother very much and I'll always miss her . . .[59]

Siblings might be placed near each other if they were working so that they could 'see something of each other', or would even be fostered in the same family.[60] How much seeing a sister could mean was well expressed by Margaret West in 1919:

I long to get near my sister and to see her more, it seems ages from my one day's outing to another although in reality it is only a fortnight I must stop now but I felt in such a mood that the only way to get over it was to write . . .[61]

Contact with natural parents was much more rare, but even without any contact children maintained emotional links. One girl who had not lived with her family for more than eight years heard about her father's death in an unfortunate way: 'A neighbour who saw the announcement in the paper bluntly told Lucy about it. Miss North said the child came running home with the news and was terribly upset and distressed.'[62]

The majority of girls wanted to have contact with their families, no matter how little interest the family had displayed in them. The Department believed that contact brought problems, and that a ward's real family might have a very unsettling influence. Mistresses frequently wrote to the Department complaining that a girl 'couldn't rest content' until she had found her mother, or would be satisfied by nothing except 'going to her people'.[63] Very often letters from a service home would complain that a girl could not concentrate on her domestic duties because she had visits from her family or received too many letters.[64] In such circumstances the Department usually wrote to the offending relations warning them 'of the impropriety of their past actions' and formally forbidding 'further unauthorised Communication'.[65]

One inspector wrote in 1932 of the way in which contact changed wards: 'Girl very cheeky and self-willed at times – especially after she has seen her mother'.[66] And a girl's employer complained in similar vein in 1924:

She is a very altered girl I regret to say since she met her brother. Her ambition is to get to town, she is discontented, insolent abusive etc, by the way she is carrying on lately . . . You would not think it possible for a girl to alter so.

He still writes such loving letters to her and longs for the time they will be together begs her to come down.[67]

Problems might occur if a state girl was unduly influenced by contact with her real family who might be understandably hostile to the Department.[68] A natural father who 'induced' his daughter 'to forsake her guardian's home' and go out with him for the day would earn a severe reprimand from the secretary.[69] Very often seeing her own family might make a state girl feel unsettled, and a few were even persuaded to abscond.[70]

Foster-mothers and employers often wrote ruefully to the Department of their charges having had 'a taste of her old life which caused her downfall'.[71]

Knowing about one's background was not just important for what it revealed about parents: it also told a girl something about herself. One girl wrote to the secretary seeking information about her parents after years of being under the care of the state:

I think it is time that I should know about them, what they are or what they were I am old enough now to know all about them Am I left alone in this wide world to get my own home, it makes anyone feel as if they don't know what to do or where to go being left like I am . . .

> I remain one of your
> Motherless and Fatherless Child.[72]

This desire to know about one's family seemed 'only natural' to most state girls, even if they were quite happy with their foster or service home.[73] One kindly mistress wrote to the Department about the reaction of her service girl when informed that her father had died, stating that the 'poor girl', when read the letter, had burst into tears, 'and also she thought it was very hard that she could never see her father again for she remembers him well and the things he used to do for them'.[74] Death in the family often served as a cruel reminder to state girls that they had been taken from their own family, that blood was thicker than water. When Jasmine Smith learnt that her sister had died of consumption in April 1906, she declared she had been promised:

that if she was very ill she would ask you to let me go and see her. Ruby herself in the last letter dated April 10th said that she was getting on all right. Next thing I hear she is dead and buried. It is more than I can bear. My brothers and sisters are all I have and yet you let one of them die and say not a word to me about it. Oh Mr Gray was it kind not to let me see her. It might have comforted her a little to have me beside her.

  Don't you think that we suffer the same as you in higher positions in life do and yet what would you feel like were a dear one of yours left to die alone and you were not allowed to come to her, not even told that she was so ill. Do let me come back I feel as though I cannot stay here now.[75]

This tragic case was a genuine error on the part of the State Children's Department who themselves had not known of the girl's transfer from the Consumptive Home at Belair to the hospital where she died.

  A family might petition the Department to have a girl returned but the home would have to be exceptionally respectable before a girl would be removed from a good service home.[76] Girls with no contact or little information went on worrying about their natural parents in the hope that they would some day be reunited, loved, and provided with a family background in an age when one's 'people' were of supreme importance.

when I was in army home the officers used to tell me it was no use troubling about them they were all right. I dare they say they would be allright but I should like to see them. If you cannot tell me where my brothers are would you kindly tell me where my dear sister Nellie is.[77]

'Discovery' of a family might make a girl angry:

And now I want to know how it is that you never told me I had a mother because I have had a letter from her stating that I am her daughter which she has been look[ing] for she has been paying money into the State for me.[78]

I had two half brothers, by the name of Farrell if I remember rightly both taken into the department at the same time as myself. I have never heard anything about them since. Could you tell me anything about them. I would be glad to know where they are.[79]

Other girls had to resign themselves to having nobody, a resignation most found 'awful hard'.[80]

State girls might long to return to their families because they felt they were needed at home either for the help they could give or the extra wages they could bring in:

She has to work hard to keep herself and three children and more often than not she is unable to do so for she is very delicate and often ill and there is nobody to do anything to help her, the other children are all under twelve I am the eldest and therefore instead of being an anxiety to her, I feel that I should be more of a help. I do what I can to help her now but still it is not what I could do if I was with her. I have been brought up to her trade and when I was at home I earned from 15/- to £1-0-0 per week but it is not of the money I am thinking . . . Sometimes I fear that she will live but a little while and it is my duty to do what I can to atone for the past . . . since I have been under the care of the State I have felt a different girl and things that once led me astray have no power over me at all . . .[81]

[my Grandparents] are getting old and feeble and need my help and I do so want to be with them. If you have no fault to find with me why can't I go because here I am working with strange people whereas there is a good home waiting for me, when I am free my people may be dead . . .[82]

There were always some girls who knew nothing about their real family and wondered in their letters to the Department, who their family were and if they would ever see them again. It is not hard to see that these letter-writers were also asking, 'What am I? Who am I?'

I was wondering if my mother and father was living, for I did not think there would be any harm done by asking for I think it is nice for a girl to know if her parents are living or not for I often think of them. I seen in the paper the other day where Mrs David South's daughter was engaged to be married she was the only

A desire to know about one's family seemed only natural to most state wards. In asking about family, girls were also asking 'What am I? Who am I?'. Two state girls, 1913.

174

daughter so I knew she was not my mother, but I thought she might be some relation.[83]

Another girl wrote:

but its hard for me, because I have asked where they are and nobody seems to know, And before I ever got married I would like to know what kind of girl I am. I'd never like to marry a receptable [sic.] boy and and to think I have nobody it would be pretty hard. Do tell me?[84]

Many other girls expected to learn something of their family when they were released, and sometimes were told a little by the secretary:

Coral is to come and see the Secretary re her release. Girl is very curious re her heredity F/M said – is making herself quite ill with uncertainty re same.[85]

As I have now reached the age of 18 years I would like to know something about my parents, I haven't any desire to go to them, or even have anything to do with them but I do think I'm old enough to know who I am.[86]

Australians' views about poverty were changed to some extent by the depression. As Ronald Mendelsohn has stated:

In 1930 the Australian people were still treating the unemployed as suspect; certainly unenterprising, probably lazy and work-shy. By the mid-1930s most were perceived to be victims of an inefficient economic system.[87]

This may be the reason why in the late 1930s the Department seems to have adopted a more liberal stance towards the poor and towards contact between a ward and her natural family. In 1934 one girl wrote gratefully: 'I was so pleased to [have] met my brother at the state Department last Friday and it was a big surprise to me'.[88] A girl's wish to see her sister might be treated with sympathy and tact by an officer of the Department by 1938:

Mary is very anxious to see her sister Beth. I told her to see Miss Jamieson re this when next in Town. She seems very attached to Beth and wept re not seeing her for so long. She is perfectly happy in this home . . .[89]

And other contact with suitable natural relatives might even be encouraged. F.G. Byrne wrote to one girl in 1937:

Some time ago your mother made a request to the Department that permission should be given for you to keep in touch with an aunt, a Mrs Hart of Prospect, whom she suggested you could go to see sometimes on your afternoon off.

I asked an officer to see Mrs Hart and I find that she is quite willing to take some interest in your life and do what she can to help you, and I am granting you permission to go out and see her just whenever it is convenient to your mistress for you to be off duty, and as long as your aunt invites you. I am hoping by this means to establish a friendship which may mean quite a deal to you in after life.[90]

The new policy of cautious contact brought many problems and difficulties. Foster-parents might feel threatened if a loved child they had come to regard as their own suddenly expressed a strong desire to meet another family. Eileen Jones wrote in 1936 appealing for

permission to see any of my parents but most of all to see my sister Ruth who I think has since had her name changed to Alice I do not know where she is for I have not see her since she was 4 she would be 12 now. I hope my wish will be granted. I am now 14 and I am attending the __ School . . .

My mother never sees me nor does my father so I think it would be lovely for me to meet them all once again.

In this case, even though Ruth's foster-mother was opposed to any contact at all between the sisters, the Department persisted, arguing that

whilst not being unmindful of your wishes with regard to the child's future life, realising that it is but natural for you to want to cling to this child as your own, nevertheless the Board feels that it is the right thing for the sisters to be allowed to meet and given the opportunity to know each other if they so desire.[91]

This is very different from the policy of 1887.

Many girls continued trying to keep up contact with families even when they received little response in return.[92] Sometimes pain and disillusionment followed, sometimes a slow realization that others meant far more than oneself:

I was very pleased to hear that I had a sister, I have wrote several letter to her and had no reply. I wish you would tell her to write for I am so anxious to hear from her, for I don't remember ever seeing her, but I suppose I [will] see her some day.[93]

Sometimes a girl might complain to the inspector: 'Ann says she has written to her sister Pauline five times and has not had an answer except a card in return for the Xmas present she sent Pauline. She is feeling very hurt about this'.[94] A year later, in 1938, Ann wrote sadly to her sister:

I have seen mum but she does not seem very pleased to see me, and I am very broken-hearted these days as I have no body now no good mistress to comfort me when I get down in the dumps. I think I have told you all the news so Goodnight and God-Bless you.

I remain
Your ever-loving sister
Ann Trench

Think of me by day
Think of me by night
Think of me when far away
And *don't* forget to write.[95]

With such friendlessness and isolation it is not surprising that many girls were moody or easily upset by little things that 'a cheerful girl would take no notice of'.[96] The sort of minor crisis that continually happened was well described by one housewife in 1932:

Mrs Lyons telephoned to say that Raelene Smith had been very rude to her this morning it seems that she and Raelene overslept and the men got up and made their own breakfast and because they did not set a place for her (Raelene) she went outside and would not come in for any breakfast – told Mrs Lyons she was going back to the Dept and packed her box.
Mrs Lyons does not want to part with girl.[97]

There was a minority in whom depression and moodiness spilled over into mental instability, into bizarre practices such as refusal to wash or eat. A girl might be

subject to fits of melancholy when she threatens to take her own life and at other times seems to become hysterical . . . also seems subject to delusions [but is] fond of children and good to the babies and her work is well done.[98]

By the mid 1920s psychological tests could clearly indicate when a girl was 'lacking in emotional control rather than in intelligence'.[99] In some girls, despair and loneliness even led to attempts at suicide.[1]

According to Harriet Stirling, president of the State Children's Council between 1923 and 1926, the most 'critical' time for state girls was between the ages of eighteen and twenty-one and for this reason they very often had their sentences extended.[2] The Department knew that most girls longed to be released and that they considered themselves quite mature enough to be able to cope. As one girl wrote in 1917:

if this one wish of mine were granted I have no intention of going home to live with my Mother, Oh no that is not so, that I do not wish to do, although I love my Mother what ever her faults may be and would not like to hear anyone say anything about her for she is my Mother . . . [my sister] is so good to me and I think the world of being so good to bring me to live with her I was never so happy ever since I was taken from my Mother as what I am now Only this afternoon did I take a class of little children to teach so therefore Mr Houlgrave I try to aim for the pure and clean things in life and seeing that my Sister and I are so fond of each other and I have a nice place to work at getting on so well there would be no harm in asking to be released for I was the only girl in our family that was ever under your care and now that I am older and know right from wrong I long to be released Oh Mr Houlgrave I do truly hope that this wish may be granted, for believe me I will always strive to do right.[3]

Often when a girl heard that she was not going to be released there would be a stormy time as she adjusted to the news:

you struck me a hard blow when you told me I was extended for two years and all the time I was looking forward to my freedom . . . every time it comes to evening I think another day near my freedom you dont know what it is to be tied down and seeing everyone enjoying themselves . . . [4]

I must say it will not make me any better, I think if a girl can't take care of herself at 20 she never will. I quite looked forward to being released but never mind, it only makes me unhappy, as regards that holiday I would rather not have it I have had enough of homes without being stuck in one for a holiday.[5]

As Appendix 5 shows, only about 11.5 per cent of wards were released back to parents in the 1890s. By the 1920s only about 4 per cent were successful.[6] In investigation, the importance of sobriety in applicants was stressed.[7] Of a sister who applied in 1914 it was reported, when her application was refused:

Mrs Jackson is a very gay young woman and is very fond of going to some place of amusement with a gentleman friend and when Ruth was with her she was left at home in the evenings to care for the children. Mrs Jackson does not attend church and did not make arrangements to send Ruth.[8]

A foster-sister who applied for a state girl was refused because, despite being married and eminently respectable, she was almost the same age as the girl applied for and hence would not be able to wield 'authority' over the younger girl.[9] The ward's present home and what would be lost if a girl were returned, were sometimes described. Sometimes it was decided that more time under the control of the state was necessary before a girl could be considered 'safe'. One girl whose stepmother and father applied for her in February 1919 eventually gained her release in December 1920. What the Department really looked for when considering a girl's release was an effective agent of social control. In this case it was a new step-mother:

Mrs Slee quite understands that Carol is a difficult girl to manage but said that she understands her disposition and ways, as she had her for a while after her mother's death. The girl would share a bedroom with Mrs Slee's two girls aged 11 and 6 years. This is a very nice room and Carol would have a single bed and the little girls the double one.

The house contains 4 rooms and back verandah. The house is nicely furnished and was very clean although Mrs Slee had only moved in about 1 week.[10]

Another girl was released to her brother and sister-in-law, the latter being 'a nice sensible woman' according to Miss Kentish.[11] Girls were also released 'on probation' to relatives who might after several years apply for the girl's absolute release if her conduct had been exemplary.[12]

The girl with an extended family, with respectable aunts or older sisters willing to 'have a try' with an erring girl – to control her in the way that society deemed proper in the 1920s and 1930s – this was the girl who might be released from the state.[13] Girls themselves were expected to show great stability and maturity if they wanted to be released before the age of twenty-one. If a girl felt her character had been slurred she might protest – as one girl did in 1928 when her sentence was extended after she reached nineteen years of age:

I do not see that you have just reasons for terming me lazy. I have never refused to work for anyone. Certainly, I did complain of having to work saturday afternoon, but I had reasons for doing so you cannot expect a girl to be contented at a place where the work has no system with it and that was the case at Mrs Jones. If I am lazy as you say how do you account for Mrs Smith keeping me I can assure you that there isn't any room for lazy people on this place. Last year you wrote me a letter which led me to think that if I put up a fair game you would release me at 19. I kept my word and all I received in return was a letter reproaching me for what had nothing whatever to do with this last 12 months.[14]

The Department had to consider not only whether a girl would return to poor associates, or parents who might be living 'in one room in considerable squalor', but also whether family or friends would seek out a girl and lead her into bad practices.[15] So it was important that a girl had someone to turn to, whether her natural family or foster-parents: The secretary, when writing to a girl advising her of her release, stressed, 'that I shall always be pleased to hear from you or to help you and advise you whenever you may be in difficulty'.[16]

Best of all was the girl not likely to need help again because she had a protector, either husband, family, or relative. And there were of course girls who did not want to see their family or leave the employment they were in when released.[17] One girl told Miss Novice, an inspector, that

she did not want to go anywhere near her home. She remembers the home and having lived differently for so many years would not now like to return to the former conditions. She would rather live her own life in the future and carve a career for herself.[18]

The policy change that occurred in the late 1930s affected the area of extension of sentences. By 1937 a girl would be given a much longer explanation of the reasons behind her release or extension. She might be told how the Department's Board had deliberated. She might in some instances even be allowed to decide her fate for herself:

The Board at its last meeting again considered your case, and, having in mind that you were so bitterly disappointed at not being released from departmental care, it spent some time in debating what should be done now that you have had the matter fully explained to you.

I think if I read your letter rightly that you do understand the Board is trying to act in your best interests in the matter.

I have been authorised to tell you that, after much consideration, the Board still thinks it would be wise for you to remain nominally under the control of the department until you are 19, though it is willing to lift any reasonable bar and permit you to do much as you like with regard to the regulations governing children under control. If in spite of this, and the knowledge that, when you ask to be allowed to visit your people the request is likely to be granted, you still wish to be entirely free from the Board, I am to suggest that you should write a letter, say in four weeks' time, asking for your release, when the Board is likely to favourably consider the request.

Now surely you must be satisfied that there is no intention to be harsh with you in view of that intimation and I shall look forward with some degree of anticipation to seeing just what you will decide when the four weeks are up. Whatever it may be, I want you to believe that the Board and the Department and its officers still desire and remain,

Your sincere friends,
F.G. Byrne,
Secretary.[19]

Mary Nolan wrote back:

in spite of all you are willing to do, I still wish to be released from Departmental care. I am old enough to take care of myself now, and I shall continue with Mrs Parsons as long as she likes to keep me, I will behave myself just the same as I would under your care . . .[20]

The sort of life that meant a girl might be absolutely released was one of quiet domestic orderliness, feminine pursuits, and firm control by parents:

Jane's conduct has been quite satisfactory as reported by the mother.

Jane has interested herself in dressmaking and has made quite a nice costume for herself since her return home. Mrs Lennox says Jane does not associate with her former companions and is quite content to remain at home. She is interested in several kinds of handwork particularly knitting and has made several very pretty and useful articles.[21]

Jane Lennox was thus a 'good girl' by the standards of 1939 Australia.

For state girls there was only one escape from authority: to abscond. A number of girls did abscond from their employers. On any one day there were likely to be two to eight girls who had run away and were hiding somewhere in South Australia (see Appendix 4). Most absconders felt that the safety valve of writing to the secretary would no longer do:

I wish to be removed as I can never do anything right here and Mrs Fraser says I dont wash the pots clean or anything else so if you dont remove me I'll remove myself by absconding let me know full particulars as soon as Possible.[22]

Or as one girl put it to her sister:

Very likely I will go to the Reformatory or Probationary School but still that will not worry me because I will run away from there and come home again if the Secretary does not let me go. I will get on alright without the State's help.[23]

The sorts of conditions that could lead even a patient girl to abscond were well described by Mary Sneddon after she ran away in 1907:

you never give me one word of encouragement from morning till night Mrs Smith you please look back you know how many times you could have spoke kindly to me instead of being cross with me . . . please don't give me too black a character because I have friends and a sister I love and don't want to disgrace. I hope you will not have another girl from the State because we girls have hearts and feelings and are not machines.[24]

Often when a state girl absconded, an account of her activities over the last few days would be sent to the Department by her astonished, annoyed, or sometimes even sorrowing employers.[25] A girl herself, after being recaptured, might reflect on the incident that had been the last straw:

I would never have left Mrs Wright the way I did had she let me come back the right way. I said Mrs Wright I want to go back to town I don't like it here and she said I have a form to fill in to keep you till you are 21 if I like then I said I will write in and ask Mr Kelsh if I can go back to town and Mrs Wright said its no [use] of you writing in to go back as the State will simply ignore your letter so I made up my mind I would stay not with her to sling off at me.[26]

A police inspector might explain an absconding by saying that a girl's mistress had 'a very long tongue' and was 'continually nagging', 'enough to drive any girl away'.[27] How it felt to be nagged was eloquently described by one girl who ran away in July 1902:

not a day passes without Mrs Roth is growling about something and very often throws out nasty sneers at me. Sir I would not mind it so much if I was one of their own but as I am without a Father or Mother . . . I cannot complain about my clothes or food as I have plenty of both But growling is terrible. I left Mrs Roth on Thursday night when I was having tea Mrs Roth was growling at me before tea and I just poured out the tea and went out side, I was thinking to go then, but I thought I would go in and see if she was any better. But I just commenced my tea and she started again. But Sir I did not give her any cheek I just got up and walked strait outside and went to a neighbour place, and they were quite willing to keep me . . .[28]

The Department tried to make it very difficult for a girl to abscond. State girls, apart from being closely supervised, normally had very little money. Nevertheless, girls might slip out at night or disappear after carrying lunches out to the men in a paddock.[29] Very often they disappeared with nothing; as one inspector was told, 'only what she was wearing: Blue Serge dress white sailor Collar and White Sailor hat'.[30]

If a girl was caught after absconding she usually had to make a statement to the Department about her activities. Any expenses incurred in arresting her came out of the office portion of her wages. Some girls' activities were innocent enough: many who absconded in the city had a network of relatives and friends whom they visited, and one girl even went with a relative to a Butchers' Picnic.[31] Other girls formed liaisons with young men of a more or less questionable kind, or so it seemed to the Department.[32] Some so 'disgraced themselves' that they were sent to the Reformatory when apprehended:

last evening Lucy Frost was brought here by 'Jack Hill' a young man with whom she has been seen several times. I find also that on Sat. and Sunday night she was with Rose Matters also __ both she and Lou Kelly slept in the wash house at the back of Mrs Macks . . .[33]

She has been sleeping on the beach and under the jetty at Largs and has been in the company of the very lowest characters of the Port. Mary admits to having been immoral with three men on Sunday – and with two others on the journey to Edithberg on Monday and Monday night. Her story is of a disgusting nature . . .[34]

The words of the girls themselves sometimes reveal rather a different picture of absconding, even allowing for bravado:

Dear Ellen

I wonder if you have heard about me yet. I am in Broken Hill living with my sister Vi. Mr Gray took a second [sic.] when he thought I was going to stay at this place so I just took My clothes and Cleared.

Now Ruth and my other Sister are up here and we have a bonzer time I went to a dance the other night and I was up at every Dance I have such a bonzer boy. He is going to travel with the band to Sydney and he wants to take me my word that will be the time. Mr Gray will never get me again. I have to laugh when I think about him trying to keep me for another 2 years and I wont have to do that now I am over the border its oh what a change alright I am off to another dance next Wednesday I went to the Theater Tuesday night and it was lovely plenty of life up here . . . [35]

It was difficult to survive, once having absconded. Girls went hungry, slept under trees, were sheltered by friends, and assaulted by male acquaintances. Some girls got away, right out of the state or so much into obscurity that they were never caught. But most seem to have stayed in the city, sleeping where they could: in the houses of friends or in summer in the parklands bordering the city proper.[36] Some made much of their freedom in letters to friends:

I seem to go out too much to write, and out every day and when we come home straight in the water just like ducks we are. I am having a glorious time mix bathing 13 of us went in together the other night five boys eight girls, I have learnt our to float, and my cousin he is trying to show me how to swim, I would love to be able to.[37]

For most girls, absconding was an act of rebellion in itself. They acted in an unplanned manner once they were free, and in such a drifting state they were very easy prey. As one girl testified in 1915:

I am an inmate of 'The Haven' Probationary School. I ran away from the above on Sunday February 21st about 8pm or 8.30pm. Betty Jones was with me. We went down towards Norwood, we went up the Parade and returned to the Parklands opposite the Wesleyan College and slept under a tree. The next day we went to the gardens. We had nothing to eat that day. We slept that night in the same place as on Monday night, and so far we had not spoken to any one, and had nothing to eat since the Monday night. On Tuesday we wandered about again and got some peaches out of a garden (we got a cap full) – that night we slept in the Park-lands behind the zoo. Wednesday we went over to the Racecourse – we saw people there and several spoke to us but we never answered them. We had a drink on the Race-course but had nothing to eat . . . That night we slept in the

Park-lands near the Olive trees – two boys were with us I only know their names to be John & Blue. I do not know who they are. We were standing near the Brittania Hotel and they came and spoke to us. John was with me during the night and Blue was with Betty. John had connection with me. They gave us some sandwiches. One went for them and the other stayed with us. Thursday we wandered about again. We had nothing to eat that day. I do not know where we went on Thursday night, but Friday we stayed down in the Parklands, and had nothing to eat all that day, we stayed out under a tree. We saw John and he gave us some cake to eat but he did not stay. Blue did not come near us. We did not tell them we were State Children but we told them we had run away from the Probationary Home. Saturday we stayed about the Park-lands and had some of the cake left to eat that John had given us the day before.[38]

This existence of hunger and isolation went on for several more days until at John's urging the girls contacted the father of one of them.

Adelaide was a small city, the mecca towards which country absconders headed when they ran away. The officers of the Department distrusted the many attractions of the city. It seemed to confirm their prejudices about the poor and, increasingly in the 1920s and 1930s, the young. Over the years the officers built up a very good knowledge of the city and its inhabitants, a knowledge shared with the police and revealed in Departmental comments. Consequently, a policewoman, Miss Annie Ross, might write to the secretary about a disturbance being caused by 'an old state boy living apart from his wife'.[39]

Many suburbs were distrusted as slums because they were built-up areas without gardens. None was so strongly disliked between the wars as the south-east and south-west of the City of Adelaide. This was an area of 340 acres, much of it covered in small row or single-storey terrace houses of two or three rooms, old houses mostly with yards less than 20 feet wide and complicated with sheds sometimes housing another family. The city as a whole (including North Adelaide) covered 3 268 acres and in 1921 had a population of 39 552, including 13 738 people under twenty-one. It had a residential density of 12.10 persons per acre, four times as much as the average population in South Australia. Of these residents, 85 per cent were tenants, which was more than twice the average for South Australia as a whole.[40]

There was an atmosphere of community living and closeness about the city that to some extent came solely from the physical environment. Attached cottages meant that a neighbour could hear if a child was being 'knocked against the wall repeatedly', and it was impossible to have a family dispute in a lane such as Churchill Street without the general uproar attracting the police or an officer of the State Children's Department.[41] There were well-known meeting places in the city: hotels, the market, the Beehive corner; all places where an absconder might be sighted and returned to the Department.

It seems an appropriate contrast to end this chapter with those girls who were grateful to the state for having rescued and protected them. Life for many state girls was hard and for a few it was brutal, but there were those who believed their lives had been improved by the intervention of the Department. There were many girls who earned rewards for good behaviour at the Central Depot, or who wrote to the Department thanking them for Christmas presents. Two girls wrote in the mid 1930s:

I am writing a few lines to show my appreciation of your kindness to me during my stay at Central Depot. I received the cheque for £1 April 20th and I am very pleased with it.

I will show that I appreciate it by not spending it foolishly.[42]

I have great pleasure in writing a few lines, to thank you for the Christmas present, which you so kindly gave me.

I was quite thrilled with it and I do want to show my appreciation of your kind gift by doing everything in my power to please you, such as behaving myself and obeying the rules of the Department which are set before me.[43]

Many girls looked back over their lives when they were released and reflected on what the Department had done for them.

Adelaide was a small city, the mecca that country absconders headed for when they ran away. There were well-known meeting places in the centre of the city: hotels, the Beehive corner, the market. This picture shows the central market in 1923.

I have always tried to please the Dept, and I hope, Sir, that I have given satisfaction. I can assure you that I will always endeavour to do my very best, wherever I may be.

I wish to thank the Dept for all their kindness and consideration shown me, for which I am very grateful indeed.[44]

I will do my best in this world it is hard to fight but others have done it and so I can I have good health at present and plenty of strength so you have made me that girl since a baby healthy and happy and I have learnt the ways of life and I know what road to take for my Lord has taught me and I wish to thank you all for helping me and keeping me through life . . .[45]

Another girl whose feelings were more ambivalent, wrote back to the Council after she had successfully absconded:

I am glad to be able to tell you I am doing well but with no thanks to the State Childrens Department if anybody ought to have the credit it is Miss Bubb [Matron of the Girls Reformatory, Redruth from 1916 to 1922] for noone could be better to the girls than her still you have good rules . . . but I found I could not tolerate the bad ones any longer so had to break them.[46]

Perhaps the whole range of experiences can be captured best in the actions of two state girls of different generations who talked together in 1918:

The day she came she would not stay in the country. I done all I could to try and make her happy, but nothing seemed to please her She has a terrible set on the State and I told her that I was a State girl myself one time and that if she tried to work herself up that she had no need to be ashamed of the State in fact I am proud of it. At about 2 o'clock on Friday I said Come and lay down in the passage with me Maud it was so hot in the bedrooms. She said alright but went in to her bedroom and at about ½ past four I sent my little boy to tell her to come and have a cup of tea but she had packed her box and gone.[47]

CHAPTER 8

Reformers and Reformed 1860–1940

1860–1914

Theory

'Boarding-out' was the term given to the first attempts to foster children. It was a system of boarding and, as the emphasis on the financial aspects in the term might suggest, it sprang from a mixture of compassion and expediency. Consideration of the emotional needs of children came much later. It was a practice of placing poor or neglected children in ordinary homes among ordinary families and paying the *de facto* parents a sum to cover the child's expenses. In order to be boarded-out a child had first to become a ward of the state.

In the last century and a half there have been three major stages in the history of child welfare, and all three have been intimately linked with reformers' views of childhood and the function of the family. Boarding-out is the second 'wave' of child-saving movements, the first being the reformatory movement, and the third the probation system and modern foster-care practices.[1]

The first wave in the history of child welfare began in England in the mid 1840s and resulted in the setting up of industrial schools and reformatories. The 1834 Poor Law Amendment Act or New Poor Law, as it is often called, had established a system of poor relief in which outdoor payments for the able-bodied had been abolished and in which the poor were to be maintained within the grim walls of the workhouse.[2] The aged, the infirm, the simple, and the young were all confined to one institution. The same applied to prisons, where child criminals were exposed to even more corrupting influences. Those who began in the 1840s to advocate separate institutions for the juvenile destitute and child criminals, claimed that reformation was impossible without proper classification. In prisons children would merely learn adult vices; in the workhouse they would absorb the 'miasma' of pauperism. It was argued by those in favour of reformatories, therefore, that child criminals should instead be punished 'with short terms in prison and then committed to reformatories for several years 'reformative training'.[3] Parents were, where possible, compelled to contribute weekly sums to the upkeep of their children. Children were still regarded as culpable and were to be punished for their misdeeds, only they were to be punished in a different way.

Industrial schools were for destitute children, not criminals. They had a greater age range of children and housed both sexes in a manner similar to orphanages. Parents were required, where possible, to contribute. Access to their children was harshly controlled and their rights as parents were completely relinquished. Within industrial schools children had to adhere, at best, to a dreary spartan regime, eating dull stodgy food, playing in barren yards, and themselves performing much of the work of the institution, the older girls acting as unpaid domestic servants under the guise of 'domestic training'. Religion and authority were given heavy emphasis. Occasionally, upper-class visitors might call and distribute tracts or fruit.[4] At worst, industrial schools could be places of excessive corporal punishment, neglect, ill-health, and death, infectious diseases being impossible to contain with so many small children. Older children in industrial schools might be apprenticed out to tradesmen or factories, a practice that had its origins in the Elizabethan Poor Law regulations of 1601. For apprenticing a child an employer would be paid several pounds.[5]

All the Australian colonies followed the philosophy of the English Poor Law despite differences in dates of settlement and the different origins of the populations of each colony. By 1860 children were confined in institutions in every colony.

As happened everywhere else, so in South Australia disease continually took its toll of the young inmates of industrial schools. This was particularly so in the early years when accommodation was makeshift. In 1864, when children were still being cared for at the Destitute Asylum in Kintore Avenue, an epidemic of scarlatina occurred. In 1867, in the course of five months, sixteen of the unfortunate children died under circumstances of neglect and squalor in the Grace Darling building at Brighton.[6] Clearly something would have to be done with the colony's poor and neglected children.

Thus reformatories and industrial schools were built in the 1860s, the Australian colonies adopting

the English system of reformatory and industrial schools with little adaption to colonial circumstances and no attempt to re-think the principles or to introduce any new treatment. They did not even incorporate all the principles adopted in European examples. For example, they largely ignored the family system (arranging the institution in small groups in cottages rather than large barrack style buildings) on which much emphasis had been placed by such prototype institutions as Mettray Agricultural Colony founded in England in 1849. Thus the system of institutions in New South Wales and South Australia was similar, if not inferior, to those of Britain and Europe.[7]

In fact, in the 1860s, when in South Australia it was proposed to build a vast expensive industrial school at Magill, it was opposed by concerned individuals who knew that cottage homes were now advocated and used in parts of Europe and England. A deputation proposed to the South Australian government that boarding-out be attempted instead.[8] But it was not successful. Arthur Blyth, the Chief Secretary, saw industrial schools as the next step.[9] A large three-storey industrial school was therefore built at Magill on a site that was to be used in one way or another for the next 120 years.

Those who believed in boarding-out as a superior alternative to keeping children in institutions had a sense of mission. They were not deterred, and Caroline Emily Clark was even given permission to board out a few children under her own auspices, though disaster and ineptitude surrounded her early efforts.[10]

In order to understand why boarding-out eventually became the dominant method of care for dependent children it is important to understand what it was, what it might degenerate into, and what it was hoped to achieve.

Boarding-out was begun as a radical alternative to keeping children in large institutions such as the Magill Industrial School for destitute children, a vast institution built in Adelaide in 1867.

The moral foundations of the idea of boarding-out had been laid by English social reformers such as Frances Power Cobbe who argued in *Frasers Magazine* in 1864 that, '*Every* child is naturally dependent – the king's son no less than the beggar's . . . [thus] *he* cannot morally be made to bear the stigma of pauperism'. Neatly encapsulating the blend of compassion and expediency in the early reformers' thoughts, she went on:

As a matter of right, no child ought to bear the stigma of pauperism; and as a matter of public interest for the future of the community every dependent child ought to be separated and removed as far as by any means may be possible from pauper moral influences and pauper physical and social degradation.[11]

The sisters Florence and Rosamund Hill, enterprising British social reformers and Unitarians, studied the tentative efforts of Mr Greig of Edinburgh in the 1840s and became active proponents of this system of child care. It was partly because of their activities that the English Poor Law Board decided in 1870 to permit the boarding-out of children in the unions under its control.[12] These developments were being closely followed by those concerned with social reform in Australia, particularly by a cousin of the Hill sisters, Caroline Clark, and her friend and ally Catherine Helen Spence, both staunch members of the South Australian Unitarian Church. In 1872 South Australia began the system by boarding-out six children, followed by Tasmania in 1873, Victoria in 1874, and New South Wales in 1880. The other two states, Western Australia and Queensland, began the system much later in the 1900s.[13]

Those who urged and initiated these reforms reveal in their writings their belief that South Australia itself was a gigantic experiment. It was believed that the colony had 'led in so many things'[14] that the second half of the nineteenth century in South Australia could fairly claim to be 'a glorious age of progress'.[15] Mistakes in method inevitably occurred even in a new country but they could be more quickly rectified, according to the Hill sisters, because they were less 'deeply rooted in the social life of the people'.[16] Catherine Spence wrote that

we took hold of the growth and development of South Australia and identified ourselves with it. Nothing is insignificant in the history of a young community and above all – nothing seems impossible.[17]

Caroline Clark, who recovered from consumption in the dry warm South Australian climate, wrote of the vice of inherited pauperism:

Consumption is hereditary; yet in this fine climate many people escape its penalties, and we may hope to escape the taint of pauperism if we take the right means to set about it at once.[18]

This is the voice of an elite; the correctional voice of a small group who wanted to rid their society of a threatening growth. This aspect of the new scheme was constantly under-emphasized by Caroline Clark and Catherine Spence and their contemporaries and, more surprisingly, by most later writers on boarding-out.[19] One writer did describe the South Australian Unitarians as 'an intellectual elite' and later concluded that 'their political temper was, in South Australia, predominantly conservative',[20] but it is necessary to further emphasize where their class position placed their reforms. It is important to see past their rhetoric to what actually happened.[21]

There is a widely accepted view that South Australian Unitarians were a radical minority, yet this acceptance is very much based on their own or their descendants' views.[22] Certainly they considered themselves a radical and embattled religious grouping and they were (even in the paradise of dissent) an extremely small sect. However, their radicalism was not even a legacy of radicalism, but an image of the group as threatened and radical, which tended to prevent innovation and re-examination.[23] It is important to independently evaluate statements they made about the boarding-out system and to appreciate what was actually meant in terms of the issues and conditions of the times.

At the heart of the philosophy of boarding-out was a double-sided notion of the family, at times pejorative, at other times prescriptive. The class which it was hoped could be eliminated by boarding-out was the pauper class, which was seen as a drain and danger to the state. Seeing the families of the respectable poor as the 'sweet soil' which nurtured humble and industrious young people, reformers urged that children who might inherit the vice of pauperism be transplanted into respectable homes and be 'absorbed amongst other children and go to ordinary schools and take a share in ordinary work'.[24] Accordingly, some families were to be broken up and others were to be augmented in order that the state might be more stable and less vulnerable to the depredations of the pauper class and the associated criminal class. Among Victorians, not least social reformers, fear of the pauper class was widespread.[25] In order to survive, particularly in an age of universal suffrage, it was argued, the state needed to house and educate the poorest classes and if possible diminish the generation of their number. As Caroline Clark noted:

The workhouse of England has become not merely the refuge, but the nursery, of pauperism. It is an acknowledged fact that most of the children reared within its walls come back to it sooner or later as men and women, and their children and grand-children follow them.[26]

This same notion, separation of adults and children, lay behind two other reforms initiated by people concerned for children in South Australia in the 1870s. In 1876 Townsend House, an asylum for blind

Caroline Emily Clark (1825–1911) who began the boarding-out system in South Australia in 1872.

children, was founded and moves were made towards establishing the Adelaide Children's Hospital. Thirty-five years after the founding of the hospital it was still being asserted (in a publicity brochure) that 'if you spend a shilling on the child, it may save a sovereign on the adult'.

In the 1860s Frances Power Cobbe and others had proceeded from a vigorous philosophical analysis about society to conclusions about the duty of citizens to the poor. During the next five decades, after reforms such as boarding-out had been achieved, there were few admissions that perhaps a different analysis of society was needed to explain the persistence of poverty.

The State Children's Council, which after 1887 administered the care of state children, was mainly concerned with the results, not the causes of poverty. Like their American counterparts of a slightly earlier era, they

thought of this improvement [in society] for the most part in negative terms: elimination of sickness, crime, mental ills and pauperism. They were not thinking particularly of the creation of a sounder social structure that might slough off such ills.[27]

The annual reports of the State Children's Council were, like the reports by other boards in different states, 'planned to sell the program',[28] and while they might relate some of the difficulties the new methods had to surmount, they tended to concentrate on the encouraging example and the sentimental story.

The Council was reluctant to consider large issues and over the years it showed a curious ambivalence when these intruded themselves. Thus, while the annual report for 1894–95 did admit that increased destitution was a 'sign of the times' (referring to the economic depression which made many families unable to afford to keep those children boarded-out with them), in 1905 they argued that much poverty could be avoided if the poor could be 'uplifted, taught their duty and enabled to do it'.[29] After receiving the police report on the upsurge of juvenile crime, truancy, and larrikinism in 1904, the Council, while admitting that it only dealt with results and not with causes, was prepared to add that it thought the root cause was 'selfishness' – something beyond the curative power of any legislature.[30]

In 1907 the Council held a convention in Adelaide to discuss the care of state children. There it was reiterated that to 'save' a child not only benefited the child, it also meant that the reformer did not, as the chairman of the Council put it, have to 'look on helplessly while the vicious seeds germinate and produce a harvest, and to reserve our money and our effort for the punishment of the full-fledged criminal'.[31] It was thus a scheme as much of self-interest as of charity.

But because boarding-out was intended to produce from the 'vicious seeds' of pauperism a healthy, happy, and industrious class of domestic servants and 'respectable poor', it was not merely the creation of hypocrites. The Council was unselfconscious about motive and saw no moral dilemmas in a scheme being intended to benefit both a child and its own class. There can be no doubt about the class from which the Council was drawn.[32] In addition, Council members employed state children in their own homes, and this was not regarded as extraordinary even as late as 1926.[33] While Council members could talk in 1907 of their work of 'love' with 'a forlorn child', they could also congratulate themselves on 'how much the SCC has done to relieve the PAINFUL DEARTH OF DOMESTIC SERVANTS'.[34]

So unselfconscious was this blend of idealism and self-interest that the latter can be quite easily missed at a first reading. But it is important that it be delineated and exposed. Compassion is an unchanging factor in attitudes to children; the change that emerges is in class attitudes. In the first forty years of boarding-out these attitudes were revealed many times.

When in Australia in 1875, the Hill sisters gave a clear idea of the type of foster-home they regarded as the best. Having visited several homes where children were boarded-out in South Australia, they approved heartily of the 'humble' wooden cottage and noted that in a home of 'higher social pretensions' the children were ill at ease and seemed to feel they were lodgers in the household. They also mention the fact that the work at the Girls' Reformatory seemed too light to them and not a good preparation for later life as servants.[35]

In 1885, giving evidence to the Destitute Commission, Thomas Sadler Reed, the chairman of the Destitute Board, seemed convinced that the foster-homes he had seen in New South Wales were far superior to those in South Australia. This drew forth some precise fury from the commissioners who stoutly defended South Australian homes and thought it was much better for a child to go to a 'bush home' and a family of the labouring classes. They could see no reason why a child 'thrown' onto the state should be brought up in a style better than other children of the same 'rank' whose parents were dutifully supporting them.[36]

In 1889 a country visitor wrote in her report to the Council that in her opinion the 'service girls' (female wards over thirteen years of age who worked as domestic servants) are so 'fussed and petted over' that they forget what their station in life is. In this case the Council defended the girls, arguing that while it had to be fair to foster-parents and employers, it had to *protect* (that is, be a parent to) the children in its charge.[37] A visiting committee in 1889 mentioned the fact that the children did not seem to realize that they were servants and regarded themselves as visitors. It was suggested by a future member of the Council that those who visited foster-homes should not be concerned overmuch with small matters such as tidiness, because

when children are placed out in the homes of poor people such people as probably their own parents would have been, we cannot insist to the same extent on these minor matters as we would about our own children in our own homes.[38]

Boarding-out was not intended to give a child the chance to rise by merit, to demonstrate the domination of environment over inheritance, as the modern reader may at first assume. Rather, it was intended to give the dependent child the same opportunities that an independent child from her own rank in society would enjoy. The children of the poor and degraded would be placed with 'such people as probably their own parents would have been: the honest industrious and independent poor'.[39] In 1907, Caroline Clark, looking back, wrote that one reason for the initial realization of the superiority of boarding-out over institutional life was that children from the Destitute Asylum 'were to be sent out as little servants to help others when they could not help themselves, it may be imagined how useless they would be'.[40]

Boarding-out thus imposed on children from the pauper class an ideal of childhood but it was not the middle-class ideal in every respect; rather, it was the middle-class perception of a working-class ideal. Like middle-class children, state children were supposed to be dutiful, passive, protected, and controlled, but unlike middle-class children, they had a childhood abruptly curtailed at thirteen when they went to work. Even before thirteen years of age they were supposed, above all, to be *useful*.

Poor children could be considered by contemporary reformers as children different from middle-class children in any case, and this was part of the reforming Victorians' views about the pauper class. To some extent boarding-out was predicated on the notion that working-class family ties were weak. 'Their' children did not have feelings like 'our' children, therefore it was believed they could be transplanted to new homes. As Nigel Middleton has pointed out in writing about the care of children in Britain in the years 1900–50: 'One widespread belief was that working-class parents wished to abandon their children for someone else to bring up; there was little appreciation of the bonds binding this type of family'.[41]

During the years 1890–1910, the Council did become increasingly concerned with what might now be called 'deviance' among the city's young. Almost always, as Anthony Platt has noted of the USA, this was behaviour previously ignored by the authorities, and behaviour 'primarily attributable to the children of lower-class immigrant families'.[42]

In 1891 the annual report noted that it seemed 'destitution is on the increase, parental control is becoming more lax, juvenile crime is making great strides, and immorality is spreading among the young'. In 1895 the Council again noted how many children 'frequent the more crowded thoroughfares and the parks' and stressed how this could lead in many cases to 'criminal practices or immorality'. By 1897, as the economic depression deepened, the Council had, at the request of the government, made a special inquiry into the increase in juvenile crime and in this instance linked what they called 'the enforced idleness of parents' with the increased amount of juvenile crime.[43]

Another explanation must surely lie in the slow but progressive extension of behaviour which could be defined within the ambit of 'juvenile crime'.[44] Throughout the development of South Australia there had been periodic depressions bringing with them increased unemployment and destitution. The poverty of the 'casual poor' must therefore have been apparent before. But only in the two decades after 1890 did juvenile crime and larrikinism begin to preoccupy South Australian reformers. When looking at the sorts of behaviours that concerned the Council – betting, smoking, sexual immorality, bottle collecting for marine store dealers, access to obscene publications, the selling of matches and race cards by children under thirteen, the roaming of the streets by children of both sexes after 8 p.m. – it can be seen that prohibition of these activities all served to emphasize the dependent character of poor children and to more clearly demarcate the world of the child from that of the adult.

The forms of behaviour considered 'respectable' in children were continually narrowed by legislation throughout this period.[45] Children were not supposed to 'wander about the streets' even if a small home and cramped garden made it a great temptation to do so. They were supposed to attend school and not dawdle on the way home; they were not supposed to be out after dark. They were not supposed to fight or swear in the street and, though it was no fault of their own, they also attracted attention if dirty and poorly dressed. The activities of girls were even more strongly controlled. Daughters were not supposed (if they wanted to remain 'respectable') to have any social or financial independence, although they might have to work of course. In fact, middle-class reformers were apt to disapprove of working-class girls who did *not* work.

For a poor child to escape being noticed by the police or officers of the Department therefore required concern and vigilance on the part of parents, and a rock-like determination to avoid the temptations of drink and petty criminal activities. It required parents to have and to maintain authority over their children.

These were just the qualities reformers looked for in foster-homes. When affection or family failed, they argued, children in danger should be removed and replanted among the respectable. The Council always preferred country to city foster-homes in their public statements ('a plain home upon some South Australian farm'),[46] but even in the 1890s nearly half the foster-homes were in the suburbs of Adelaide. Sobriety, industry, and respectability were the qualities looked for in foster-parents. The 'tone' of the home had to be good, though this in no sense implied prosperity. The personality and influence of the foster-mother was of primary importance. This elevation of the family, of work, of parental authority, was an inherent part of the whole ideology of the proponents of boarding-out. It was the other side of that dichotomy which stamped some families as dangerous, improvident, and pauperized.

R.J. Lawrence argues in *Professional Social Work in Australia* that voluntary social effort in Australia was weak in the nineteenth century because there was no 'leisured class' with the time and money to help the less fortunate.[47] This assessment seems to have been based on examination only of the eastern states, because in South Australia it was precisely such a leisured class which initiated and maintained the early effort in boarding-out and the whole cluster of reforms and philanthropic institutions which characterized South Australia in the 1870s and 1880s. The early philanthropists were well-to-do members of the middle class by South Australian standards.[48] The women in such a social group had the time, the education, and the money to devote much of their energies to social effort. Between 1887 and 1920 half the personnel on the State Children's Council were women and the visiting committees were overwhelmingly composed of female members, as was the earlier Boarding-out Society. A great part of the time-consuming work of boarding-out was performed by energetic and earnest ladies of a type peculiar to the late nineteenth century, though not in any sense peculiar to South Australia.

In the USA it has been pointed out that it was women from 'the higher circles' who helped take 'some of the roughest edges' off late nineteenth-century capitalism:

upper-class women were very important between 1890 and 1920 in bringing into existence a more humane and paternalistic social system. If their role is less obvious since that time, it is perhaps even more persuasive ... they fought especially for these measures on behalf of their feminine counterparts from the other side of the tracks but much of their activity also benefited male workers.[49]

Connected with this issue is the myth that boarding-out was a 'women's movement'. To the extent that large numbers of women were involved this is true, but it is apparent that the positions of real power were held by men. The powerful and pivotal position of Council secretary was always a male public service stronghold, and all the members of the earlier Destitute Board, the ministries, and the parliaments of the day were men. Although women gained early political recognition in Australia, they were not intended to *enter* business, politics, or the public service. Charitable work was another matter; in some circles, as Lawrence points out, it even conferred a social cachet. Thus, while at first glance it was a ladies' movement, real power was wielded by the gentlemen.

The 'child-savers' in South Australia, however, were not women such as the founders of the Juvenile Court in Illinois, 'bored at home and unhappy with their lack of participation in the "real world" '. They were not women who dissociated themselves from radical movements such as the suffragette movement, but they were alike in another important respect. Like their fellow reformers in Illinois, 'they vigorously defended the virtue of traditional family life and emphasised the dependence of the social order on the proper socialisation of children'.[50]

Without proper upbringing, without education, the social order might be under threat from class divisions within it. Fear of 'the mob', the pauper class enraged, was a concept that might easily be transplanted from nineteenth-century urban England to Australia. If universal suffrage was to be granted then the people would have to be 'educated' so that they could use it wisely.[51] And education in its fullest sense began at a mother's knee, in the family.

Enshrining of the 'family' is therefore central to the ideology which could justify removing children, forever, from 'unsuitable' parents and paying strangers to act as parents towards them.

It should be emphasized here that boarding-out in the 1890s and 1900s was a system of fostering different from that of modern-day theory. Children who were boarded-out were not intended, in the vast majority of cases, to have any contact with their parents again. As already mentioned, they were expected to completely forget their natural parents and their early environment. If they were told anything about their origins, or why they came under the care of the state, it was not until they reached the age of eighteen or later. Siblings might be fostered in the same family, it is true, but the 1887 Regulations were quite specific about parents: 'Relatives shall not have access to children placed out, except in the case of a child becoming seriously ill, or under special circumstances, with the sanction of the council'.[52]

The child must be prepared for her responsibilities as a citizen. And in the case of pauper children this meant removing them to a home where they would be taught the value of work and thrift. This view was based on what the historian Leonore Davidoff has called 'domestic peace and salvation'. She argues that this cluster of beliefs remained deeply part of 'a secular morality' until long after World War I.

The essence of domesticity in the daily round, the weekly and seasonal rituals within the home, emphasized the cyclical and hence timeless quality of family life in opposition to the sharp disjunctive growth and collapse of commerce and industry.[53]

How did this affect the policies of the State Children's Department?

In theory there was a clear distinction between foster-homes and service homes, the former being for the state child under thirteen, and the latter being the home and place of employment for children over thirteen. But in reality there was often very little distinction, the qualities which were looked for in one being the standard for both. Over the years the Department managed to establish a wide knowledge of suitable families throughout the state and this network of respectable families became both foster-parents, employers, and reliable sources of opinion about other families. The Department was able to write, for example, 'Mr Jones is a brother of Mr Jones of Gumeracha where our boys and girls have always had a good home and training'.[54]

The influence that a woman was supposed to have in either sort of home was the same: to set a reforming example in every aspect of her life by strict adherence to certain codes of behaviour. To quote Davidoff again:

It was felt that in some way their own personal behaviour would stand as examples to the working class even in the minutiae of living ... [which to] most women really meant their servants ...[55]

Female wards who were working as live-in domestics were in need of just as much guidance as children who were boarded-out: being at 'a dangerous age', they might in fact be in need of more care.

The nuclear family was not the only sort of household thought suitable for wards. Wards were sometimes boarded with or sent to work for widows, spinsters, or childless wives. The main thing was that pauper influences should be replaced by habits of obedience, industry, and personal cleanliness, that great touchstone of respectability.

Factory work was regarded as totally unsuitable for state girls, but apprenticeship as a servant was ideal because it enabled a moral guardian to maintain complete control over a girl's development and inculcate habits of deference and piety. After the age of twenty-one state wards were no longer under the control of the Council, and it was then hoped that the reformative power of boarding-out would reveal itself, and they would become good 'anonymous' citizens, not 'known' to the police.

About 1902–14 one can detect the tentative beginnings of a long, slow drift away from the above view of poverty and a move towards something more modern.

In some instances this found expression as 'an imperial anxiety', a fear about the survival and fitness of the British (or Australian) race compared to other nations, in particular Germany and Japan. In England this change in thinking led variously to the St Pancras School for Mothers (1907), the endowment of motherhood, and the eugenics movement.[56] In Australia it found expression in concern about the declining birth rate and the establishment of the Commonwealth Maternity Grant in 1912.

In South Australia, as in the reforming 1870s and 1880s, there was a cluster of innovations reflecting the new views. In 1902 the Queen's Home, a maternity hospital, was opened after two years of fund-raising and genteel agitation. In 1909 the first infant welfare centre opened in Adelaide – the beginnings of the Mothers and Babies Health Association. In 1914 McBrides Hospital for unmarried mothers opened in Medindie. Between 1915 and 1917 the movement which later led to the opening of Mareeba Hospital for infants and young children at Woodville was under way, and in 1928 the Northcote Home for Mothers and Babies opened near Grange. In education, the new views led to the establishment of domestic arts classes for girls in all primary schools by 1907, and to compulsory drill for boys. In 1915 it became mandatory to attend school every day. Later still the new 'ideology of motherhood' led to 'scientific mothering' as advocated by the child-rearing reformer Dr Truby King.

The gradual adoption of aspects of the probation system can also be traced back to this shift in thinking about poverty. The third 'wave' of child welfare reforms has its earliest genesis in these years. Probation was permitted in South Australia from 1887 but was not understood until long after that, and 'the number it applied to was very small'.[57] Like the reforms described above, probation systems aimed to support the family, not to break it up. Children were visited by Departmental officers and not, in most cases, removed from their own families. All the institutions established in South Australia's second 'flowering' of philanthropy were intended to support and educate the ordinary family in its roles and in times of crisis. It is true that probation did not always mean that children were placed with their own parents, but as the system was slowly adopted more children came to be placed on probation with their natural parents. Probation could be just as prescriptive as boarding-out, and could mean that many things in a family were supposed to be altered. Although it helped in the greater social control of female adolescents by forcing them to accept the authority of their parents, probation did indicate the beginning of the end of a notion of class so hierarchical that the break-up of families could be justified. True probation systems most clearly demonstrated that poverty was no longer always considered a crime, that some faith might after all be placed in a child's natural family and in her ties with it.

The 1909 Interstate Congress of Workers in the Field of Dependent Children, held at the University of Adelaide, attracted participants from all over Australia. In their speeches is caught the tension between the old and new views of poverty. Probation was much discussed and advocated; whether it was fully understood is a moot point. Catherine Spence pointed out that South Australia lacked a probation officer, while the Chief Probation Officer from Victoria proudly asserted that in his state 'Probation has come to stay'.[58] There was also much discussion of infant mortality, of eugenics, and the fecundity of the 'unfit'. The old view that poor children were a 'burden and a menace to society' if not boarded-out still had many adherents. Most heat was aroused over Dean Latham's insistence that dependent children in Western Australia were quite happily cared for in small institutions rather than being boarded-out. Old battles, it seemed, were still not won.

About 1908 the State Children's Council began the State Children's Advancement Fund, a charitable fund intended to help children who showed 'special ability' to pursue their education, perhaps even to university level. Children with any aptitude were supposed to be helped to proceed to secondary school. There were many other advances in child-care practices in the next four years, although South Australia was not the most progressive state.[59] The appointment of a medical officer, reduction of the infant mortality of state children, and the appointment of a dentist for state children were all advances. But just as at the 1909 Congress, there was still oscillation between old and new views.

The Commonwealth Maternity Grant was greeted sourly by the Council in 1913 and a protest against its passing was lodged by the Council. The Council thought 'it was not required, and that its tendency will not be for good'.[60] In contrast to this reactionary judgement, the Council in 1910 had reported passing a resolution making it compulsory for all state children to pass 'at least the third class standard' before 'they are allowed to leave school'. And in 1914 they recommended that boys be removed from the huge Magill Reformatory to cottages with a man and wife in charge – a forward-looking policy still advocated as an ideal sixty years later. They also wanted consolidation in South Australia of the acts relating to children.

Apart from a preoccupation with the 'problem' of half-caste children,[61] the main issue which reappears in the half decade before 1914 is that of a payment to mothers. At the 1909 Congress some delegates from New South Wales wanted to adopt this advanced policy but South Australia was content to claim that few children were taken from their parents for reasons of poverty alone and that rations were available from the Destitute Board. Advocates of the policy wanted cash payments (not rations) to widows, deserted wives, and respectable single mothers. In 1909 it was a radical proposal and it supported the family. By 1911 the Council was still considering the issue, believing the matter was 'not at present adequately dealt with'. In the following year the same 'somewhat momentous issue' was considered but management was still left with the Destitute Board.

In 1913 the Council's annual report 'congratulated' the state on the smallness of the increase in the number of state children, adding:

when it is remembered that during the whole year eight persons have been constantly, and two more intermittently, looking for children whose circumstances might warrant the interference of this department in order to save them from disaster. That so many have been discovered, and in so many instances sufficiently helped without taking the children from their homes, is a matter for rejoicing.[62]

This statement encapsulates the 'new' views about poverty which lay behind the reforms the Council was now advocating. But 1914 was to be dominated by other events.

Practice

In this section I want to look at three aspects of boarding-out in South Australia. First, whether the state was as innovative as early reformers claimed; secondly, whether boarding-out degenerated into 'a system of juvenile servitude'; and thirdly whether the children 'of the poor and degraded' were helped 'to rise'.

1   After careful comparison of the statistics published by the Destitute Board and the State Children's Council with Victorian figures from the same years, it is apparent that while South Australia may have been first in the field of boarding-out by perhaps twelve months, the scheme was taken up with far more skill and enthusiasm by Victoria.[63] In 1872 South Australia boarded-out six children and in the following year twelve children. Victoria began the scheme a year later it is true, but in 1873 boarded-out 650 children under thirteen years of age from that state's appalling reformatories and industrial schools. South Australia's much vaunted 'law of the land' is not apparent if one looks at the statistics. Table 9 clearly shows the desire of the Destitute Board and its chairman, Thomas Reed, to pay lip-service only to the elements in the community advocating boarding-out.[64]

Certainly many children in care would be removed from a vegetable existence in institutions, but the greatest number would be placed out without any subsidy at all, some would be licensed to service, and a considerable number would remain in the Industrial School. The scheme which the reformers had so proudly set out to imitate was genuine 'boarding' of children in a suitable home, based on Mr Greig's experiments in Edinburgh. It is also obvious from Table 9 that every year more children were in employment than were genuinely boarded-out, and that most children were placed out without any subsidy at all under the misnomer of 'adopted or licensed for adoption'.[65]

Allegations of mistreatment and proselytizing in the state's reformatories had led to a Royal Commission being set up in 1883.[66] In its final report the Commission said they were astonished 'that young children have been so unwisely dealt with for so many years'.[67] By this they meant that so many children had been kept in institutions instead of being boarded-out. They maintained that the Industrial School system and boarding-out were not compatible. Yet in South Australia they found the existence of both systems and this had meant that

Table 9 Children boarded-out in SA, 1873–83

	1873	1874	1875	TO 31 DECEMBER 1876	1877	1878	1879	1880	1881	TO 30 JUNE 1882	1883
Total no. placed out	280*	280	267	277	273	306	322*	458*	405	474	450
Adopted	124	161	174	176	183	205	216	188	270	279	259
Boarded-out under subsidy	55	39	24	23	25	33	50	81	61	104	96
Household service	41	42	36	49	35	32	24	45	37	39	42
Other employment	55	38	33	29	30	36	36	44	37	52	53
Total no. of visitors and reports	523	554	553	409	401	440	515	638	737	1883	2285
Remaining:											
In Industrial School	39	51	62	109	118	134	142	111	100	108	132
In Boys' Reformatory	16	23	14	9	26	16	31	53	47	29	60
In Girls' Reformatory	10	9	6	4	3	7	7	5	8	21	9
In Destitute Asylum	4	4	5	8	3	8	12	11	14	6	6

Sources: Half-yearly and annual reports of the Destitute Poor Board in *South Australian Government Gazettes*.
*I cannot explain these discrepancies in the original totals.

203

the expansion of the boarding-out system has been checked and the Industrial School has become a mere receptacle for children until they can be boarded or licensed out ... a glutted depot for the boarding-out system.[68]

The Commission pointed out that 'adoption' was not *in theory* an inadequate method of child-care:

Under proper safeguards there may be no objection to this so long as the child merely gives such service as a child of the house would be expected to give and is not made a drudge. But such a relationship is perilously liable to abuse and might readily degenerate into a system of juvenile servitude not to be tolerated in any civilized community.[69]

That this degeneration had occurred in South Australia they found to be the result of the Destitute Board's having been in existence for many years and to its having 'a tendency to rest satisfied with old methods' and to 'adhere to routine'.[70] In New South Wales and Victoria the comparable departments had recently been reorganized and were therefore trying out 'new lines of action'.

Early reformers could admit by 1907 that they had been very much aware that the correct system of boarding-out had been corrupted by Thomas Reed's mistaken parsimony. Caroline. Clark wrote that they were often 'extremely vexed' with his practice of taking boarded-out children from good homes when he found people willing to take them for nothing. Catherine Spence thought that this parsimony was the direct cause of there being, by 1885, '103 [children] in the Industrial School [and] an epidemic of ophthalmia'.[71] But during the years between 1872 and 1885 Clark and Spence shirked controversy, and the Boarding-out Society of which they were members was able to write in 1875 of Thomas Reed's 'unremitting care'.[72]

In Victoria, in merely eleven months, and largely as a result of the determination and energy of Charles Pearson, reforms in the system of child care which had begun well a few years earlier (but had since been impeded by an official very like South Australia's own Thomas Reed) were rapidly completed. The official, Mr Neal, was suspended and then given a subordinate position under a new departmental head, industrial schools were emptied of over 200 children, two professional visiting agents were appointed, normal wages were allowed to children in service, and despite all this the budget was cut. The touch of ruthlessness necessary to carry through such a programme placed Victoria 'far in advance of the sister-colonies and of older countries'.[73]

South Australia lacked anyone with the energy and determination of Charles Pearson. Although much testimony was given against the chairman of the Destitute Board, Thomas Reed was not retired until 1889, the Royal Commission having tended to let the evidence speak for itself rather than formally condemning him in their conclusions.

The abuses with which the system was riddled by 1885 are rightly greeted with horror by other writers for they make appalling reading. But I cannot share the view that the State Children's Act of 1886 began a new epoch in South Australia for children needing care and protection.[74] Certainly many abuses would be rectified but there were still a great many power-holders uninterested in child welfare.[75] The State Children's Council could not succeed in making the government or the Chief Secretary agree to its requests for a separate reformatory for girls and boys (both still being kept at Magill), higher salaries for clerical staff, and more ready acceptance of its recommendations for release or extension of sentences.

Throughout 1888 the Council corresponded most unsatisfactorily with the Chief Secretary, and resigned en masse in 1889. Although most of the requests over which the Council resigned were not acceded to, it was largely re-appointed.[76] The reasons for this are complex but three may be suggested as being of prime importance. First, there were among the members 'great searchings of heart' about whether they should have resigned.[77] Second, for the women of the Council, at least, it must have been very unpleasant to be 'agin the government', at odds with one's own social class. Third, the work itself was of such vital interest to those involved in it that it seemed more important to carry on the work than to resign from it forever.

In 1911, after Caroline Clark and Catherine Spence had died, their portraits were hung in the offices of the State Children's Department and they were revered for over a quarter of a century. Yet evidence is strong that so anxious were the early reformers to publicize the virtues of the boarding-out system that they tended to simplify or ignore the comments of those who wanted to point out some of the difficulties.

In 1906 Miss Evelyn Penny, one of the most perceptive of the Department's inspectors, wrote a long report on her impressions of her first twelve months of work. Parts of this report were reprinted by Catherine Spence in Children of the State, where she indicated at the beginning that she would 'like to quote the whole' but for reasons of space would only take extracts.

The extracts from the report were quoted with certain pessimistic sections omitted, many qualifying phrases deleted, and without indication that all this had been done.[78] Two long sections headed 'Reticence of the Children' and 'Prejudice of the General Public' were left out completely. Miss Penny's strong impression that state children were happier when placed out with people who had no children of their own and the poignant words of some of the children to this effect were also left out. Catherine Spence was careful to leave the reader with a rose-coloured picture.

Other instances of the Council's extreme sensitivity to criticism are not

Catherine Helen Spence (1925–1910), Caroline Emily Clark's friend and ally.

hard to find. In 1924 the Council's immediate past secretary, James Gray, embarked on a history of the Council. He had been an inspector with the Department since 1887 and secretary of the Council from 1904–17. He had given thoughtful critical evidence on the difficulty of getting children to talk to the inspector to the 1885 Destitute Commission and at the 1909 Congress had spoken in favour of children on probation not having to come before the court. Perhaps the Council thought he would be too critical, for when he wrote to the secretary asking if he might have access to the Department's correspondence, the Council replied that requests for specific information would be considered, but that apart from published material and Catherine Spence's book, *Children of the State*, the bulk of source material was not available.[79]

Other writers have lately shown that South Australia did not lead the world in child care after 1896, in particular that: 'developments regarding Children's Courts were similar, adaptive rather than innovative', and that 'Boston has the credit for establishing the first in camera courts for children'.[80]

2   One of the ways in which boarding-out could easily 'degenerate into a system of juvenile servitude', to quote the 1885 Destitute Commission, was if children were made to work too hard by their foster-families or if they were neglected or beaten. There can be no doubt that children boarded-out were expected to be 'useful'. But how useful, and were they to be boarded-out simply because of their usefulness? Thomas Sadler Reed evidently thought so. The half-yearly report of the Destitute Board (31 December 1878) commented on those children left in the Industrial School:

it happens rather unfortunately that the tender ages of the children in the school, and their consequent inability to be of any service to those who might otherwise adopt them is a stumbling block in the way of getting them homes.[81]

Early reformers had emphasized that the success of boarding-out depended on children being able to confide in lady visitors or inspectors. But even after the just thunder of the final report of the 1885 Destitute Commission it was still not easy for children to complain of overwork or ill-treatment. All children, it is true, were to be regularly inspected. According to the 1887 Regulations, a member of the district visiting committee was to carry out an inspection every six weeks. In addition, public school-teachers were required to report on each state child every three months.

Despite this, one of the recurring criticisms directed against the Council in the thirty-five years after 1887 was that the children could not say what they really felt to the visiting committees. One year after the Council was formed the annual report recorded the Port Pirie Visiting

Committee's view that employers should express 'a little more sympathy' towards the child and stressed that lady visitors should try to be regarded as the child's 'friends'. In Evelyn Penny's report, referred to earlier, she wrote:

On the whole I feel that children who are placed in homes where the foster-parents have no children of their own are happier and are treated with greater affection than those who are placed amongst other children.[82]

In support of this opinion I may mention that a lady visitor told me that she had known of one instance where the children of the house and their parents sat at one end of the table and the State Children at the other end 'below the salt', where they partook of different food and were in other ways made to feel that they were outcasts from the family.

She goes on to detail how impressed a New South Wales visitor was with the quality of homes she visited, but she still felt obliged to say:

there are homes that might be greatly improved, where one instinctively feels that the children are regarded as a business transaction, where the clothes are kept at the barest limit, and the children though apparently well-fed and not ill treated do not get much affection. I can safely say these homes are in the minority.

Evelyn Penny thought that one of the main difficulties in ascertaining whether the children were 'really happy' was, however,

the reticence of the children themselves. Perhaps this is partly due to the fact that I was a stranger to them, partly because they know their own misdemeanours will be reported to the Inspector and lastly because they fear a scolding from their foster-parents if they make complaints.

One has to guard against a merely mechanical catechism, and yet there is neither the time nor opportunity to obtain the information one requires in most cases indirectly.[82]

Under these conditions it is easy to see that girls might remain silent rather than complain. And it must be remembered that these were children under thirteen years of age.[83]

In 1908 Evelyn Penny asked an older girl whether she had really been happy in one service home where she had been several years before:

I made a point of asking her whether she had really been happy at Mt Gambier. She told me that she had disliked her place very much, that Mrs. Kelly had a violent temper and had once thrown a tin dish at her head and had often shaken her and pinched her. I asked her why she had never complained to me and she said she was far too frightened to tell me...[84]

One girl wrote of being 'nervous and confused' when being questioned. She had written to her brother complaining that she did not have time to eat her meals.

when Miss Grant [a lady visitor] was asking me if I had time enough to eat my meals, being confused at the time I said 'Yes' which seems as a falsehood after saying I had not time enough. This has been troubling me very much ... Miss Price [her employer] came in my room at the time this conversation was going on and made me more nervous and confused.[85]

If girls in service found it sometimes hard to complain, how hard was it for children under thirteen?

3 As late as 1911 the State Children's Council still perceived its purpose as being 'to ameliorate the conditions of the people, and especially and first the poor and degraded, by helping their children to rise'.[86] This is a very ambitious statement, one that modern community welfare departments would not essay. The idealism inherent in it must be measured against the resources that were in reality provided to enable the children of pauper families to 'rise'.

In practice the children of the 'poor and degraded', as earlier chapters have detailed, were placed with the 'respectable' poor, and after the age of thirteen were sent out to middle-class families as domestic servants and farm labourers. Very often they were completely unskilled, a situation difficult for the employer as well as the child. Occasionally girls would be allowed extra schooling, particularly if they were backward at school, or if they were too dull or too delicate for service. In the 1930s it became the Department's policy to allow foster-children the chance to earn their living by working for their foster-parents.[87] Some girls managed to find work in the locality of their foster-homes so that all connections were not broken, but most girls went to work as live-in domestics at thirteen years of age.

Many commentators have written on the slowness of girls who were sent out from English workhouses to be servants.[88] State wards in South Australia also had little idea of household work; the multitude of complaints from their mistresses testify to that. As girls could not leave their employer at will but were often returned as unsuitable, they were not apprenticed in any real sense. The work they might have learnt in state institutions was not likely to enable them to cook and sew for a living outside it. Girls would have to adjust anew to each different mistress's ways. The amount of instruction they received varied immensely with the number of tasks they had to perform and also, of course, the energy and intelligence of the girls themselves. In the early years of the scheme the only alternative occupation available to young girls was dressmaking. This was dominated by the 'sweating' system, as

Table 10   Occupations of state wards 1919–30

Occupation	1919	1920	1921	1922	1923	1924	1925	1926	1927	1928	1929	1930
Poultry Farmer	–	–	–	–	–	–	–	–	–	–	2	1
Fruit-grower	–	–	–	–	–	–	–	–	–	–	3	2
Engineer	–	–	–	–	–	–	–	–	–	1	1	–
Tailoress	–	–	–	–	–	2	1	–	1	–	3	2
Butcher	–	–	–	–	–	–	–	–	–	–	–	2
Plasterer	–	–	–	–	–	–	–	–	1	1	1	–
Telegraph Dept	–	–	–	–	–	–	–	–	1	1	–	–
Motor Mechanic	–	–	–	–	–	–	–	–	1	4	–	–
Cabinet-maker	–	–	–	–	–	–	–	–	2	–	3	2
Assistant Cook	–	–	–	–	–	–	–	1	–	–	–	–
Telephonist	–	–	–	–	–	–	1	1	–	–	–	–
Carpenter	–	–	–	–	–	1	1	1	–	1	–	–
Baker	–	–	–	–	–	1	2	–	–	–	–	–
Greengrocer	–	–	1	–	–	1	–	–	–	–	–	–
Clerk	–	–	1	1	–	–	–	–	2	3	3	1
Waitress	–	–	–	1	–	–	–	–	–	–	1	1
Furniture Mkr	–	2	11	–	–	–	–	–	–	–	–	–
Factory hand	–	5	11	1	19	15	12	9	14	6	1	3
Blacksmith	–	1	2	11	1	–	–	–	–	–	–	–
Messenger	–	5	–	–	–	–	6	4	1	–	–	–
Milliner	–	2	–	1	–	–	–	–	–	–	–	–
Teacher	1	–	1	2	1	1	1	–	–	–	–	–
Bookmaker	3	–	–	–	–	–	–	–	–	–	–	–
Postal Dept	–	–	–	–	2	1	–	–	–	–	–	–
Railways	7	3	3	–	–	1	1	4	2	3	2	–
Dressmaker	4	3	2	2	1	1	–	1	1	–	–	–
Nurse Probation	–	–	–	1	3	1	2	–	–	–	–	–
Office Boy	1	1	2	–	–	–	–	–	–	–	–	–
Tailor	–	–	–	–	–	2	1	1	–	–	–	–
Shop Assist.	9	2	9	8	3	7	1	2	14	4	11	5
Sheep Farmer	5	2	4	9	3	–	3	3	2	1	2	–
Labourer	16	19	20	21	20	21	18	24	21	24	12	8
Dairy Farmer	17	7	8	12	10	10	10	10	7	4	6	6
Gardener	21	17	26	24	30	14	21	35	12	9	3	9
Farmer	114	103	77	78	98	102	97	74	78	72	43	47
Domestic	191	217	177	181	190	209	192	161	131	118	91	90

Source: State Children's Department, *Annual Reports*.

the 1892 Shops and Factories Commission amply shows. Young girls were particularly liable to exploitation under dubious apprenticeship schemes,[89] and it is likely that being a dressmaker sometimes served as a cover for prostitution[90]

The Council's annual reports reveal that in the years 1890–1913 only four state girls were sent to an occupation other than domestic service, the principal occupation of working-class women. The correspondence of the Department also reveals that they were sent out untrained and unapprenticed. As Table 10 indicates, no more than a handful of state girls became anything other than domestics before 1922.

By the 1930s things were little different. The year 1930, the last year for which detailed statistics are available, saw ninety girls placed out as domestics and ten in other occupations such as shop assistant or tailoress. No figures are available for 1930–40 although the 1940 annual report states:

Amongst the girls, some are taking up music, accountancy, and positions in the Commonwealth and State Government Departments. Several are entering the nursing profession, whilst other girls are employed in offices, shops, and factories. Some are learning dressmaking and tailoring. Information is being received constantly by the department concerning suitable and happy marriages that have been made by girls who were previously under control.[91]

After 1914 girls increasingly disliked being placed out as domestic servants. Their letters of complaint illuminate the reasons why the Council thought domestic service an ideal occupation. The State Children's Department regulations stated that employers were expected 'to do all in their power for the moral and religious training of the child'.[92] In this lay the great advantage. Factory work or dressmaking could not provide this moral oversight and it would also expose a girl to undesirable companions and the dangerous freedom of the factory girl.[93]

The way a girl could 'improve' herself in domestic service was by specialization. To some extent this depended on age (censuses indicate that housekeepers were usually found in the over thirty-five age brackets) but it also depended on skill and the ability to resist 'outside' or menial work. Girls continually tried to raise their status by refusing to clean boots, chop wood, or feed pigs or horses.

One division of domestic labour that many girls aspired to was 'nurse-girl' – the Australian equivalent of nanny. Even when labour-saving devices were gradually absorbed into the household in the 1920s and 1930s, the isolated character of child care did not change, and this was one area where a state girl could still be employed.[94] The other specialized branch of domestic service that absorbed a few refined or delicate girls was the socially ambiguous position of 'companion'.

The State Children's Advancement Fund did not make any significant differences to the lives of state girls between 1914 and 1940. Great care was always taken to ensure that money spent on any secondary education would not be wasted. To set this in perspective, it should be mentioned that even in the 1920s only about 5 per cent of all children received a secondary education of any sort.[95] But it should also be mentioned that the Repatriation Commission was dismayed in 1925 to learn that not all state wards who were beneficiaries under the Soldiers' Children's Education Scheme had been placed 'in some skilled trade or calling which will warrant continuance of assistance'.[96] Other states did a little better. In Victoria at this time extra subsidy was paid to boys over fourteen to enable them to be apprenticed, and in 1926 state wards in Tasmania had two years training in domestic skills before being sent out.[97] Thus, although in the nineteenth century domestic service was really the only occupation for unskilled females, it can be seen that it was continued by the Council through the 1920s and 1930s despite a small broadening of opportunities. This was because of the Council's belief that despite its being an occupation without security or advancement, it was a proper occupation for state children. Approved service homes were held to compensate for the 'admittedly low wage' many children earned and it was believed that allowing children to find their own situations would be 'the death knell of all discipline'.[98]

The strengthening hostility that this course produced among state girls who saw contemporaries working in factories or shops in the 1920s and 1930s was usually countered by the staff of the State Children's Department, and later the Children's Welfare and Public Relief Department. Girls were taught that to work slowly in return for wages was, in fact, stealing. They were taught that equality was incompatible with gratitude and respect. There was a vague and oft-quoted category of being disrespectful 'in speech and manner' and there was a massive distrust of the modern city miss with her 'finery'.[99] Only right at the end of the 1930s did the Department start to hesitate over its policy of ensuring that girls 'knew their place'.

Adelaide in the 1920s and 1930s continued to be a society where wealth and status were discreetly displayed. The wives of rich men rode in cars and might dance at night in 'the floating palais' on the Torrens River.[1] The sons of the rich went to St Peter's College. To help the poor they established St Peter's College Mission in the heart of the city. At least one state girl worked as a house and dining room maid at St Peter's College in the late 1920s, a small piece of a much larger pattern.[2]

Domestic service for state girls was the crowning achievement of the nineteenth-century reformers' dream: to eliminate pauperism and at the same time not make dependent children a drain on the public purse. Girls would not be supported by the state and yet in effect they would be supervised by a deputy parent responsible to the state until they were twenty-one years old.

The world had to move, in particular industrialization had to occur in South Australia, before the state would be forced to abandon such a successful practice.

1914-40

The Department at Work

By 1900 the staff of the State Children's Department (excluding institutional staff) had increased from the five appointed in 1887 to thirteen. This included the powerful position of secretary, three inspectors, five clerks, an enquiry officer, two junior clerks, and an inspectress for licensed foster-mothers. At the Central Depot there were a matron and two assistants. By 1914 this welfare bureaucracy had more than doubled, with the increase mainly in the clerical support area. There were now one more inspector, nine more clerks, and a telephone operator. There were now also two probation officers. In addition there were a staff of six for licensed foster-mothers, the responsibility for whom had been transferred to the Department in 1895. This department of civil servants was under the control of an honorary board of twelve, of whom more will be heard later.

It has been argued that because a professional attitude to social work developed so late in Australia, the entire field of social services remained identified with the concept of the rich advising the poor.[3] England began to diverge from this in the 1890s with the establishment of a Women's

The State Children's Department, Adelaide, circa 1905.

213

University Settlement in the East End of London, and the setting up in 1912 of a Department of Social Science and Administration. In the late 1890s similar developments occurred in the USA, with the first professional course for social workers beginning in 1914. As R.J. Lawrence says:

By the time the social work training movement appeared on the Australian scene, a general pattern of administration of social provision had become set, and in fact it remained little changed during the 1930s. Paid Commonwealth and State male public servants, drawn from the general public service pools, were administering social legislation. There was little recognition that persons working in this or any other part of the public service needed special ability or training. Most non-government social agencies relied upon unpaid, voluntary work, which usually meant women attending to the execution of policy, and men, employed elsewhere, sitting on boards and committees in their spare time, helping with financial and general policy matters.[4]

This is certainly true in the case of South Australia. The men in power in the Department rose from the ranks. So also did the women in some cases but not as far or as often. Neither had social work qualifications of an academic type.

John B. Whiting, the first secretary of the Department, had been on the staff of the Destitute Poor Department since 1873, as had the first inspector, James Gray (first appointed 1883). Celestine Houlgrave, the second inspector, was appointed to the State Children's Department in 1889. In 1903 James Gray became secretary and remained in that position until 1918 when Celestine Houlgrave was appointed. The latter retired in 1927 when the State Children's Council was amalgamated with the Destitute Board to form the Children's Welfare and Public Relief Board. His successor, Frederic John Prestige Kelsh, had first been appointed in 1892, and Francis Gordon Byrne, who was appointed secretary from 1931–38, had first entered the public service in 1906. The secretary's was a powerful, highly-paid position. The secretary attended Council or Board meetings and was the nexus between the honorary body and the paid staff.

It is interesting to note that nursing qualifications were held by many female Departmental staff.[5] In 1925 there were twenty-five female staff and at least six of the thirteen non-clerical positions were filled by women with nursing qualifications. In 1938 it was stated that all inspectors of children boarded-out were 'trained nurses'. The female staff were, of course, paid less than male staff and no woman ever rose to the top three positions in the Department. Some undoubtedly ascended the public service ladder through an intense interest in their work. Kate Cocks had to 'bide her time' doing clerical work until she was given the chance to show her 'capabilities'.[6] And another female staff member was appointed

Fourth Probation Officer in 1920 after ten years as the Department's telephone operator.

The way in which information was gathered by the officers of the State Children's Department and the Children's Welfare and Public Relief Department illustrates a great deal about attitudes to the poor and poverty in the years between the wars in Australia. Changes in attitude only came right at the end of the 1930s.

Morality and mission lay at the core of the methods of the Departmental staff. They were supposed to be women of high standards (such as ideal mothers and nurses) and to have an uplifting influence on the children and families with whom they came into contact. In this they were like the secretary and the Council but being in touch with day-to-day realities also gave them a more pragmatic approach. A report by Evelyn Shaw in 1927 exemplifies this:

I found like the previous inspector that these people are really making an effort to improve their home conditions – An iron cot has now been procured for the little girl, and although their bedding, and outfits leave much to be desired – still they are making an effort.[7]

A careful distinction was often made between children who were merely grubby or untidy, and children who were dirty: 'The place is very untidy and I should say that Mrs Rowatt is a very indifferent manager. Still nothing serious enough to warrant an interference'.[8] Miss Lee, faced with the difficult decision of whether or not to remove a ten-year-old child from a happy foster-home because of the unexpected pregnancy of the single daughter of the house, while admitting that in ordinary circumstances such a home would not be recommended, argued that it was 'a misfortune that might happen in any home' and that as the state girl was 'already in the home and is very happy', she should stay.[9]

The officers saw an important part of their role as being work 'of a preventive order', inducing neglected families to 'pull themselves together' so that the committal of their children to the state could be avoided.[10] They had contacts in the police force, with teachers and with foster-mothers. State children were supposed to be visited at least three times a year and this meant that in country districts greater reliance had to be placed on teachers and police to report to the Department should anything untoward occur in the intervals between visits. Teachers would often write or contact the Department about children who appeared neglected, were away too often, or were reputed to be maltreated. As the recipients of snippets of local gossip, teachers might also sometimes undertake to warn the offending parent when rumours began to be circulated.[11]

Visiting was done by trap, train, tram, bicycle, and later by car. In 1901 an inspector, Thomas W. Perkins, reported that he had ridden his bike over 800 miles in merely three months service with the Department.[12] 'Adventures' travelling in remote country districts were not uncommon.[13] Very often a poor family would be brought to the attention of the Department because the local police felt the children were not getting 'a fair chance'. Sometimes after several visits from inspectors, an understanding would be reached with local police that if things 'went wrong' again they would report it promptly to the Department in Adelaide.[14]

Adelaide in these decades was sufficiently small for the officers to have an exhaustive knowledge of families, something out of the question for welfare departments in larger cities. Very often a case of suspected neglect, not bad enough for prosecution and committal of the children to the state, could be left to 'develop', so sure was the Department that it would hear of the deterioration.[15] Sometimes the officers would know of the family when the report reached them because the home was already under surveillance or had been in the past or, as in one case, because a woman before her marriage had been, 'in my sister's home and was an unprincipled girl of very indifferent parentage'.[16] Unlike the Council, the officers actually encountered the child beaten or starved, or the father on the verge of *delirium tremens*.[17] They also had to use tact and discrimination to assess the large number of anonymous letters they received as many of these turned out to be merely the result of quarrels with neighbours.[18] Not all were. Of course there were indifferent and callous families known to the Department.[19] A child aged six and weighing 24 pounds was removed in 1927 after two separate letters had been written to the Department by concerned neighbours. But this was one of the more dramatic cases.

Although some families undoubtedly felt hostile to the Department and were, indeed, threatened by it, a few appealed to it to help them control errant daughters. One father wrote in 1918:

You mention you could get Lois a place at 10/- a week too much Money is no good to Lois.

Spend it on Novels Chewing Gum and picture shows and any other folly she can find.

If you can find her a place, With a Strict Master and Mistress, A lot of hard work and her food and clothes, and make her go to Church and Sunday School. This might be some good to her.[20]

Other inquiries came from parents who found their daughters pregnant, or from husbands and wives who hoped the Department might curb an erring partner. The staff of the Department also had to deal with children abandoned to relatives;[21] or a sister who might write in desperation of her brother's neglect of his children.

However, despite their practical approach, officers of the Department

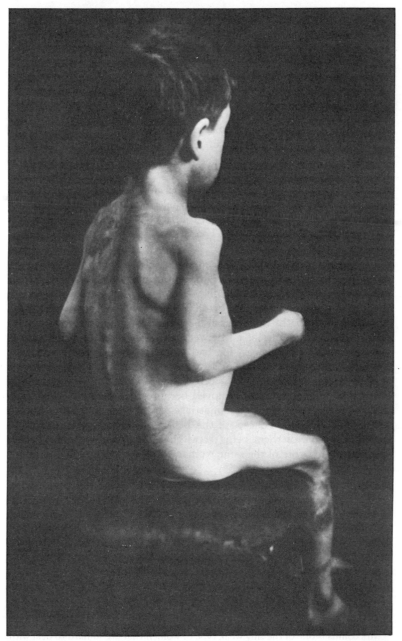

This child, aged six, weighed 24 pounds when made a ward of the state in 1927.

sometimes clung to beliefs more at home with Victorian charity than twentiety-century social welfare. Certain families were regarded as hopeless: they would not 'try' or they had no 'spark of feeling' left.[22] Between the wars in Australia these poor families were often condemned. Little sympathy was extended to families who were 'bad' enough to lose their children, and in most cases they were regarded as devious if they tried to reclaim those children. Increasingly in the 1920s it could be noted dispassionately that it was 'difficult to get work' in certain areas, or that a breadwinner out of a job exacerbated family poverty.[23]

The appearance of poverty in children would certainly be noted precisely:

I saw the children . . . coming home from school and they were miserably clothed; only Cathy had boots on. The twins were bootless and hatless and looked pitiful objects and they were shivering with the cold. Paul 13 yrs was in rags too his coat was thin and full of holes he had no boots or hat.[24]

It might even be conceded that a family was 'extremely poor through no fault of their own'.[25] But Departmental officers still perceived their work as a mission; they still felt they had the right to walk into a house and, without asking, open windows if they felt the need for 'ventilation'.[26] And despite sympathy there was also the condemnation which forbad, in most cases, any contact at all between the state child and her natural parents. It was especially easy for 'bad' women to be dismissed: they were not often considered capable of reformation. One boy whose sister had applied for his return from a 'good subsidy home with very good kind honorable people', was not removed because Miss Kentish considered, 'This woman's character before marriage was not good. She was known to the Port Adelaide Police. All the Bell family were undesirable and I cannot conceive of them being good guardians to any child'.[27] Three years later she wrote of the same woman:

Mrs B. was such a bad girl before marriage that it is hard to conceive of her as being a suitable guardian for her brother . . . The girls of the family went to the bad and the boys were found in abject neglect. Having had such a bad start in life I am specially anxious they shall now have every chance.[28]

High standards were expected of mothers:

It struck me that Mrs Collins did not really care for her children.
    She seemed delighted when I suggested that her husband fostered them and she took work. She evidently wants to go free.
    Mrs collins is one of the silly weak type of women that are so hard to deal with. She is only a girl herself in Appearance.[29]

218

A working-class mother who drank, even a little, was to be immediately suspected.[30] Sometimes heredity was blamed.

I fear heredity is at work in this lad. There is a wild streak in the family. All the girls go astray, some of them many times. Mrs Robins is perhaps one of the best of them.[31]

the illegitimate child of Mr Teague's daughter, a very bad girl. In my opinion . . . inherits very unfortunate traits from her.[32]

This home has always been very unsatisfactory . . . The Mother's relatives are most undesirable people most of them are addicted to drink and also immoral.[33]

Officers sometimes revealed a fear of what later came to be called 'the culture of poverty'. Poor families and their associates were monitored by the Department.[34] In a number of cases these families were the second or third generation who had been 'known' to the Department, an indication of the smallness of the community.[35] Very often 'bad' families seem to have been very large families. They might live in the city where there was poor housing, or in poor localities: 'right opposite a low class hotel where I have seen and heard drunken brawls on more than one occasion', as Miss Lee remarked.[36] Although they might be seen as trying to improve, little understanding of their economic difficulties was shown.

Not all poverty of course was in the towns. There was much rural poverty, especially along the Murray River.[37] While the local police might be quite sanguine about the conditions under which some of these children lived, the inspectors could not be:

words fail me in describing it and that nothing has been done to alter the loathsome and filthy condition of things since the last visit . . .

No attempt has been made to send the children to school. Vivienne aged 3½ I unearthed from the filthy rags forming the bedding. She was wailing in a heart-rending way and seemed beside herself with fear. She was dirty insufficiently clad but apparently well fed. She immediately burrowed under the rags again, more like a dog than a child. The two other girls were in the garden with Blue aged 22 years seeing our approach they made for the scrub. We hunted for them but could not find them.[38]

The home is a four-roomed iron and bag humpy and I found it in a most deplorable state of filth and neglect. The sleeping accommodation is miserable indeed. The bedding consists of rags and dirty old rugs for blankets. The dining room was littered with rags and dirt.

The younger ones look ill-nourished and they were in a very dirty condition . . . They have sores on their feet caused by chilblains breaking into running wounds.[39]

Parents often objected, to no avail, to the way the Department treated their children. One father asked angrily in 1922:

If you think it a proper thing to do too go to school and give Nettie a good talking to and threatening to take her away if she is not out of the house by Friday. I do not as I am the one to see this girl goes to school regular is Clean and has decent clothes on has her meats regular.

Fancy asking the child for an explanation why I have not been in to see you when you have only to come to the house . . . [40]

Another parent thought it desperately unfair that families should be broken up because of a father's drinking; she argued that the Department should 'punish him instead of the children it is wrong very much about the children think of me and the children dont parte them from me . . . please think of me and the little ones'.[41] But despite the protestations of some parents, families were broken up. If a family was regarded as hopeless then its children would be boarded-out and urged to 'forget those things' they had witnessed in their own homes.[42]

There is another aspect of the Department's influence between the wars which further supports Lawrence's arguments about the 'cleavage' in social administration. He sees a duality:

On the one hand there was an approach through broad legislative measures, sponsored by political parties and administered by government, largely male officials; on the other was an approach through numerous small voluntary organizations, catering for individual needs, sponsored by a wide variety of citizen groups or churches, with detailed work largely in the hands of unpaid women in the higher income groups.[43]

Ladies visiting committees continued to back up the work of the Department in South Australia throughout the 1920s and 1930s. Their role was not as important as it had been in the nineteenth century and their numbers diminished during the depression. By 1940 there were only seven 'lady visitors' and by 1946 there were none.[44] There had been more urgent work for 'ladies' in the war. Their survival at all, the fact that there was no professionalism to challenge their existence, nor indeed any widespread feeling against the notion that social work was merely 'one class advising another', needs to be remembered when considering the upheaval of 1926.

Upheavals: 1926

In 1926 for the first time startled South Australians heard the voice of the 'reformed' talking about their reformers, the voice of the poor talking about upper-class ladies, even, it was claimed, the voices of children:

220

I have heard what the kiddies say and it is not very complimentary to the ladies. Some of the ladies think it is a frightful thing for a boy to steal some fruit from a garden. In cases such as I have mentioned, where incompetent justices have been allowed to sit, it is dangerous, and it explains how so many children have been put into institutional life. If the ladies are so gone on doing a job (my own personal opinion is they like to see their names in the newspaper as detailed to sit at the court) they can look after the youngsters on probation.[45]

This was the assertive voice of Albert A. Edwards, politician and firebrand. Born in 1888 in the West End of Adelaide, he was widely believed to be an illegitimate son of the South Australian politician Charles Cameron Kingston. He was raised as a Roman Catholic and began his working life at the market and on racecourses. He had a long association with the West Adelaide Football Club. In 1914 he was elected to the Adelaide City Council and in May 1917, as an anti-conscriptionist, he won the seat of Adelaide in the House of Assembly.

In parliament Edwards belligerently defended persecuted Germans, the city's poor, bookmakers, underpaid teachers and police. It was soon remarked that 'if he keeps on bringing in dirty linen he will have to find a bigger basket'. [In 1920] Edwards' revelations of appalling conditions in city slums were crucial in bringing the Adelaide City Council under the auspices of the town planning bill. He also argued for advances for workers to build homes; for the establishment of a fair rents court; the licensing of bookmakers and against temperance moves for a prohibition referendum.[45]

'Bert' or 'the king' as he was known, was also interested in prisons and reformatories. He had been appointed to the State Children's Council in 1925 and in 1926, after writing to the press, appeared before a Royal Commission on Law Reform with sensational allegations against the Council. A year later the Council was abolished. But what had changed? In order to answer this it is necessary to look at the Council as it was in the 1920s.

In the ten years before 1927 there were twenty members of the State Children's Council although there were only twelve at any one time. Three of these members (in a sense) inherited the 'family seat' on the Council as there had been a member of their family on the Council in an earlier decade. Martha Crompton remembered in 1956:

After my Aunt retired from the SCC my mother was elected to her seat and after my mother's retirement I followed on, very feebly I'm afraid in the days when Harriet Stirling was president ...[47]

Harriet Stirling, the president of the Council from 1923-27, had been preceded by her father Dr E.C. Stirling, who was president of the first

Council from 1887–90. She had been a member of the Council since 1906. The age of the members is also a factor of importance. Of the twenty people who were members during the period 1917–27, one, P. McMahon Glynn, had been on the Council since the end of the nineteenth century and another, the secretary, Celestine Houlgrave, had begun as an inspector in 1889. Another two members of the Council had been on it since before 1910, eight other members had been appointed before 1918, and the two most important members, Harriet Stirling and Celestine Houlgrave (who together with any other member of the Council could form the 'Emergency Committee'),[48] had been appointed for twelve and thirty years respectively. In 1923, during a parliamentary debate, the Attorney General, Tom Price, asserted that the Council could now be called 'the State Children's Liberal Union'.[49]

In answer to a question from the Royal Commission on Law Reform about whether there were any 'poor women appointed women justices', Agnes Knight Goode, a member of the Council and a prominent Liberal, answered that she was 'one of the poor women', indicating rather a lack of touch with the realities of poverty in South Australia in the 1920s.[50] Examination of the members of the Council from 1887–1927 shows that almost all its members were appointed from the middle and upper classes. In the 1920s parliamentarians and professional men were also appointed.

The president, Miss Harriet Stirling, came from an eminent South Australian family. With Dr Helen Mayo, she had founded the Mothers and Babies Health Association in 1912. Yet by the 1920s she was thought to be old-fashioned. Mr W. Hall, Magistrate of the Children's Court, Adelaide, arguing against the appointment of women justices, told the Royal Commission on Law Reform of her delicacy:

A larrikin of 18 years was charged with having used indecent language, and the constable blurted out in court the words he used. Miss Stirling was shocked and felt quite embarrassed. She took no further part in the case – she could not. I dealt with the fellow without consulting her.[51]

Hall went on to say that he did not feel 'the same embarrassment' when sitting with a woman of the world such as Mrs Goode, as he did when sitting with a single woman.

The chairman of the Royal Commission on Law Reform, F.W. Birrell, who had been a member of the Council from 1917–24, argued to Harriet Stirling that he and Walter Hutley, Mr Claridge, Mr Webb, and Dr Gilbert Brown, had resigned because they found that they could not accompany the lady members on all the necessary visits to institutions. Behind these various arguments was a common feeling that the Council was dominated by 'ladies' ill-equipped either to set policy or to act as justices or counsellors to children. There can be no doubt that it was a surviving group of 'ladies and gentlemen' of the nineteenth century. In

Edwards' view ladies and 'tea and cake and knitting' had meant that a number of 'capable gentlemen' had resigned from the Council.[52] But to see whether his vociferous criticisms had any effect they must be set in context.

The Royal Commission on Law Reform had been set up in 1923 to recommend changes in the law and legal practice. It heard evidence on a range of topics and presented a report every year until 1927. Most of the testimony against the State Children's Council was presented in 1926, although there had been some discussion in 1923. Many witnesses argued that children could not readily communicate their grievances to the secretary, and almost all witnesses agreed that more officers were needed in order to visit the children properly.[53] Walter Hutley, Agnes Knight Goode, and W. Hall believed that children were often unable to write about maltreatment. Walter Hutley, who had been a Council member from 1914–23, and president for the last two years of this period, argued that better facilities should be provided so that children could complain to the nearest local probationary officer instead of having to send 'everything to the SCC through the secretary'. He thought 'the whole procedure in regard to the SCC' wanted reviewing'.[54] In his opinion three probationary officers for the whole state were inadequate, and he advocated the setting up of a state-wide system of honorary probationary officers.[55]

Agnes Knight Goode admitted that it had only recently been decided to provide stamped envelopes to state children, and that up until a month ago they had had to ask their employer or foster-parent for stamps and envelopes – undoubtedly a deterrent to the free communication of grievances. She stated that children could write to the Council without having their letters perused but admitted, in answer to a question as to whether that right could be carried out, that some children were 'perhaps too timid to take things into their own hands'.[56] Hall thought that the Council was not aware of 'everything that goes on' because communications, particularly from country children, did not reach them.[57] Hall argued that when children were ill-treated 'it is difficult for a complaint to reach the State Children's Council, unless subterfuge is employed because letters have to go through the children's employers'.[58]

While Harriet Stirling might defensively claim that no complaint went unheeded,[59] it seems that many complaints were suffered in silence because the children were cut off from their protectors. Harriet Stirling freely admitted that her officers were overworked and that children were in theory supposed to be visited every four months, 'but it is not done as often as that, because when an inspector becomes ill or takes her long leave the work gets behind'.[60] She thought the only way the system could be improved was by having more inspectors. Agnes Knight Goode was even more forthright, stating that there were really only three officers able to inspect because one had to stay in the office to do paper-work, 'and they are becoming elderly. It will be unfortunate if we have no young women training under them. There is no eight hours business about them; they are much over-worked'.[61] Other criticisms of the workings of the Department were made by Belinda Shannon Christophers and by J.C. Genders. But none carried the bite and hostility of Edwards' remarks.

Edwards' remarks were fuelled by class hatred; they were more than academic. He claimed that:

Every public man knows that a number of these [extended sentences] are protested against by the parents with very little hope of success. I asked in one case why the extension was to be granted and I was told that the child had come from a very unsuitable home. I asked when the home was last examined and was told that it had not been examined since 1912, and so this child was to have three years tacked on to the sentence and the parents deprived of that child for that period without any further enquiry being made concerning the home.[62]

Some of Edwards' most serious charges concerned the deplorable state of the Magill Reformatory. He claimed it was 'the worst of its kind in Australia'.[63] As well as a wealth of detail about conditions there, he alleged it was 'a travesty' to think that boys had a chance to learn trades while in the reformatory.

If members could only see those workshops they would see the comedy of the thing. An aged enthusiast comes along a couple of times a week, and attempts to teach the boys woodwork, and even at the bootshop where only an elementary knowledge is necessary for the repair of children's institutional boots, the work cannot be finished.[64]

Edwards' appearance before the Royal Commission had followed his questions in the House of Assembly on the same topics in 1925. They were questions set in the larger context of the Labor Party's support for the Maintenance Bill.[65] This bill was to pay at state level a weekly sum to needy mothers with children. It will be remembered that the Council had been discussing this in 1913. Agnes Knight Goode had raised it in 1923 when giving evidence to the Royal Commission on Law Reform. The Labor Party had supported such a measure for some time, and the Labor MP John Gunn had raised it in the House of Assembly in 1920. The fact that other states already had such a measure was emphasized. The strict means test to be applied to women eligible for the benefit was also stressed.

Despite this, the bill met bitter opposition in the Legislative Council and was returned in 1924. In 1925 when the bill was brought forward again it was linked with a proposal that the Destitute Board and the State Children's Council be replaced by a smaller more workable body. This bill was also rejected by the Legislative Council and there was much criticism of the rejection of philanthropy implied in the proposed abolition of the Council.[66]

The Maintenance Bill in slightly altered form was re-introduced in 1926. The proposed new board was now to have five members, two of whom were to be women. This change may have been the result of the defence of women's voluntary work mounted by Agnes Knight Goode and Harriet Stirling, the president of the Council. The latter attempted to refute Edwards' charges both to the Commission and in a report to the Chief Secretary, dismissing him as someone 'who often protested against every system'.[67] She argued that the carpentry shop at Magill Reformatory turned out 'beautiful work'. In regard to apprenticeships she stated that the Council was 'experimenting with a few boys'.[68] She readily admitted that she, Mrs Hone, and Agnes Knight Goode had employed state children in their homes at times.[69] Hall and Edwards' criticisms of 'meddling' women justices and their derision of 'ladies' charitable work were strenuously refuted.

When the Maintenance Act was finally given assent on 16 December 1926, it became possible to make a payment to mothers. But Edwards' insistence on less state surveillance of illegitimate children, notification of extension of sentence, and better access to information for parents of state children being included in the bill came to nothing. All these provisions were deleted from the bill by the Legislative Council. The Legislative Council also insisted on the exclusion of members of parliament from the new Board and on provision for women justices in the Children's Court. The payment to mothers was to be reserved for the 'deserving' and any woman who received such payments had to allow the officers of the new Department to visit her children just as if they were 'state children boarded-out'.[70] The chairman of the new Board was to be a public servant. More importantly, at least half the members of the new Board were to be women. Harriet Stirling, Mrs Hone, and Mrs Austin Hewitt, who were all Council members, were appointed to the Board of the new Children's Welfare and Public Relief Department.[71]

Upheavals: 1938

The Committee appointed by the government to inquire into Delinquent and Other Children in the Care of the State presented its report in September 1939.[72]

The Committee had been appointed on 15 June 1938 as a result of the alleged flogging of a boy at Edwardstown Industrial School. It visited all the institutions under the control of the Children's Welfare and Public Relief Department and received submissions from individuals and community groups interested in children's welfare. It also visited Sydney and Melbourne, and studied child welfare practices and legislation in Great Britain, the USA and, interestingly, Scandinavia.

The report was humane and innovatory. It was scathing about many of the institutions for children, condemned the attempt at probation that it found operating in South Australia, recommended provision for proper medical and psychological examinations, the setting up of a Children's Council, and the establishment of properly constituted Juvenile Courts. In its preface the report stated:

By initiating the boarding-out system in the eighties of last century, South Australia, at that time, led the world in the enlightened treatment of neglected children. Since then our advance has been tardy, and our neglected and delinquent children are not being granted the means of development and rehabilitation which are provided in other States and other countries. We trust that this report will prove useful in providing the Government with data which will support and reinforce its endeavours to give the children under its immediate care the special attention and training of which they are in special need in view of their unfortunate start in life.[73]

In part I of the report, the effect of environment in causing problems in the neglected or destitute child was firmly established. Punitive and repressive methods used in the past were condemned, and while punishment was not entirely dismissed, re-education and the welfare of the child rather than 'the vindication of the majesty of the law' was advocated. Specially trained and qualified staff were needed to work in institutions whose regimes fostered trustworthiness and self-responsibility rather than discipline and 'mental and physical distress'.[74]

In briefly discussing this detailed and informative report, emphasis will be given to those sections of the report which were a summary of 'existing conditions in South Australia'. It was noted that 'the underlying principle upon which the department operates, is that all children, whenever possible, are placed in private homes'. While supporting this policy, the report added that there was 'need for more expert help in determining' when children should be transferred to foster-homes and in finding suitable foster-homes and employers.[75]

The system of controlling delinquents had failed in several 'fundamental' ways, according to the report.[76] Children's courts were attached to police courts and, more seriously,

The failure to comprehend the principles underlying the system of 'probation' is shown by the fact that voluntary probation officers are still appointed by the sheriff, and are therefore controlled (so far as there is control) by the Gaols and Prisons Department. Thus both child and parent conceive the idea that 'to be placed on probation' is equivalent to being 'placed in the hands of the police'.[77]

While admitting that the 'probative work' which the Department under-
took might be valuable, the Committee found it 'fulfils neither in scope
nor in function "probation" as now understood'.[78]

The continuing use of solitary confinement of children as a punishment in institutions or pending a court hearing, the Committee
considered anathema to all modern principles of child care.

Failures of the present system lay in its making no adequate provision
for interrogation of children or for Children's Courts. Acknowledging
that South Australia had been one of the first places where charges
against children had been heard separately, the Committee went on to
argue that:

progress otherwise has been slow, and, except for the appointment of a special
magistrate, to hear children's cases at Adelaide and Port Adelaide, little more has
been accomplished. No legislation dealing with the function, procedure or powers
of children's courts exists.

At present if the magistrate thinks that detention is necessary, he has no option
but must send a child of eight or over to the reformatory, if he is found 'guilty' of
certain offences. The child may be conveyed to court in a police van. He may have
his finger prints taken. He may be questioned and cross-examined out of the court
and in it. He may be ordered a whipping by the court, the actual manner of
administering such whipping being set out in the Children's Probation Act. A
conviction is recorded against him. The press may attend sittings of the Children's
Court. Reports may be printed in the daily papers . . . There is need for a
thorough revision of the present system.[79]

The Committee was most critical about the institutions for state
children. It might have been 1938, there had been a depression, but once
again other states were found to be doing better. The Central Depot in
Gawler Place they found 'most depressing'. Children who were
'refractory are placed in cells, the only light being that from an outside
electric light in the gangway'.[80] Seaforth, at Somerton, they found to be
attractive and well-run but,

Like many receiving homes elsewhere it is used partly as a dumping ground for
adolescent girls who, by reason of their subnormality or instability cannot retain a
situation found for them. Such girls need a separate home or institution where
they can receive proper training.[81]

The Edwardstown Industrial School was unattractive, with 'inadequate
and out of date' kitchen and domestic arrangements, and to add to the
dour prison-like atmosphere, two cells with locks and bars were a feature
of the garden 'or what passes as such'. The methods in use at the Boys'
Probationary School at Mt Barker left 'much to be desired'. The Girls'
Probationary School was less harshly criticized but it was noted that the

only training given was in domestic work. At Magill Reformatory the inconvenience of the buildings and the need for more training in industrial occupations was noted. The main building should, the Committee argued, be destroyed or else reduced to two storeys. The two girls' reformatories were not as severely criticized, but the Committee thought that, 'In most of our institutions, private and State, the inmates are made to do far too much work and much of it is definitely soul-destroying'.[82] Children confined in such institutions would have difficulty in not acquiring 'a grudge against the rest of the community'. Enduring the regimes in use would produce 'mutinous feelings' in even an 'unusually quiet' child, the Committee suggested.

The education of any abnormal child should not be the province of the Children's Welfare and Public Relief Department, the Committee argued. There should be a training school set up under the control of a special branch of the Education Department. The training that girls received for domestic work was inadequate:

The teaching of domestic science (not by the drudgery of making beds, scrubbing floors and doing laundry work) should be an important part of the training of girls in these institutions. Girls gain very little from the weekly half-day visit of a trained domestic science teacher from the Education Department.[83]

The Committee recommended sweeping changes in all institutions except Seaforth. Noting that New South Wales had two child guidance clinics, they also recommended the establishment of a child guidance clinic, regarding this as 'the most important of our recommendations'.[84] Juvenile Court proceedings ought to be made private and informal by law and children should not be questioned by the police at their place of work or at school. Children should not be transported in police vans or by uniformed police, and the Central Depot in Gawler Place should be closed down. Quietly criticizing the work of the Department in regard to probation, the Committee recommended the appointment of a fully trained chief probation officer from England or the USA as there were no facilities in Australia where such an officer could qualify.

Abscondings were to be fully investigated. The boarding-out system, with more care taken over placement and proper provision for reconsideration of placement, was given full approval.

Over the next few years a number of changes were adopted to lessen the stigma of being a state child. Children were no longer sent out with conspicuous 'boxes': suitcases were supplied instead. Clothing was sometimes bought instead of being made by girls in institutions. A myriad of small changes brightened the state's institutions. But it had been pointed out by witnesses, 'that almost invariably children did not want to be known as 'State' children because of the fear of ostracism'.[85]

The Committee could recommend little to change community prejudice. South Australia did not employ a psychologist in the Department until 1943. Other major changes had to wait for the post-war years beyond the scope of this story.

Reform on a pedestal, the South Australian example would seem to show, soon acquires verdigris. The only statues that have a patina are those accessible enough to be polished by the touch of children's hands.

APPENDIXES

I
Members of the Council and Board
1887–1940

Members of the Council 1887
Dr E.C. Stirling
Miss B.A. Baker
Mr J. Smith
Mrs M. Colton
Miss C.H. Spence
Mrs C.H. Goode
Miss K. Howard
Miss C.E. Clark

1895
Thomas Rhodes
Lady Colton
Lady Downer
Mrs J.W. Farr
Mrs A. Finlayson
Miss B.A. Baker
Miss C.E. Clark
Miss C.H. Spence
Dr J. O'Connell
Dr R. Robertson
Mrs A.K. Goode
Mr J.A. McPherson

1905
Thomas Rhodes, Esq., J.P.,
   President
Lady Bonython
Lady Way
Mrs T. Brown
Mrs M.H. Bensly
Miss C.E. Clark
Miss C.H. Spence
R.S. Rodgers, Esq., MAMD
C.H. Goode, Esq., JP
P. McM. Glynn, Esq., BA, LLB,
   MHR
E.W. Hawker, Esq., BA, LLB

1915
C.W. Hamilton, Esq., MD, ChB,
   JP
Lady Bonython
Lady Holder
Mrs S.M. Crompton
Mrs Austin Hewitt
Mrs Walter Wragge
Miss H.A. Stirling
H. Davenport, Esq.
P. McM. Glynn, Esq., BA, LLB,
   MHR, KC
W. Hutley, Esq., JP
J. Marshall, Esq., JP
N.A. Webb, Esq., LLB

1925
Miss H.A. Stirling, JP, President
Miss M. Crompton
Mrs A.K. Goode
Mrs Austin Hewitt, JP
Mrs L. Hone
Miss D. Vaughan
E. Anthoney, Esq., JP
G. Brown, Esq., MB, ChB
G. Cooke, Esq., MP
A.A. Edwards, Esq., MP, JP
Hon. P. McM. Glynn, Esq., BA,
   LLB, KC
J. McInnes

Members of the Board 1935
Mr F.J.P. Kelsh, JP
Mrs Austin Hewitt
Mrs L. Hone
Mr J.H. Hobbs
Mr P. O'Connor
Mr A.W. Pettit
Mr C.M. Reid
Miss H.A. Stirling
Miss D. Vaughan

1940
Mr F.G. Byrne, JP, Chairman
Mr W.T. Collins
Mrs M.R. Hewitt, MBE
Mr J.H. Hobbs
Mrs L. Hone
Mr B.P. Martin
Mr A.W. Pettit
Miss H.A. Stirling, OBE
Miss D. Vaughan

II
Permanent Staff
of the Departments
1887–1940

1887

State Children's Department   (under Act 210, 1881 and Act 387, 1886)

Title of officer	Name in full	Date of present appointment
Secretary	John B. Whiting	15.12.86
Inspector	James Gray[a]	1.10.83
Clerk	Theo. Boothby	1.1.87
Clerk	H.E. Fesenmeyer	1.1.87
Clerk	Lucy Duval Hood	25.4.87
Medical Officer	W.T. Clindening, MRCS[b]	1.7.87

GIRLS' REFORMATORY
Matron
Wardswomen (4)[c]
Hospital Nurse[c]

INDUSTRIAL SCHOOL
Matron
Cook (1)[c]
Needlemistress (1)[c]
Nurse (1)[c]
Gardener (1)[c]
Labourer (1)[c]

REFORMATORY HULK

Superintendent	J.F. Button[c]	1.5.85

Shoemaker (1)[c]
Schoolmaster[c]
Assistant Wardsman[c]
Tailor (1)[c]
Wardsman[c]

[a] Actual expenses paid when travelling.
[b] Also Medical Officer Permanent Force, £45 per annum, and Medical Officer Destitute Poor Department, £525 per annum.
[c] Allowed quarters, rations, fuel, and light.

1890

State Children's Department

Title of officer	Name in full	Date of present appointment
Secretary	John B. Whiting	15.12.86
Inspector	James Gray[a]	1.10.83
Second Inspector	Celestine Houlgrave[a]	5.8.89
Clerk	Theo. Boothby	1.1.87
Clerk	H.E. Fesenmeyer	1.1.87
Clerk	Lucy Duval Hood	25.4.87
Medical Officer	W.T. Clindening, MRCS[b]	1.7.87

GIRLS' REFORMATORY
Matron[c]
Sub-Matron[c]
Wardswomen (4)[c]

INDUSTRIAL SCHOOL
Matron
Cook (1)[c]
Needlemistress (1)[c]
Nurse (1)[c]
Gardener (1)[c]
Laborer (1)[c]

REFORMATORY HULK

Superintendent	J.F. Button[c]	1.5.85

Deputy Superintendent[c]
Carpenter and Wardsman[c]
Tailor[c]
Cook[c]

[a] Actual expenses paid when travelling. Department, £525 per annum.
[b] Also Medical Officer Permanent Force, £45 per annum, and Medical Officer Destitute Poor.
[c] Allowed quarters, rations, fuel, and light.

1910

State Children's Department

Title of officer	Name in full	Date of present appointment
Secretary	James Gray	1.7.03
Medical Officer	Bedlington Howel Morris[a]	1.8.99
Dentist	Roy Lancelot Sims	1.5.09
Inspector	Celestine Houlgrave	1.7.03
Second Inspector	Thomas William Perkins	1.2.08
Third Inspector	Evelyn Emma Penny	20.2.05
Fourth Inspector	Beatrice Thompson-Searcy	1.1.10
Clerk	Frederick John Prestige Kelsh	8.5.1900
Clerk	Annie Novice	8.5.1900
Clerk	Annie Esther Sara	7.6.1900
Clerk	Howard Henry Bishop	26.4.05
Clerk	Helena Adelaide Austin	1.4.06
Shorthand Writer and Typist	Rebecca Wilson Mildred	29.3.10
Junior Clerk	Francis Gordon Byrne	1.11.06
Junior Clerk	Victor Edwin Cox	1.7.07
Junior Clerk	Garrett Peter Cronin	22.4.09
Telephone Operator	Myrtle Fanny Rebecca Treloar	7.11.10
Enquiry Officer	Henry Curnow	1.8.10
Probation Officer	Kate Cocks	1.4.06
Second Probation Officer	Alice Martha Kentish	1.4.09
CENTRAL DEPOT		
Matron	Rosalie Clare Bayly[c]	3.8.08
Needlewoman	Eliza Ophel[d]	1.12.1900
Assistant Needlewoman	Louisa Stopp[d]	1.10.09
Attendant	Mary Lester[c]	3.4.08
Attendant	Myrtle Annie Maria Gilpin	1.2.10
GIRLS' REFORMATORY		
Matron	Elizabeth Annie Price[c]	25.3.10
Sub-Matron	Mary Mackereth[c]	1.1.87
Wardswoman	Bella Tyrie[c]	13.1.91
Wardswoman	Maggie Ethel Scott[c]	8.1.06
Wardswoman	Mary Florence Stafford[c]	1.7.09
Wardswoman	Minnie Conlon[c]	1.2.10
INDUSTRIAL SCHOOL		
Matron	Frances Louisa Sheppard[c]	1.12.1900
Sub-Matron	Emily Rigby Weir[c]	1.9.10
School Teacher	Isabella Mary Macdonald[c]	1.7.10
Nurse	Jessie Gregg[c]	18.4.06

Nurse	Annie Ross[c]	1.6.09
Nurse	Dora Elizabeth Hanson[c]	15.10.10
Nurse	Rosetta McKeevor[c]	1.9.10
Cook	Annie Aldermann[c]	2.12.07
Assistant Cook	Olive Hocking Kirkwood[c]	8.6.10
Gardener	Edward Slattery[b]	1.2.98

BOYS' REFORMATORY

Superintendent	James Freeman Button[c]	1.1.87
Schoolmaster	William Chapman[c]	13.2.05
Assistant	Elizabeth Annie Button[c]	1.10.08
Assistant	Frank Burton	1.5.10
Gardener	William Edward Lewis[c]	1.7.01
Gardener	John Hill[c]	1.11.09
Cook	Margaret Langrehr	23.6.10

LICENSED FOSTER-MOTHERS
AND LYING-IN HOMES

Inspectress	Sarah Moule	1.1.99
Assistant Inspectress	Eva Allen	4.1.10
Assistant Inspectress	Charlotte Nairn	1.2.10
Clerk	Gertrude Marian Austin	1.1.10

[a] Also Medical Officer Destitute Poor Department, £500 per annum; Yatala Labor Prison, £125 per annum; and Adelaide Gaol £25 per annum.
[b] With rations.
[c] Rations, quarters, fuel, and light allowed.
[d] Special allowance in lieu of quarters, etc.

1925

State Children's Department

Name of officer	Date of birth	Title of office
Houlgrave, Celestine	19.8.55	Secretary, State Children's Council and Collector, IDPR Act
Kinmont, Edward, MB, ChM, MD	7.4.70	Medical Officer
Kelsh, Frederick John Prestige	13.8.76	Accountant and Receiver of Revenue
Byrne, Francis Gordon	22.5.89	Chief Prosecuting Officer and Asst Collector, IDPR Act
Philcox, Claude Joseph Owen, ACUA	6.9.08	Prosecuting Officer
Leaney, Herbert Edgar	1.9.91	Cashier
Bean, Spencer Allan	7.5.87	Ledgerkeeper

McMaster, Elizabeth Withers	—	Clerk
Siebert, Joseph Augustine	16.2.95	Clerk
Brandenburg, Robert Edmund	22.9.90	Clerk
Mildred, Rebecca Wilson	—	Clerk
Novice, Annie	—	Clerk
Austin Helena Adelaide	—	Clerk
Reed, Frederick Cecil Garnet	2.11.94	Clerk
Alderman, John Kevin	5.7.99	Clerk
Cooper, Harold Frank	13.5.82	Clerk
Mullins, Leslie Howard	26.10.86	Clerk
Colquhoun, Lindsay John	24.12.01	Clerk
Cormack, Ada	—	Clerk
Overbury, Rose Barnard	—	Clerk
Robertson, Annie Isabel	—	Clerk
LeMessurier, Eunice Irene	—	Clerk
Withers, Hilda Sylvia	—	Clerk
Duffield, Mollie Lindley	—	Clerk
Chaston, Neta Amelia Margaret	—	Shorthand-Typiste
Shaw, Evelyn Charlotte	—	Inspector
Penny, Evelyn Emma	—	Inspector
Lapidge, Elfrida Jane May	—	Inspector
Nairn, Charlotte	—	Inspector of Licensed Foster Mothers and Maternity Homes
Copley, Sarah Louisa	—	Inspector of State Children
Palmer, Elizabeth	—	Asst Inspector of Licensed Foster Mothers and Maternity Homes
Baker, Hettie Chaston	—	Asst Inspector of Licensed Foster Mothers and Maternity Homes
Smith, Sydney Wallace	17.5.73	Inquiry Officer
Kentish, Alice Martha	—	Probation Officer
Lee, Edith Florence	—	Second Probation Officer
Randell, Florence	—	Third Probation Officer
Treloar, Myrtle Fanny Rebecca	—	Fourth Probation Officer
Ophel, Eliza	—	Needle Worker
Arnold, Charles Henry	20.3.86	Superintendent and Teacher, Boys' Reformatory
Lewis, William Edward	12.12.62	Senior Attendant, Boys' Reformatory
Beaumont, Lancelot William	15.6.1900	Farm Overseer, Boys' Reformatory
Stinson, Katie Valerie	—	Matron, Industrial School

Taylor, Susannah	—	Sub-Matron, Industrial School
Lester, Mary	—	Matron, Central Depot
Craig, Margaret	—	Sub-Matron, Central Depot
Howland, Arthur Stilville	6.7.89	Representing Officer

1939

Children's Welfare and Public Relief Department

Name	Date of birth	Title of office
Byrne, F.G.	22.5.89	Chairman
Reily, H.J., AFIA, AAA, AAIS	23.11.83	Accountant and Receiver of Revenue; also Accountant, Unemployment Relief Council
Lewis, C.G., MSM, ACUA, FAIC, FAIS, FCI	30.7.93	Secretary
Wilson, C.E.C., MB, BS	27.9.75	Medical Officer
Mugford, F.K., MB, BS	16.11.99	Assistant Medical Officer
Hayter, H.E., AFIA, AAIS	2.2.03	Officer-in-Charge Prosecuting Branch
Adams, H.G., AFIA	24.9.95	Bookkeeper
Bean, S.A.	7.5.87	Paying Officer
Landers, T.E.	13.8.91	Inquiry Officer
Brandenburg, R.E.	22.9.90	Checking Officer
Colquhoun, L.J.	24.12.01	Clerk
Reed, F.C.G.	26.11.94	Clerk
Siddle, J.C.	24.10.95	Clerk
Lewis, L.T.	7.7.84	Clerk
Matthews, G.R.	12.10.10	Clerk
Victory, W.G.	3.1.14	Clerk
Glastonbury, A.A.	10.2.15	Clerk
Weiss, A.A., AFIA	24.7.17	Clerk
Arthur, B.B.	17.10.18	Clerk
Jamieson, Jessie	12.9.81	Boarding Out Officer
McIntyre, Ellen	21.10.92	Clerk
McMaster, Elizabeth W.	26.4.87	Clerk
Cormack, Ada	3.2.82	Clerk
Overbury, Rose B.	12.10.85	Clerk
Robertson, Annie I.	12.7.95	Clerk

Hay, Margaret H.	4.9.05	Clerk
Marsh, Annie	10.12.95	Clerk
Giuliano, Josephina	6.10.05	Clerk
Smith, Thelma I.E.	8.10.11	Clerk
Robin, Alethea O.	12.1.92	Shorthand-Typiste
Alexander, Florrie D.	7.10.14	Typiste and Clerk
Anderson, Jean T.	14.12.87	Clerk
Campbell, Hazel J.	14.10.08	Clerk
Jolly, Roma B.M.	14.9.16	Shorthand-Typiste
Leaby, Constance M.	19.3.11	Shorthand-Typiste
Roach, Kathleen	8.11.84	Clerk
Robertson, Grace	6.10.97	Clerk
Shaw, Evelyn C.	13.3.86	Inspector
Hecker, Ivy E.	12.3.92	Inspector
Jackson, Harriet	5.8.00	Inspector
Pile, Ellen B.	1.9.91	Inspector
Lee, Edith F.	23.7.80	Senior Probation Officer
Curtis, Mildred J.	21.5.02	Probation Officer
Marshall, Gladys M.	15.3.06	Probation Officer
Shaw, Margaret P.	4.10.97	Probation Officer
Palmer, Elizabeth	5.7.79	Inspector of Licensed Foster-Mothers and Maternity Homes
Przygoda, Irene F.	28.3.91	Assistant Inspector of Licensed Foster-Mothers and Maternity Homes
Lapidge, Hilda A.I.	8.8.84	Assistant Inspector of Licensed Foster-Mothers and Maternity Homes
Bampton, Jane K.	1.1.97	Assistant Inspector of Licensed Foster-Mothers and Maternity Homes
Stopp, Louisa	19.3.81	Officer-in-Charge, Clothing Outfit
Arnold, C.H.	20.3.90	Superintendent and Teacher, Boys' Reformatory, Magill
Thomson, V.G.	8.7.86	Senior Attendant, Boys' Reformatory, Magill
Evans, D.L.	27.5.93	Overseer Attendant, Boys' Reformatory, Magill
Queale, Lily	20.8.91	Matron, Central Depot
O'Loughlin, Elizabeth M.	22.1.89	Sub-Matron, Central Depot
Byrne, A.N.	9.2.78	Superintendent, Edwardstown Industrial School
Miller, Lilian J.	15.11.82	Matron, Edwardstown Industrial School

Sources: *South Australian Parliamentary Papers*, 1887, 1890, 1910, 1925, 1939.

III
Male and Female
Committals
1905–40

Year	Neglected		Destitute		Uncontrollable		Convicted of offences		Admitted temporarily		
	F	M	F	M	F	M	F	M	F	M	
1905	38	19	1	27	5	15	4	43	—	1	
1910	58	53		26		13	2		—	2	
1915	53	57	32	36	8	15	1	24	6	3	
1920	56	49	23	25	12	22	4	59	22	22	
1925	19	45	15	25	15	14		1	2	51	
1930	22	14	11	19	11	16	11	165	8	27	
1935	29	22	14	10	9	9	8	136	10	21	
1940	27	28	12	21	12	15	10	136	6	25	
Total	302	287	147	189	79	119	53	696	80	152	2104
Percent.	14.3%	13.6%	6.9%	8.9%	3.7%	5.6%	2.5%	33%	3.8%	7.2%	100%

Source: State Children's Council, and Children's Welfare and Public Relief Department, *Annual Reports*.

Tabular (Council) categories grouped for this table:

Neglected	Unfit guardianship, illegitimate.
Convicted of offences	Default of fine, receiving, larceny, unlawful assault, fraudulent intent.
Admitted temporarily	Pending trial.

IV
Location of Children
1890–1940 (30 June)

Year	Total no. of wards	Female wards	Females (placed out in State)	Lying-in Home and House of Mercy, etc.	Minda and Lunatic Asylum F	Minda and Lunatic Asylum M	Absconded F	Absconded M
1890	867	376	N/A	4	1	—	—	—
1895	1124	535	475	1	2	2	—	2
1900	1248	608	504	2	5	1	3	14
1905	1260	608	495	2	3	3	—	11
1910	1479	695	583	2	4	10	2	21
1915	1735	799	666	1	8	11	5	25
1920	1843	853	726	1	6	14	8	19
1925	1773	802	658	4	18	21	8	32
1930	1354	557	441	1	10	16	5	27
1935	1042	431	352	2	8	5	1	13
1940	1082	378	313	4	9	10	—	15

Source: State Children Council, *Annual Reports*.

V
State Children
Discharged
1888–92

Year	Over age	Sentence expired	Released to parents	Released to relatives	Died	Absconded	Hospital	Married	Total
1888	61	16	15	4	6	9	9	1	121
1889	83	13	20	—	4	—	—	—	120
1890	78	—	15	—	5	—	—	—	98
1891	89	8	15	—	7	—	—	—	119
1892	76	3	—	15*	10	—	—	2	106
Total	387	40	65	19	32	9	9	3	564
Percent.	68.6%	7.0%	11.5%	3.3%	5.6%	1.5%	1.5%	.53%	100%

Source: State Children's Council, *Annual Reports*.
*This category is just stated as 'released' for this year.

VI
Females in Specified
Classes of Industry
1901–47

Females in Specified Classes of Industry as a Percentage of Total Females in Industry, Australia, Censuses 1901–47

Industry order	1901[a]	1911	1921	1933	1947
PRIMARY PRODUCTION					
Agricultural, Pastoral, Dairying	6.04	4.09	2.17	3.37	3.42
Other	0.02	0.02	0.09	0.06	0.11
Total	6.06	4.11	2.26	3.43	3.53
MANUFACTURING AND CONSTRUCTION					
Articles of Dress	20.24	22.74	17.12	13.15	11.95
Other	3.14	5.68	9.19	10.49	16.91
Total	23.38	28.42	26.31	23.64	28.86
TRANSPORT AND COMMUNICATION					
Transport	0.35	0.38	0.62	0.78	2.19
Communication	0.69	0.87	0.96	1.23	2.28
Total	1.04	1.25	1.58	2.01	4.47
COMMERCE AND FINANCE					
Property and Finance	1.90	1.91	1.38	1.85	3.39
Commerce	8.14	10.66	14.44	17.42	19.64
Total	10.04	12.57	15.82	19.27	23.03
PUBLIC AUTHORITY (NEI) AND PROFESSIONAL					
Health	3.54	4.37	5.81	6.13	7.84
Education	7.20	6.84	7.79	6.16	5.37
Other	2.04	2.43	4.83	6.08	7.59
Total	12.78	13.64	18.43	18.37	20.80
ENTERTAINMENT, SPORT AND RECREATION	0.28	0.33	0.51	0.68	1.15
PERSONAL AND DOMESTIC SERVICE					
Private Domestic Service	30.61	26.80	21.42	21.39	5.84
Hotels, Boarding Houses and Restaurants	12.12	10.17	11.37	8.23	9.08
Other	3.69	2.71	2.30	2.98	3.24
Total	46.42	39.68	35.09	32.60	18.16

Source: *Commonwealth Parliamentary Papers*, 1947, Vol. 2, p. 42.
[a] Includes pensioners and retired persons whose previous industry was recorded on Census Schedules.

NOTES

ABBREVIATIONS

	Correspondence of the State Children's
CSCD	Department
CCWPRD	Correspondence of the Children's Welfare and Public Relief Department
F	Files relating to children under Departmental supervision and released in the 1940s and 1950s. (It is not possible to divulge the surnames of persons quoted in these files. Each surname is therefore entered here simply by its initial and the date. Bona fide researchers with Departmental permission may consult the master list in the author's possession.)
SCC	State Children's Council
Annual Report	Annual reports of the State Children's Council (1887–1927) and of the Children's Welfare and Public Relief Department (1928)
Mandates	Court Mandates committing children to the custody and control of the Council
Service Application Boarding-out Application	Application for a child to board or for service
Release Application	Application for the release of a child from the Council's control

PREFACE

1 John Burnett, *Useful Toil: Autobiographies of working people from the 1820s to the 1920s*, Allen Lane, London, 1974, p. 111.

2 Such comments or statistics were published in the *Annual Reports* in 1900, 1913, and 1918. In 1897, alarmed by a suggestion that reformatories were mere 'feeders' of the jail, Caroline Emily Clark had Sheriff Boothby extrapolate 'the total number of female prisoners admitted to Adelaide Gaol for the 5 years ending 31 December 1896'. Of this total, 18 (1.3%) were former Reformatory inmates, a small percentage, but in fact far higher than in the general population. Thirty-one women (2.2%) were black, a tragic disproportion that persists to this day. See CSCD 1897/337, 22.4.97.

In 1939 in giving evidence to the *Committee of Inquiry into Delinquent and Other Children in the Care of the State*, the chairman of the Children's Welfare and Public Relief Board, F.G. Byrne, produced statistics showing that in the years 1928–38, 'over 75 per cent of the children who passed through the reformatories were reasonably conforming to the law'. See *South Australian Parliamentary Papers*, 1939, Vol. 2, No. 75, p. 43.

INTRODUCTION

1 CSCD 1891/184, 11.2.91.
2 CSCD 1901/1387, 14.11.01.
3 CSCD 1890/957, 4.11.90.
4 CSCD 1891/774, 21.8.91.
5 CSCD 1900/140, 6.2.1900.
6 CSCD 1896/253, n.d.
7 T.H. Kewley, *Social Security in Australia 1900–1972*, Sydney University Press, 1965.
8 Release Application 1918/4, 16.6.20, Miss Kentish to Secretary.
9 Mandates, C. 1918/20, C576, Box 11, Miss Kentish's comments.
10 Release Application 1919/5, 21.2.19, Miss Kentish to Secretary.
11 'Report of the Royal Commission on the Basic Wage', 1920, *Australian Parliamentary Papers*, 1920–21, Vol. 4, pp. 529–646.
12 For a discussion of this act, see Ch. 8, pp. 224–5.

CHAPTER 1   THE CHILDHOOD OF STATE WARDS 1887–1914

1 CSCD 1890/700, 13.7.90.
2 CSCD 1890/761, 5.9.90. This child was removed and the foster-mother prosecuted.
3 'Regulations of the State Children's Council, 1887', *South Australian Parliamentary Papers*, 1887, Vol. 3, No. 38.
4 The expense of visiting later curtailed the number of remote country homes.
5 *Annual Report* of the SCC, 1887.
6 CSCD 1891/530, 29.5.91, Millicent Visiting Committee to Department.
7 CSCD 1900/798, 27.7.90.
8 CSCD 1911/59, n.d.
9 'Extracts from Regulations of the State Children's Department', C.H. Spence, *State Children in Australia*, Vardon & Sons, Adelaide, 1907, p. 144.
10 It began merely one year after the Council was formed, the 1888 *Annual Report* stressing that lady visitors should be regarded as the child's 'friends'.
11 CSCD 1890/924, 27.10.90.
12 Any expenses incurred in capturing an absconding child were to be taken from the child's savings. 'Regulations of the SCC, 1887'.
13 CSCD 1902/19, 28.12.01.
14 CSCD 1908/651, 4.5.08.
15 CSCD 1911/54, 6.1.11.
16 CSCD 1902/854, 5.8.02.
17 CSCD 1909/755, n.d.
18 CSCD 1910/315, 23.3.10.
19 CSCD 1912/101, 26.1.12.
20 CSCD 1902/1160, 13.11.02.
21 CSCD 1911/229, 14.2.11.
22 CSCD 1891/704, 28.7.91.

23 CSCD 1903/462, 24.4.03.
24 CSCD 1904/123, 30.1.04.
25 Ibid.
26 CSCD 1900/188, 19.2.1900.
27 CSCD 1906/145, 13.2.06.
28 CSCD 1912/195, 13.2.12.
29 CSCD 1909/51, 14.1.09.
30 CSCD 1890/761, 5.9.90.
31 CSCD 1890/785, n.d.
32 Ibid.
33 CSCD 1904/279, 7.3.09.
34 CSCD 1903/643, n.d.
35 CSCD 1905/230, 6.3.05.
36 CSCD 1906/273, 18.3.06.
37 CSCD 1905/402, 24.4.05,
38 CSCD 1909/767, 13.7.09.
39 CSCD 1907/365, 12.4.07.
40 CSCD 1910/301, 18.3.10.
41 'Regulations of the SCC, 1887'.
42 CSCD 1896/946, 7.12.96.
43 CSCD 1890/1096, 15.12.90.
44 CSCD 1903/485, 28.4.03.
45 CSCD 1890/754, n.d.
46 CSCD 1890/53, 14.1.91.
47 CSCD 1903/819, 16.7.03.
48 CSCD 1908/275, 5.3.08.
49 For an interesting discussion of the work expected of children, see Kerry
    Wimshurst, 'Child labour and school attendance in South Australia
    1890–1915', *Historical Studies*, Vol. 19, No. 76.
50 CSCD 1896/214, n.d.
51 CSCD 1891/466, 6.5.91.
52 CSCD 1891/193, 12.2.91
53 CSCD 1901/925, 30.7.01.
54 CSCD 1906/184, 26.2.06.
55 CSCD 1891/232, n.d.
56 CSCD 1891/533, 31.5.91.
57 CSCD 1910/1228, 9.11.10.
58 CSCD 1910/1228, 9.11.10.
59 CSCD 1907/305, 22.3.07.
60 CSCD 1896/834, 21.10.96.
61 CSCD 1891/568, 10.6.91.
62 CSCD 1890/738, 11.8.91.
63 CSCD 1903/834, 27.7.03.
64 CSCD 1910/1207, 2.11.10.
65 CSCD 1908/329, 11.3.08.
66 CSCD 1896/573, n.d.
67 CSCD 1909/755, n.d.
68 CSCD 1912/63, 15.1.12.
69 CSCD 1900/147, 8.2.1900.

70   CSCD 1900/147, 8.2.1900.
71   CSCD 1890/1131, 24.12.90; CSCD, 1901/1191, 2.10.91.
72   CSCD 1910/1202, 1.11.10; 1911/54, 6.1.11.
73   *Annual Report*, 1914.
74   CSCD 1909/44, 13.1.09.
75   CSCD 1910/307, 22.3.10.
76   CSCD 1908/651, 4.5.08.
77   CSCD 1891/230, n.d.
78   CSCD 1901/1175, 3.10.01.
79   CSCD 1901/924, 29.7.01.
80   K.R. Bowes, 'The 1890 Maritime Strike in South Australia', MA thesis, Adelaide University, 1957, pp. 6, 12.
81   C.M. Davies, 'Women in Industry: the development in the employment of women in South Australia from 1900–1954', BA Hons thesis, Adelaide University, 1956, p. 14.
82   *South Australian Parliamentary Papers*, 1892, Vol. 2, No. 37.
83   Mrs E. Rogers, needlewoman, giving evidence, Q. 2337, 'Report of the Shops and Factories Commission, *South Australian Parliamentary Papers*, Vol. 2. No. 37, p. 65.
84   Margaret Anne Buckton, shirtmaker, giving evidence, Q. 5971 and Q. 5972, 'Report of the Shops and Factories Commission', p. 155.
85   Mrs Agnes Anderson Milne, shirtmaker, giving evidence, Q. 4122, 'Report of the Shops and Factories Commission', p. 111.
86   *South Australian Directory*, 1911, p. 24.
87   CSCD 1891/356, 1.4.91.
88   CSCD 1912/133, 2.2.12.
89   CSCD 1913/43, 7.1.13.
90   CSCD 1913/43, James Gray, Secretary, to girl.
91   CSCD 1907/145, 7.2.07.
92   CSCD 1891/683, 23.7.91.
93   CSCD 1891/699, 24.6.91.
94   CSCD 1901/1175, n.d.

CHAPTER 2   DOMESTIC SERVICE 1887–1914

1   CSCD 1890/847, 4.10.90.
2   CSCD 1896/36, n.d.
3   CSCD 1904/146, 9.12.05.
4   CSCD 1911/147, 6.1.11.
5   CSCD 1901/999, 22.8.01. Despite the care taken over homes, returns were high. See Tables 5 and 6, Ch. 1.
6   CSCD 1909/740, 2.17.09.
7   R.E.N. Twopeny, *Town Life in Australia*, E. Stock, London, 1883, p. 35.
8   CSCD 1896/36, n.d.
9   CSCD 1903/852, 23.7.03.
10   CSCD 1900/769, 20.7.1900.
11   CSCD 1906/243, 12.3.06, p. 8, Evelyn Penny, 'Impressions of the work of the State Children's Department of South Australia'.
12   CSCD 1895/565, 24.7.95.

13 CSCD 1901/1314, 1.11.01.
14 CSCD 1901/1297, 27.10.01.
15 CSCD 1901/1314, n.d.
16 CSCD 1901/1305, 29.10.01.
17 CSCD 1900/404, 18.4.1900.
18 CSCD 1904/290, 11.3.04.
19 CSCD 1900/431, 26.4.1900.
20 CSCD 1896/943, 5.12.96.
21 CSCD 1912/25, n.d.
22 CSCD 1900/407, 20.4.1900.
23 CSCD 1900/404, 18.4.1900.
24 CSCD 1901/1297, 27.10.01.
25 CSCD 1891/22, 18.1.91.
26 CSCD 1913/342, 3.2.13.
27 CSCD 1912/106, 26.1.72.
28 CSCD 1905/809, 16.8.05.
29 CSCD 1912/83, n.d.
30 CSCD 1903/823, 19.7.03.
31 CSCD 1909/775, 12.7.09.
32 CSCD 1910/1226, n.d.
33 CSCD 1911/80, 12.1.1911.
34 CSCD 1905/148, 11.2.05.
35 CSCD 1902/750, 4.7.02.
36 CSCD 1902/851, 4.8.02.
37 CSCD 1890/917, 27.10.90.
38 CSCD 1897/445, 26.5.97.
39 CSCD 1891/166, n.d.
40 CSCD 1903/464, 24.4.03.
41 CSCD 1902/297, 4.3.02.
42 CSCD 1904/283, 8.3.04.
43 CSCD 1904/286, 8.3.04.
44 CSCD 1911/3, n.d.
45 CSCD 1904/373, 26.3.04.
46 CSCD 1905/280, 15.3.05.
47 CSCD 1896/598, 23.7.96.
48 CSCD 1909/792, 7.7.09.
49 CSCD 1904/382, 28.3.04.
50 CSCD 1911/273, 16.2.11.
51 CSCD 1896/613, 4.8.96.
52 CSCD 1910/309, 25.3.10.
53 CSCD 1911/232, 14.2.11.
54 CSCD 1910/378, 8.4.10. Twopeny, *Town Life*, p. 50, commented, 'Of course
    she is independent, often even cheeky, but a mistress learns to put up with
    occasional tantrums, provided the general behaviour and character are good'.
55 CSCD 1907/1910, 13.12.07.
56 CSCD 1905/76, 29.7.05.
57 CSCD 1890/719, 2.8.90.
58 CSCD 1896/836, 23.10.96.
59 CSCD 1913/112, 20.1.13.

60 CSCD 1891/22, 9.1.91.
61 CSCD 1902/261, 3.2.02.
62 CSCD 1890/92, 25.10.90.
63 CSCD 1908/467, 12.4.08.
64 CSCD 1901/1469, 8.12.01.
65 CSCD 1902/643, 2.6.02.
66 CSCD 1902/714, 25.6.02.
67 CSCD 1908/444, 8.4.08.
68 CSCD 1901/1445, 3.11.01.
69 CSCD 1902/14, 28.12.01.
70 CSCD 1891/573, 11.6.91.
71 CSCD 1903/682, 16.6.03.
72 CSCD 1891/135, 2.2.91.
73 CSCD 1896/452, n.d.
74 CSCD 1891/745, 10.8.91.
75 CSCD 1905/487, 8.6.05.
76 CSCD 1905/571, 4.7.05.
77 CSCD 1896/200, 13.3.96.
78 CSCD 1909/794, 11.7.09.
79 CSCD 1913/132, 24.1.13.
80 CSCD 1891/577, 15.6.91.
81 CSCD 1890/825, n.d.
82 CSCD 1900/126, n.d.
83 Ada Cambridge, *Thirty Years in Australia*, Methuen, London, 1903, p. 73.
84 CSCD 1905/208, 26.2.05.
85 CSCD 1908/297, 6.3.08.
86 CSCD 1905/411, 3.5.05.
87 CSCD 1897/466, 3.6.97; CSCD 1890/716, n.d.
88 CSCD 1903/787, 12.7.03.
89 CSCD 1902/430, 12.4.02.
90 CSCD 1908/435, 6.4.08.
91 CSCD 1905/363, 12.4.05.
92 CSCD 1908/377, 28.3.08.
93 CSCD 1909/702, 25.6.09; CSCD 1900/708, 7.7.1900.
94 CSCD 1901/1229, 9.10.02.
95 CSCD 1891/445, 28.4.91.
96 CSCD 1902/269, 3.3.02.
97 CSCD 1908/450, 9.4.08.
98 CSCD 1900/163, 13.2.1900.
99 CSCD 1901/1192, 22.9.01.
 1 CSCD 1907/247, 9.3.07.
 2 These wages seem on a parity with domestic servants' wages in the community. Beverley Kingston in *My Wife, My Daughter and Poor Mary Ann*, p. 46, comments on the slow decline in wages after 1887 and states that even beyond World War I 'a general servant rarely could command more than £1 a week and usually she settled for less'.
 3 CSCD 1908/657, 5.5.08.
 4 CSCD 1908/601, 27.4.08.
 5 CSCD 1908/591, 23.4.08.

6 CSCD 1907/306, n.d.
7 CSCD 1908/297, 6.3.08.
8 CSCD 1907/227, n.d.
9 CSCD 1909/752, 5.7.09.
10 CSCD 1913/181, 11.2.13.
11 CSCD 1909/792, 7.7.09.
12 CSCD 1902/683, 17.6.02.
13 CSCD 1901/1156, 25.9.01.
14 The *Annual Report* for 1908, p. 7, states: 'The demand for service girls has been very great, and has been as far as possible met. It has, however, been impossible to supply half the requirements'.
15 CSCD 1901/1290, n.d.
16 *State Children's Convention*, University of Adelaide, 1907, p. 21.
17 CSCD 1911/80, 12.1.11.
18 CSCD 1911/25, 4.1.11.
19 CSCD 1901/1274, 21.10.01.
20 CSCD 1908/305, n.d.
21 CSCD 1901/946, 8.8.07.
22 CSCD 1910/1177, 19.10.10.
23 CSCD 1911/115, 21.1.11.
24 Mr W.B. Dorman giving evidence to the Shops and Factories Commission, *South Australian Parliamentary Papers*, 1892, Vol. 2, No. 37, p. 319.
25 CSCD 1890/735, 28.8.90.
26 CSCD 1890/1057, 10.12.90.
27 CSCD 1904/896, 26.9.04.
28 CSCD 1903/867, 28.7.03.
29 CSCD 1909/792, 7.7.09.
30 CSCD 1912/80, 19.1.12.
31 CSCD 1906/155, 14.2.06.

CHAPTER 3 COUNTRY LIFE AND OTHER TRIALS 1887–1940

1 CSCD 1903/110, 23.4.03.
2 *Annual Report*, 1887, p. 3.
3 'a plain home upon some South Australian farm', 'Final Report of the Destitute Commission', Part II, *South Australian Parliamentary Papers*, 1885, Vol. 4, No. 228, p. LXII.
4 CSCD 1897/110, 7.2.97.
5 CSCD 1891/447, 29.4.91.
6 CSCD 1897/123, 1.2.97.
7 CSCD 1910/292, 8.3.10.
8 CSCD 1896/331, 10.1.96.
9 CSCD 1907/54, 10.1.07.
10 CSCD 1910/299, n.d.; CSCD 1905/454, 16.5.05.
11 CSCD 1907/50, 9.1.07.
12 CSCD 1912/49, 8.1.12; CSCD 1904/261, 2.3.04.
13 CSCD 1912/49, 8.1.12.

14 CSCD 1906/243, 12.3.06, p. 9, Evelyn Penny, 'Impressions of the work of the State Children's Department of South Australia'.
15 CSCD 1906/255, 14.3.06.
16 CSCD 1913/130, 21.1.13.
17 CSCD 1907/85, 21.1.07.
18 CSCD 1896/331, 10.1.96.
19 CSCD 1896/411, n.d.
20 CSCD 1901/1167, 25.9.01.
21 CSCD 1913/145, 27.1.13.
22 CSCD 1902/350, 23.3.02.
23 CSCD 1908/543, 16.4.08.
24 CSCD 1906/255, 14.3.06.
25 CSCD 1913/203, 10.12.13.
26 CSCD 1912/113, 23.1.12.
27 CSCD 1913/301, 18.2.13.
28 CSCD 1917/41, n.d.
29 CSCD 1901/813, 4.7.01.
30 CSCD 1901/814, 4.7.01.
31 CSCD 1913/247, 14.2.13.
32 CSCD 1910/1203, 29.10.10.
33 CSCD 1913/45, 5.2.13.
34 CSCD 1906/31, 8.1.06.
35 CSCD 1903/874, 27.7.03.
36 CSCD 1910/303, 20.3.10.
37 CSCD 1911/203, 2.2.11.
38 CSCD 1905/208, 26.2.05.
39 CSCD 1916/209, 7.2.16.
40 CSCD 1905/220, 2.3.05.
41 CSCD 1908/566, n.d.
42 Dorothy Gilbert, 'Country Life in the Later Nineteenth Century: Reminiscences by Dorothy Gilbert', *South Australiana*, Vol. XII, pp. 57–70.
43 CSCD 1902/742, 5.7.02.
44 CSCD 1891/465, 6.5.91.
45 CSCD 1904/396, 28.3.04.
46 CSCD 1896/286, n.d.
47 CSCD 1902/1252, 11.12.02.
48 CSCD 1904/225, 17.2.04.
49 CSCD 1913/74, 13.1.13.
50 F A. 13.12.34.
51 F F. 8.6.36.
52 CSCD 19/8/13, n.d.
53 F B. 9.9.35.
54 CSCD 1918/98, 26.1.18.
55 F E. 11.7.34. This letter *was* forwarded to the girl's parents.
56 CSCD 1917/126, n.d.
57 CSCD 1916/206, 6.2.16.
58 CSCD 1915/611, 9.5.15.
59 F C. 17.6.36.
60 F C. 22.2.37.

61 F B. 13.11.35.
62 F E. 24.6.36.
63 CSCD 1919/874, 21.1.20.
64 F A. 25.12.35.
65 CSCD 1915/446, 3.4.15.
66 F B. 15.3.35.
67 CSCD 1905/106, 25.1.05.
68 CSCD 1908/392, 31.3.08.
69 CSCD 1912/106, 26.11.12.
70 CSCD 1902/915, 25.8.02.
71 CSCD 1908/490, 15.4.08.
72 CSCD 1902/858, 4.8.02. The docket cover on this file has been damaged and notes on it are illegible.
73 CSCD 1903/264, 1.3.1903. A note on the file of 22.4.03 records an improvement in relations, and a note of 12.5.03 states 'child to remain'.
74 CSCD 1912/104, 26.1.12; see also 1907/51.
75 F C. 18.2.37.
76 CSCD 1897/486, 4.6.97.
77 CSCD 1906/266, 14.3.06.
78 CSCD 1907/154, 10.1.07.
79 CSCD 1901/1242, 6.10.01.
80 CSCD 1905/109, 26.1.05.
81 CSCD 1896/624, 28.7.96.
82 CSCD 1896/624, 21.11.76.
83 CSCD 1911/263, 21.2.11.
84 CSCD 1891/557, 8.6.91.
85 CSCD 1900/136, 8.2.1900.
86 CSCD 1909/775, 12.7.09.
87 CSCD 1904/944, 15.10.04.
88 CSCD 1912/25, n.d.
89 CSCD 1900/761, 19.7.1900; 1911/200, 5.2.11; 1905/576, 1.7.05.
90 CSCD 1909/777, 13.7.09.
91 CSCD 1890/1100, 15.12.90; CSCD 1910/299, n.d.; CSCD 1906/214, 28.2.06.
92 CSCD 1913/295, 24.2.13.
93 CSCD 1905/629, 16.7.05.
94 CSCD 1911/80, 12.1.11.
95 CSCD 1896/579, 11.7.96.
96 CSCD 1906/222, 21.1.06.
97 CSCD 1906/130, 10.2.06.
98 CSCD 1890/751, 1.9.90.
99 CSCD 1906/121, 7.12.06.
 1 CSCD 1902/282, 10.3.02.
 2 CSCD 1913/168, 4.2.13.
 3 Annual Report, 1917, p. 8. Statistics on infant mortality, Year Books of the Commonwealth of Australia, 1911, 1921, and 1940.
 4 CSCD 1900/765, 12.8.1900.
 5 CSCD 1890/1120, n.d.
 6 CSCD 1909/80, 23.1.09.

7   See Edna Ryan and Anne Conlon, *Gentle Invaders: Australian Women at Work 1788–1974*, Nelson, Melbourne, 1975.
8   CSCD 1908/666, 5.5.08.
9   CSCD 1907/362, 5.4.07.
10 CSCD 1901/1213, n.d.
11 CSCD 1905/771, 5.8.05.
12 CSCD 1904/853, 10.9.04.
13 CSCD 1910/263, 8.3.10; CSCD 1897/450, 29.5.97; CSCD 1904/937, 8.10.04.
14 CSCD 1904/246, 20.2.04.
15 CSCD 1904/340, 21.3.04; CSCD 1904/809, 22.8.04.

CHAPTER 4   SEX AND MARRIAGE 1887–1940

1   CSCD 1903/570, 14.5.03.
2   Boys suffered too. In 1902 it was considered normal that a boy in Magill Reformatory who had become 'mentally affected' through frequent masturbation, have a silver ring inserted through his foreskin as a deterrent. CSCD 1902/858, 1902/904. Boys were also whipped.
3   Christine Chinner, '"Earthly Paradise": a social history of Adelaide in the early 1890s', BA Hons thesis, Adelaide University, 1960, Ch. 3.
4   D.E. McConnell, *Australian Etiquette*, Melbourne, 1886, pp. 152–3.
5   CSCD 1913/142, 24.1.13.
6   CSCD 1907/28, 8.1.07.
7   CSCD 1907/186, 6.2.07.
8   CSCD 1905/278, 16.3.05.
9   CSCD 1902/503, 28.4.02.
10 CSCD 1907/190, 20.2.07.
11 CSCD 1912/148, 6.2.12.
12 CSCD 1902/538, 8.5.02.
13 CSCD 1907/277, 14.3.07.
14 CSCD 1912/169, 5.2.12.
15 CSCD 1911/110, 17.1.11.
16 CSCD 1912/169, 5.2.12.
17 CSCD 1896/536, n.d.; CSCD 1896/592, 22.11.96.
18 CSCD 1913/102, 20.1.13.
19 CSCD 1891/5, 3.1.91.
20 CSCD 1907/297, 19.3.07.
21 CSCD 1913/48, 7.1.13.
22 CSCD 1896/454, 2.6.96.
23 CSCD 1902/1169, 17.11.02.
24 CSCD 1903/6, 26.12.03.
25 CSCD 1900/739, 10.7.00.
26 CSCD 1903/529, 10.5.03.
27 CSCD 1912/14, 3.1.12.
28 Jessie Ackermann, *Australia from a Woman's Point of View*, Cassell, London, 1913, p. 282.
29 CSCD 1912/14, 3.1.12.

30 Gertrude Himmelfarb, 'The Culture of Poverty', in H.J. Dyos and M. Wolff (eds), *The Victorian City: Images and Realities*, Routledge & Kegan Paul, London, 1973, p. 731.
31 CSCD 1913/301, n.d.
32 CSCD 1898/Unfiled (loose in box, docket cover missing), 8.5.98.
33 CSCD 1907/Unfiled (loose in box, docket cover missing), n.d.
34 CSCD 1904/584, 8.6.04.
35 CSCD 1891/492, 11.5.91.
36 CSCD 1896/244, n.d.; CSCD 1897/487, 5.6.97.
37 CSCD 1890/748, 31.8.90.
38 CSCD 1891/70, 16.1.91.
39 CSCD 1910/291, n.d.
40 CSCD 1910/291, 17.3.10.
41 CSCD 1902/76, 15.1.02.
42 CSCD 1900/107, n.d.
43 CSCD 1907/41, 10.1.07.
44 CSCD 1910/255, 7.3.10.
45 CSCD 1906/163, 16.2.06.
46 CSCD 1913/43, 7.1.13.
47 CSCD 1901/1385, 19.11.01.
48 CSCD 1902/125, 27.1.02.
49 CSCD 1890/706, 13.8.90.
50 CSCD 1891/4, 4.1.91.
51 CSCD 1907/331, 28.3.07..
52 CSCD 1901/1252, 17.10.01; CSCD 1902/224, 27.2.02.
53 The most detailed treatment of prostitution in South Australia is Susan M. Horan, 'More Sinned Against than Sinning': Prostitution in South Australia 1836–1914, BA Hons thesis, Flinders University, 1978; 'Reports on Lessening the Evils of Prostitution', *South Australian Parliamentary Papers*, 1867, Vol. 3, No. 86.
54 CSCD 1909/703, n.d.
55 C.A. Chandler, 'Darkest Adelaide & Sidelights of City Life', 1907, State Library of South Australia.
56 CSCD 1901/1269, 22.10.01.
57 CSCD 1908/321, 9.3.08, 1907/138, n.d.
58 To Victorian eyes, Dora was in the classic position of peril: young, unemployed, alone, and impressionable in the city.
59 CSCD 1902/586, 10.5.02, girl's statement.
60 CSCD 1902/586, Secretary, SCD to Commissioner of Police, n.d.
61 CSCD 1903/581, 22.5.03.
62 CSCD 1891/12, 7.1.91.
63 CSCD 1891/497, 16.5.91. This case did cause some disquiet in the district; several residents wrote asking for a retrial. As far as can be ascertained they were not successful.
64 The tragic irony is that they were placed out as domestics in family homes to be controlled and protected from 'moral danger'.
65 CSCD 1906/257, 14.3.06.
66 CSCD 1891/94, 10.1.91.
67 CSCD 1909/72, 20.1.09; 1891/127, 30.1.91.

68 CSCD 1906/220, 3.3.06.
69 CSCD 1911/48, n.d.
70 CSCD 1891/127, 30.1.91; 1891/127, 30.1.91.
71 CSCD 1910/291, 16.3.10.
72 CSCD 1904/176, 12.2.04.
73 CSCD 1909/72, 20.1.09; CSCD 1891/127, 30.1.91.
74 CSCD 1902/227, n.d.
75 The Lying-in Home in the Destitute Asylum on Kintore Avenue was one of the Destitute Department's services. Women had to apply for admission shortly before confinement and if considered 'deserving' on admission, had to sign an agreement to remain in the home for six months until their baby was weaned.
76 CSCD 1912/1, 28.12.11.
77 CSCD 1912/40, 8.1.12.
78 For an account of a household coming to terms with a domestic with a child see, G.A. Alcock, 'Alice', Lone Hand, 1 April 1908, pp. 640–2.
79 CSCD 1900/424, n.d.
80 CSCD 1891/110, 24.1.91; 1891/432, 11.4.91.
81 CSCD 1900/106, n.d.
82 Neville Hicks, 'This Sin and Scandal': Australia's Population Debate 1891–1911, Australian National University Press, Canberra, 1978, p. 27.
83 CSCD 1902/619, 3.6.02.
84 CSCD 1901/1224, 7.10.01
85 CSCD 1902/790, 19.7.02.
86 CSCD 1907/53, 12.1.07.
87 Alexandra Hasluck (ed.), Audrey Tennyson's Vice-Regal Days, National Library of Australia, Canberra, 1978, pp. 106–7.
88 CSCD 1912/12, 4.1.12.
89 CSCD 1901/1381, 18.11.02.
90 CSCD 1903/361, 28.3.03.
91 CSCD 1902/258, n.d.
92 CSCD 1896/564, n.d.
93 CSCD 1902/1108, 28.10.02.
94 CSCD 1891/180, 19.3.91; CSCD 1901/1499, n.d.
95 CSCD 1913/46, 8.1.13.
96 CSCD 1909/822, 19.7.09.
97 CSCD 1904/353, 20.3.04.
98 CSCD 1891/274, 2.5.91.
99 CSCD 1902/1147, 8.11.02.
1 CSCD 1907/362, 5.4.07.
2 CSCD 1903/515, 22.4.03.
3 CSCD 1910/386, 4.4.10.
4 CSCD 1911/50, 3.2.11.
5 CSCD 1890/934, 29.10.90.
6 CSCD 1909/38, 8.1.09.
7 CSCD 1905/473, 29.5.05.
8 CSCD 1903/515, 22.4.03.
9 CSCD 1890/832, 28.9.90.
10 CSCD 1890/1098, 12.12.90.

11 CSCD 1911/91, 6.1.11.
12 CSCD 1891/687, 19.7.91.
13 CSCD 1903/759, 3.7.03.
14 CSCD 1904/186, 15.2.04; 1912/208, 15.2.12; 1891/226, 23.2.91.
15 CSCD 1905/583, 2.7.05.
16 CSCD 1908/317, 17.3.08.
17 CSCD 1902/1215, 1.12.02.
18 CSCD 1910/304, 18.3.10.
19 CSCD 1891/56, 13.12.91.
20 CSCD 1915/93, n.d.
21 CSCD 1919/688, 3.9.19.
22 CCWPRD 1929/57, 21.7.28.
23 F B. 27.1.38.
24 F C. 29.10.35.
25 F F. 7.1.36.
26 CSCD 1916/227, 14.2.16.
27 CSCD 1916/221, 11.2.16.
28 CSCD 1916/21, 3.1.16.
29 F F. 21.10.35.
30 F A. 25.4.36.
31 CSCD 1921/226, n.d.
32 CSCD 1916/550, 20.1.16, Matron, Industrial School to Secretary.
33 CCWPRD 1927/355, 9.8.27.
34 CSCD 1925/295, 24.5.25.
35 CSCD 1919/481, 23.6.19.
36 CSCD 1922/505, n.d.
37 CSCD 1926/335, n.d.
38 CSCD 1918/106, 29.1.18.
39 CSCD 1922/505.
40 CCWPRD 1928/100, 23.2.28, E. Lee, Second Probation Officer, to Board.
41 See the account of Hilary Goldner and Judith Allen, 'Prostitution in New
   South Wales 1870–1932: Re-structuring an Industry', *Refractory Girl*, Dec.
   79–Jan. 1980.
42 CCWPRD 1929/41, n.d.
43 CCWPRD 1929/78, 13.2.29.
44 CCWPRD 1928/124, 1.3.28.
45 CSCD 1918/45, 14.1.18.
46 CSCD 1924/147, 10.3.24.
47 Service Application 12045, 5.4.19.
48 Ibid.
49 CSCD 1917/83, 15.1.17, 22.1.17.
50 CSCD 1917/66, 8.1.17.
51 CSCD 1919/422, 20.7.19.
52 CSCD 1918/70, –.1.18.
53 CSCD 1922/53, 5.2.32.
54 CSCD 1914/604, 18.5.14.
55 F A. 28.2.36.
56 CSCD 1918/142, 27.1.18.
57 CSCD 1921/203, n.d.

58 CSCD 1925/346, 18.6.25.
59 CSCD 1924/172, 16.12.24.
60 CSCD 1923/534, 22.1.24.
61 CSCD 1925/263, 13.5.25.
62 CSCD 1923/534, 13.8.23.
63 CSCD 1925/157, 15.3.25.
64 CSCD 1918/32, 10.1.18.
65 CSCD 1918/224, 28.3.18.
66 CSCD 1923/457, 19.6.23.
67 CSCD 1923/461, 5.11.23.
68 CSCD 1921/258, 20.8.21.
69 CSCD 1917/110, 21.1.17.
70 F C. 1936.
71 F C. 10.7.36.
72 CSCD 1917/108, 23.1.17.
73 CSCD 1919/485, 9.4.20.
74 CSCD 1924/534, 22.5.24.
75 F A. 7.6.40.

CHAPTER 5 GROWING UP A STATE WARD 1915–40

1 CCWPRD 1928/86, 18.2.28, A. Novice, Clerk, reporting.
2 This home was reported to have 'improved' as a result.
3 See S.J. Carmichael, 'The Call to Duty: some aspects of Social Response to the Great War in South Australia 1914–1918', BA Hons thesis, Adelaide University, 1967.
4 CSCD 1915/91, 18.1.15.
5 CSCD 1919/706, 20.9.19.
6 *Annual Report* of the Children's Welfare and Public Relief Department, 1929.
7 F B. 5.11.30.
8 F A. 3.9.90.
9 F F. 20.10.30.
10 F F. 28.10.30.
11 F A. 18.11.29.
12 Boarding-out Application, 12.9.1919.
13 Ibid., 12.9.19.
14 Ibid., 27.9.19, E. Lapidge, Fourth Inspector.
15 Mandates, 6/24, C752, Box 2, 7.4.24.
16 Release Application 1920/83, 16.1.20.
17 CSCD 1925/158, 4.4.25. Subsidy for children was increased in 1927.
18 CSCD 1915/425, 29.3.15.
19 CCWPRD 1927/510, 16.5.27.
20 F A. 39.1.30.
21 F B. 2.7.30.
22 F A. 2.10.39.
23 CSCD 1925/173, 27.3.25.
24 'One or two other simple duties, including 15 minutes piano practice'; F C. 1.7.39.

25 F C. 1.7.39.
26 Hal Porter, *The Watcher on the Cast-iron Balcony*, Faber & Faber, London, 1963, p. 60.
27 F A. 8.3.32.
28 F C. 24.11.37; F C. 26.5.37.
29 F C. 3.2.30.
30 F C. 23.4.30.
31 F C. 26.10.34.
32 Boarding-out Application 12083, 25.5.18.
33 F C. 11.5.38.
34 Boarding-out Application 12063, 29.8.18.
35 Ibid. 12085, 11.3.19.
36 Ibid. 12067, 13 7.18.
37 Ibid. 12047, 20.9.24.
38 Release Application 1920/93, 30.1.20.
39 CSCD 1915/234, 16.2.15.
40 F B. 5.11.36.
41 CSCD 1916/557, n.d.
42 CSCD 1924/114, 23.1.24.
43 Dorothy Roysland, *A Pioneer Family on the Murray River*, Rigby, Adelaide, 1977, p. 58.
44 CSCD 1921/266, 12.4.21.
45 F F. 13.7.32.
46 F F. 18.1.37.
47 F C. –.12.30.
48 This child denied the nine-year-old boy's accusations. Two years later she was removed from another foster-home for swearing.
49 F A. 9.10.39.
50 F C. 18.5.32.
51 F F. 1.6.36; In 1926 Evelyn Penny thought wages should be raised as 'All children are given so much to spend in these days'. CSCD 1926/453, n.d.
52 This was especially so, when, as in the instance below, the girl was the child of an ex-state ward.
53 CSCD 1927/412, 9.8.27.
54 F A. –.10.33.
55 *Annual Report* of the CWPRD, 1939; this is an age when dress was one of the most public signs of respectability and status. See evidence relating to hats, p. 1508, 'Minutes of Evidence of the Royal Commission on the Basic Wage', Government Printer, Melbourne, 1920.
56 CSCD 1919/912, 19.11.19.
57 CSCD 1920/304, 6.4.21.
58 CSCD 1920/304, 24.2.21.
59 CSCD 1918/12, 28.12.17.
60 F C. 14.12.38.
61 F C. 28.3.33.
62 CSCD 1906/243, 12.3.06.
63 F A. 28.8.34.
64 CSCD 1922/538, 2.5.22.
65 F A. 19.3.39.

66 F C. 26.10.34.
67 Mandates B., 146/20, C648, 10.10.24.
68 F F. 3.7.33.
69 F F. 10.8.33.
70 F A. 3.6.33.
71 F A. 26.4.39.
72 One of the recommendations of the 1939 Committee of Inquiry into Delinquent and other Children in the care of the State was that greater care be taken with placement. See *South Australian Parliamentary Papers*, 1939, Vol. 2, No. 75, p. 30.
73 F A. 26.2.30.
74 F C. 11.5.32.
75 F C. 26.9.35.
76 F C. 16.12.35.
77 CSCD 1923/484, 2.7.23.
78 CSCD 1919/478, 19.6.19.
79 CSCD 1926/459, 25.6.26.
80 CSCD 1922/525, 16.8.22.
81 CSCD 1918/12, 4.9.18.
82 CCWPRD 1928/117, 26.2.28.
83 CSCD 1918/12, 18.1.18.
84 CSCD 1920/273, 25.3.20.
85 CSCD 1925/429, 21.8.25.
86 CSCD 1916/207, 7.2.16.
87 F A. 20.1.30.
88 F F. 13.10.32.
89 CCWPRD 1929/512, 15.11.29.
90 F C. 23.12.29.
91 CCWPRD 1928/82, 9.2.28.
92 Suzanne Edgar, 'Constance Davey', *Australian Dictionary of Biography*, Vol. 8, Melbourne University Press, 1981.
93 F F. 19.6.35.
94 CSCD 1925/344, 14.6.25.
95 CSCD 1914/76, 16.1.14; 1929/32, 16.1.29.
96 CCWPRD 1929, 16.1.29.
97 CCWPRD 1925/158, 6.4.25.
98 CSCD 1924/75, 10.12.23.
99 CSCD 1924/96, 12.2.24.
 1 F C. 3.6.40.
 2 CSCD 1924/264, 16.7.25, 27.8.25.
 3 Walter Hutley, giving evidence, Q. 5373 and Q. 5375, 'Royal Commission on Law Reform, 1926', *South Australian Parliamentary Papers*, 1926, Vol. 2, No. 54, p. 25.
 4 W. Hall, giving evidence, Q. 5190, 'Royal Commission on Law Reform, 1926'.
 5 Girls with mental handicap were particularly liable to sexual assault according to A.K. Goode, Q. 5297, 'Royal Commission on Law Reform 1926', p. 21.
 6 F C. 12.9.35.
 7 Boarding-out Application 12082, 5.4.27.

8 F C. 27.6.33.
9 F C. 31.10.34.
10 F C. 6.2.40.
11 F C. 30.5.40.
12 F C. 27.1.32; F C. 20.8.40.
13 Figures calculated from *Year Books* and *Reports of Factories and Steam Boilers Department*.
14 F A. 13.6.34.
15 CSCD 1915/55, 29.4.15.
16 CSCD 1924/75, 22.12.23.
17 F C. 29.1.36.
18 F F. 3.9.31.
19 Rosabelle Farmer, 'Minutes of Evidence of the Royal Commission on the Basic Wage', Q. 66582, p. 1507, and Q. 66614, p. 1508.

CHAPTER 6 GOING TO WORK 1915–40

1 Lillian Pyke, *Australian Etiquette*, Speciality Press, 1931, p. 18.
2 See Appendix VI.
3 Ackermann, *Australia from a Woman's Point of View*, p. 281.
4 CSCD 1914/21, 6.1.14.
5 F C. 17.8.32.
6 Unfortunately almost all Applications for a child for Service were destroyed in 1961. However an impression of the size of the houses can be gained from Correspondence.
7 CSCD 1918/57, 1.4.18.
8 Service Application 12077, 9.4.18.
9 Service Application 12060, 10.5.18. This application was declined on the grounds that 'it is the wish of the State Children's Council that no State Child shall be placed in a Maternity Hospital'.
10 Service Application 12044, 26.4.18.
11 Service Application 12053, 21.5.18, 'Applicant is a nice sensible woman . . .'
12 Service Application 12072, 30.4.18.
13 Service Application 12069, 6.6.18.
14 Kay Daniels, *Women in Australia: An Annotated Guide to Records*, AGPS, Canberra, 1977, Vol. I, p. 52. 'Minutes of the Girl's Industrial School', 1926.
15 CSCD 1921/256, 4.4.21, Matron, Central Depot, to Secretary.
16 CSCD 1922/366, 2.6.22.
17 But of course they had none of the security of an indentured apprentice.
18 F A. 25.4.36.
19 CSCD 1918/57, 15.1.18.
20 CSCD 1914/632, 27.5.14.
21 CSCD 1914/591, 18.5.14.
22 F A. 21.5.34.
23 CCWPRD 1929/53, F.G. Byrne to girl.
24 CCWPRD 1928/92, 17.3.28.
25 CCWPRD 1929/85, Chairman, CWPRB, to girl; F E. 8.11.33.
26 F B. 24.3.33.

27 F B. 17.10.30, Miss Kentish's words.
28 CCWPRD 1929/529, 3.7.30.
29 F C. 18.12.33.
30 CSCD 1919/907, 12.11.19.
31 CSCD 1921/258, 21.6.21.
32 See K. Mansfield, *Collected Stories*, Constable, London, 1964, p. 228.
33 CSCD 1920/162, 27.2.20.
34 CSCD 1919/480, 21.6.19.
35 CSCD 1919/929, 17.1.20.
36 Meredith Atkinson (ed.), *Australia: Economic and Political Studies*, Macmillan, Melbourne, 1920, p. 297.
37 CCWPRD 1928/127, 27.2.28; F A. 28.9.36; F C. 9.12.35.
38 CSCD 1917/24, 3.1.17.
39 F F. 18.2.37; CSCD 1915/230, 15.2.15; CSCD 1914/157, 31.1.14.
40 CSCD 1915/622, 11.5.15.
41 F F. 14.5.37.
42 F B. 20.11.34.
43 CSCD 1923/463, 30.6.23.
44 Judith Wallace, *Memories of a Country Childhood*, University of Queensland Press, St Lucia, 1977, p. 26.
45 CSCD 1924/275, 13.5.24.
46 CSCD 1917/126, 26.1.17.
47 CSCD 1915/125, 23.1.15; F A. 31.10.32.
48 CSCD 1914/135, 30.1.14.
49 CSCD 1918/8, 27.12.17.
50 CSCD 1923/463, 22.6.23.
51 F A. 11.2.31.
52 F C. 22.2.37.
53 CSCD 1924/942, 15.8.24.
54 CSCD 1919/907, 10.2.19.
55 CSCD 1918/171, 8.3.18.
56 CSCD 1921/253, 15.4.21.
57 F C. 23.3.36.
58 CSCD 1921/194, 9.3.21.
59 CSCD 1921/194, 9.3.21.
60 F C. 23.3.3.6
61 CSCD 1919/905, 10.11.19.
62 CSCD 1919/479, 3.7.19.
63 F B. 28.10.35.
64 F A. 1.9.39. Leonore Davidoff mentions the continuing irrationality of housework in 'The Rationalization of housework', in Diana L. Barber and Sheila Allen (eds), *Dependence and Exploitation in Work and Marriage*, Longman, London, 1976, p. 143.
65 CSCD 1915/629, 15.5.15.
66 F A. 23.11.36.
67 F A. 5.5.38, H. Jackson, Inspector.
68 CSCD 1914/266, 23.2.14.
69 CSCD 1917/51, 12.1.17.
70 CSCD 1922/505, 9.8.22.

71 CSCD 1921/203, 10.12.21.
72 CSCD 1919/479, 24.6.19.
73 CSCD 1923/293, 23.4.23.
74 F A. 25.1.37.
75 F C. 5.5.39.
76 F C. 27.3.35.
77 CSCD 1919/914, 18.11.19; CSCD 1914/173, 7.2.14.
78 F A. 10.3.38.
79 F F. 25.1.38.
80 F E. 16.2.37.
81 H.A. Stirling, giving evidence, Q. 5669, 'Royal Commission on Law Reform,
    1926', p. 43.
82 F A. 15.2.30, Constance Davey to Secretary.
83 CSCD 1907/250, 8.3.07.
84 CSCD 1917/61, 15.1.17.
85 CSCD, A.21.2.34.
86 F B. 5.5.38.
87 CSCD 1922/333, E. Lapidge to Secretary.
88 CSCD 1914/64, 12.1.14.
89 F A. 19.5.39.
90 F B. 6.4.37; F. 12.3.40.
91 F F. 12.3.40.
92 CSCD 1926/134, Secretary to girl.
93 CSCD 1922/333, 31.3.22.
94 CSCD 1926/453, 21.6.26.
95 F B. 16.5.33.
96 F F. 15.6.36.
97 F E. 27.12.34.
98 F E. 14.4.36.
99 F 1914/582, 17.5.14.
 1 CSCD 1916/23, 3.1.16.
 2 CSCD 1915/289, 26.2.15.
 3 F E. 14.7.36.
 4 CSCD 1921/206, 23.12.21.
 5 CSCD 1926/453, 21.6.26.
 6 F A. 6.3.35.
 7 F B. 11.10.37.
 8 F F. 24.7.39.
 9 CSCD 1914/52, 9.1.14.
10 CSCD 1914/52, n.d.
11 F A. 29.1.36.
12 CSCD 1923/300, 25.6.23.
13 CSCD 1926/467, 17.6.26, Evelyn Penny to Secretary.
14 F B. 16.5.39.
15 F A. 19.1.39.
16 F 1914/188, 7.12.14.
17 F B. 20.12.39.
18 F A. 31.12.32.
19 F C. 14.11.35.

20 F B. 19.1.39.
21 The fund also paid for such things as insurance on the Boys' Memorial Hall at the Industrial School.
22 *Annual Report* of the CWPRD.
23 F C. 27.4.37.
24 CSCD 1917/90, 23.1.17, 'Regulations as to the higher education of State children'.
25 CSCD 1915/246, 7.2.15. This girl had a contract with the Education Department which was cancelled when an incriminating letter was found in her drawer.
26 CSCD 1916/570, 24.4.16. Education Department: Teachers Personnel History Files, South Australian Archives.
27 CSCD 1917/67, 15.1.17.

CHAPTER 7   ON BEARING A STIGMA 1887-1940

1 Catherine Helen Spence, quoted by F. and R. Hill in *Children of the State*, Macmillan, London, 1889, p. 242.
2 CSCD 1925/363, 2.12.26.
3 CSCD 1911/80, 12.1.11.
4 CSCD 1897/182, n.d.
5 CSCD 1901/1428, 26.11.01.
6 CSCD 1909/792, n.d.
7 CSCD 1904/452, 20.4.04.
8 CSCD 1913/130, n.d.
9 CSCD 1906/77, 29.1.06.
10 Being accused of stealing, or being told that state girls always 'went wrong' were merely two ways.
11 CSCD 1910/117, 19.10.10.
12 CSCD 1926/138, 26.2.26.
13 CSCD 1908/351, 22.3.08.
14 CSCD 1926/453, 21.6.26.
15 CSCD 1919/905, 19.1.20.
16 CSCD 1926/317, 4.6.26.
17 F A. 29.1.37, F.G. Byrne, Secretary, to girl.
18 F A. 6.1.38, F.G. Byrne, Secretary, to girl.
19 CSCD 1922/369, 27.6.22.
20 CSCD 1924/264, 16.7.25.
21 CSCD 1926/316, 12.5.26.
22 F A. 18.6.35; F B. 5.7.32.
23 CSCD 1923/466, 30.6.23.
24 C.H. Arnold, Superintendent of the Boys' Reformatory, giving evidence, Q. 5491, 'Royal Commission on Law Reform, 1926'.
25 CSCD 1918/2, 23.12.17.
26 CSCD 1915/93, 20.1.15.
27 CSCD 1925/173, 27.3.25.

28 CSCD 1919/109, 23.1.19.
29 CSCD 1926/325, 24.8.26.
30 F E. 7.7.37.
31 CSCD 1916/221, 11.2.16.
32 F B. 10.2.37.
33 F A. 18.3.35.
34 F F. 2.2.39.
35 F E. 16.2.37.
36 CSCD 1925/281, 22.5.25.
37 CSCD 1923/483, 31.8.23.
38 CSCD 1920/178, 24.2.20.
39 CSCD 1925/429, 13.8.25.
40 F E. -.7.37.
41 CSCD 1916/563, 25.4.16.
42 See J. Fitzpatrick, *The Bicycle and the Bush*, Oxford University Press, Melbourne, 1980.
43 CSCD 1914/42, Mistress to Secretary, n.d.
44 CSCD 1914/42, Secretary to Mistress, n.d.
45 CSCD 1916/553, 20.4.16.
46 F B. 3.8.39, '[foster-mother] has bought Ruth a bike so she can ride into work – Ruth does not find it too much and thinks it has helped her in many ways'.
47 F F. 27.1.37.
48 F E. 21.10.36, and A. 18.7.33.
49 F C. 11.5.37.
50 F C. 28.4.37; F A. 16.8.35.
51 F B. 1939.
52 F A. 28.6.36 and A. 19.6.39.
53 F F. 28.2.38.
54 F A. 17.3.37.
55 CCWPRD 1929/55, 26.1.29.
56 'Regulations of the SCC, 1887'.
57 There seems some reason for scepticism that the system, in fact, functions very differently. In a letter to the writer (19.6.80) Andrew Peake pointed out that even though the theoretical basis of modern foster-care is that it be short-term care and that contact with natural parents be encouraged (Community Welfare Act, Section 37, and the Department for Community Welfare's stated policy in *Foster Care*, Adelaide, 1976, p. 3), foster-care very often becomes long-term care with minimal parental contact. See *Quarterly Data Review*, Jan.–March 1977, Jan.–March 1978.
58 CSCD 1914/13, 31.2.14.
59 F A. 23.2.37.
60 CCWPRD 1928/119, 20.2.28.
61 CSCD 1919/907, 12.11.19.
62 F C. 18.11.38.
63 CSCD 1903/184, 9.2.02; CSCD 1890/916, 27.10.90.
64 CSCD 1902/522, 2.5.02.
65 CSCD 1908/489, n.d.
66 F B. 13.10.32.
67 CSCD 1924/104, 12.2.24.

68 CSCD 1900/184, 19.2.1900. Some parents quite clearly wanted financial support from absent daughters when applying for their release: 'She was always a good girl in bringing her wages home'.
69 CSCD 1927/406, 11.6.27. 'Your influence over Mary is most detrimental', Secretary to father.
70 CSCD 1919/46, 14.2.19.
71 CSCD 1919/121, 2.9.19.
72 CSCD 1903/247, 23.2.03.
73 CSCD 1891/654, 13.7.91.
74 CSCD 1901/843, 11.7.01.
75 CSCD 1906/343, 9.4.08.
76 An appropriate form of social control was sought after. See Release Applications.
77 CSCD 1906/81, 27.1.06.
78 CSCD 1904/953, 16.10.04.
79 CSCD 1909/748, 5.7.09.
80 CSCD 1902/45, 17.1.02.
81 CSCD 1904/257, 27.2.04.
82 CSCD 1912/153, 3.2.12.
83 CSCD 1925/173, 1.2.25.
84 CSCD 1923/461, 8.2.24.
85 CSCD A. 13.9.37.
86 CWPRD 1929/57, 8.6.28.
87 Ronald Mendelsohn, *The Condition of the People: Social Welfare in Australia, 1900–1975*, Allen and Unwin, Sydney, 1979, p. 100.
88 F C. 22.2.34.
89 F B. 5.5.38.
90 F A. 15.10.37.
91 F B. 4.8.36, F.G Byrne to foster-mother.
92 F A. 13.2.34; B. 22.2.30.
93 CSCD 1925/173 1.2.25.
94 F F. 19.2.37.
95 F F. 26.2.38.
96 CSCD 1918/119, 8.2.18.
97 F A. 23.11.32.
98 CCWPRD 1927/408, 25.8.28.
99 CSCD 1925/274, 24.7.25, Dr Fry to Secretary.
1 CCWPRD 1929/26, n.d.
2 Harriet Stirling, giving evidence, Q. 5623, 'Royal Commission on Law Reform, 1926', p. 41.
3 CSCD 1917/96, 21.1.17.
4 CSCD 1922/390, 11.6.22.
5 CSCD 1926/451, 6.7.26.
6 A sample of 100 Release Applications between 1918 and 1921 showed that about 12.5 per cent of all families applied for their children back. Of this 100, 40 were unsuccessful, 37 were released on probation, 8 were absolutely released, 3 were cancelled, and the rest were variously deferred.
7 Release Application 95, 1.3.20.
8 CSCD 1914/622, 20.5.14.

9 Release Application 16, 2.6.21.
10 Ibid., 62, 7.12.20.
11 Ibid., 90, 2.2.20.
12 Ibid., 91, 2.8.23.
13 Ibid., 99, 15.3.20.
14 CCWPRD 1928/91, 11.3.28.
15 CCWPRD 1929/31, 15.1.25.
16 CSCD 1921/259, 7.5.21.
17 CSCD 1911/41, 8.1.11. 'If my mother or sisters should happen to inquire my whereabouts I would be awfully obliged if you gave them no satisfaction'; CSCD 1905/273, 8.3.05, where the girl asked the Department whether her family were 'suitable people to go to'.
18 CCWPRD 1927/470, 14.2.28.
19 F F 31.7.37.
20 F E 31.8.37.
21 F B. 9.8.39.
22 CSCD 1919/874, 19.1.20.
23 F A. 4.12.33.
24 CSCD 1907 (docket number lost), 27.11.07.
25 CSCD 1916/19, 4.1.16.
26 CCWPRD 1928/53, 29.1.28.
27 CSCD 1902/376, 4.4.02.
28 CSCD 1902/831, 30.7.02.
29 CSCD 1901/1297, 27.10.01; CSCD 1900/192, 21.2.00.
30 CSCD 1904/213, 19.2.04.
31 CSCD 1901/1189, 4.10.01.
32 CSCD 1918/21, 5.1.18.
33 CSCD 1900/408, 24.4.1900.
34 CSCD 1903/144, 31.1.03.
35 CSCD 1910/298, 22.3.10.
36 CSCD 1890/1014, 27.11.90.
37 CSCD 1914/176, 10.2.14.
38 CSCD 1915/260, 21.2.15.
39 CSCD 1925/313, 28.5.25.
40 All information from *Commonwealth Censi* and *South Australian Year Books*.
41 CSCD 1920/173, 11.2.20; CSCD 1925/313, 28.5.25.
42 F A. 11.5.35.
43 F E. 27.12.34.
44 CCWPRD 1929/31, 15.1.25.
45 F A. 23.1.37.
46 CSCD 1919/708, 1.2.21.
47 CSCD 1918/98, 26.1.18.

CHAPTER 8 REFORMERS AND REFORMED 1860–1940

1 In a letter to the writer, Andrew Peake suggested a fourth wave of child welfare: 'the introduction of voluntary help for families rather than help after legal action has been taken for neglect or delinquency'.

2 Michael Rose, *The Relief of Poverty*, Macmillan, London, 1972, p. 8.
3 Susan Magarey, 'The Reclaimers: a Study of the Reformatory Movement in England and Wales 1846–1893', PhD thesis, Australian National University, Canberra 1975.
4 Nigel Middleton, *When Family Failed*, Victor Gollancz, London, 1971.
5 Ibid., p. 311.
6 'Report of the Select Committee of the Legislative Council on the Destitute Poor', *South Australian Parliamentary Papers*, 1867, Vol. 3, No. 91.
7 Leonora Ritter, 'Boarding-out in Australia', *Journal of the Royal Australian Historical Society*, September 1978.
8 It was believed, too, that boarding-out would be cheaper.
9 Brian Dickey has described these early years in more detail in a book being written on the history of social welfare in South Australia.
10 See C.E Clark, 'The Boarding-Out Society', in Catherine Helen Spence, *State Children in Australia*, Vardon & Sons, Adelaide, 1907, Ch. 2.
11 *Frasers Magazine*, September 1864, pp. 381–2.
12 While in Australia they lost no opportunity to advocate boarding-out. F. and R. Hill, *What We Saw in Australia*, Macmillan, London, 1875.
13 Jill Roe (ed.), *Social Policy in Australia: some perspectives 1901–1975*, Cassell, Melbourne, 1976.
14 Catherine Helen Spence, *An Autobiography*, W.K. Thomas, Adelaide, 1910, p. 106.
15 Florence and Rosamund Hill, *Children of the State*, Macmillan, London, 1889.
16 Ibid., p. 8.
17 Spence, *Autobiography*, p. 101.
18 C.E. Clark, 'The Boarding-Out Society', p. 14.
19 See, for example, Jeanne F. Young, *Catherine Helen Spence*, Lothian, 1937, p. 108; Elizabeth S.L. Govan, 'A Community Program of foster-home care: NSW 1881', *Social Service Review*, Vol. XXV, No. 3, September 1951, p. 375; J. Ramsland, 'The Development of Boarding-out in Australia', *Journal of the Royal Australian Historical Society*, Vol. 60, Pt 3, September 1974; Ritter, 'Boarding-out in Australia'.
20 Susan Magarey, 'A Study of Catherine Helen Spence', MA thesis, Australian National University, 1971, pp. 104, 116.
21 This argument was first advanced in Margaret Barbalet, 'State Children: Theory and Practice in South Australia 1918–28', MA thesis, Adelaide University, 1973.
22 Susan Magarey, 'A Study of Catherine Helen Spence'; the reputation of Annie Martin's School, p. 110 rests on evidence from descendants of the family.
23 For an account of the quickly acquired orthodoxy of the rest of the Hill family, see Deborah Gorham, 'Victorian Reform as a Family Business: The Hill Family' in Anthony S. Wohl (ed.), *The Victorian Family: Structure and Stresses*, Croom Helm, London, 1978.
24 F. and R. Hill, quoting C.H. Spence in *Children of the State*, p. 242.
25 The best description of this fear I have come across is in Gareth Steadman Jones, *Outcast London*, Peregrine Books, London, 1976.
26 Clark, 'The Boarding-Out Society', p. 14.

27 Frank J. Bruno, *Trends in Social Work*, Columbia University Press, New York, 1957.
28 E.S.L. Govan, 'A community program of foster-home care: NSW 1881', *Social Service Review*, Vol. XXV, No. 3, Sept. 1951, p. 375.
29 *Annual Report* of the SCC, 1905.
30 Efforts were made, however, by C.E. Clark and C.H. Spence in 1905 to stop the practice of sending boys to the Reformatory for a short time if they were unable to pay a fine, but the government of the day declined any action.
31 Thomas Rhodes, Chairman's Address, State Children's Convention, Adelaide, 1907.
32 See Appendix 1 for a list of Council members.
33 Harriet Stirling, President of the State Children's Council, giving evidence, Q. 5585, Royal Commission on Law Reform, 1926, stated that she, Mrs Hone, and Mrs Goode, had all employed state children in the past.
34 Rhodes, Chairman's Address.
35 F. and R. Hill, *What We Saw in Australia*, Macmillan, London, 1875, p. 146.
36 'Final Report of the Destitute Commission, 1885', Pt II, Children Under the Care of the Government, *South Australian Parliamentary Papers*, 1885, Vol. 4, No. 228, p. LXIII.
37 *Annual Report* of the SCC, 1889.
38 James Smith, quoted in Hill, *Children of the State*, p. 241.
39 'Final Report of the Destitute Commission', p. LXIII.
40 Clark, 'The Boarding-Out Society', p. 17.
41 Middleton, *When Family Failed*, p. 45.
42 Anthony Platt, *The Child Savers*, University of Chicago Press, 1969, p. 139.
43 *Annual Report* of the SCC, 1898.
44 See Constance M. Davey, *Children and their Lawmakers*, Griffin Press, Adelaide, 1956, p. 23.
45 Susan Magarey, 'The Invention of Juvenile Delinquency in early Nineteenth Century England', *Labour History*, No. 34, May 1978.
46 'Final Report of the Destitute Commission, 1885', Vol. 4, No. 22, p. LXIII.
47 ANU Press, 1965.
48 Catherine Helen Spence was probably the poorest member of this group. The third Council included Lady Colton, Lady Downer, Lady Bonython, and Lady Way.
49 G. William Domhoff, *The Higher Circles*, Random House, New York, 1970, p. 35.
50 Platt, *Child Savers*, p. 78.
51 C.H. Spence thought this the best argument for universal education. See Magarey, 'A Study of Catherine Helen Spence', p. 140.
52 'Regulations of the SCC', 1887.
53 Leonore Davidoff, 'Landscape with Figures', in J. Mitchell and A. Oakley (eds), *The Rights and Wrongs of Women*, Penguin, Harmondsworth, 1976, p. 156.
54 Service Application 12039, 6.7.18.
55 Leonore Davidoff, *The Best Circles*, Croom Helm, London, 1977, p. 40.
56 Anna Davin, 'Imperialism and Motherhood', *History Workshop*, Issue 5, Spring 1978.

57 Andrew Peake, 'The State Children's Council 1886–1895: Welfare Development – Innovation or Imitation', Development of Social Work Essay, Flinders University, July 1980, p. 12.

58 In 1911 a printed brochure outlining the work of the SCC stated that the work of probation was 'comparatively new'.

59 See Brian Dickey, 'Care for Deprived, Neglected and Delinquent Children in N.S.W. 1901–1915', Journal of the Royal Australian Historical Society, Vol. 63, No. 3, Dec. 1977.

60 Annual Report of the SCC, 1913.

61 In 1911 the SCC assumed control of all the state's 'neglected illegitimate, aboriginal half-caste, quadroon and octoroon children', Annual Report of the SCC, 1911. The 1910 Annual Report gives examples of classic contemporary racism.

62 Annual Report of the SCC, 1913.

63 Dr J.M. Tregenza first suggested this comparison to me.

64 Reed's parsimony resulted in the maximum amount of instability for children.

65 This was not adoption in the modern sense, but merely placing a child without any subsidy at all.

66 Sometimes known as the Way Commission after its chairman, Chief Justice Way.

67 'Final Report of the Destitute Commission, 1885', Vol. 4, No. 228.

68 Ibid., p. XLV.

69 Ibid., p. L.

70 Ibid., p. XLIX.

71 Spence, Autobiography, p. 23.

72 Reports of the Society for the Supervision of Children Placed Out, 1875.

73 George Guillaume, quoted by John Tregenza in Professor of Democracy, Melbourne University Press, 1968, p. 168.

74 Davey, Children and their Lawmakers, p. 17.

75 A clear majority of children from the total number under the Council's control were boarded-out from 1887–1906.

76 Dr Stirling and James Smith declined re-appointment.

77 Spence, Autobiography, p. 31.

78 For the report, see CSCD 1906/243, 12.3.06.

79 CSCD 1923/287, 13.2.24.

80 Peake, 'State Children's Council', p. 22.

81 South Australian Government Gazette, 31.12.78.

82 CSCD 1906/243, n.d.

83 Some children were even less able to complain as they were illiterate or mentally handicapped.

84 CSCD 1908/377, 28.3.08.

85 CSCD 1902/742, 1.7.02.

86 Annual Report of the SCC, 1911.

87 See Chapter 6.

88 See, for example, Pamela Horn, The Rise and Fall of the Victorian Servant, Gill & Macmillan, Dublin, 1975, p. 34; Frank Huggett, Life Below Stairs, John Murray, London, 1977, p. 110.

89 See the 'Report of the Shops and Factories Commission'.

90 Susan M. Horan, '"More Sinned Against than Sinning"', BA Hons thesis, Flinders University, 1977–8, p. 15.
91 *Annual Report* of the SCC, 1940.
92 'Regulations of the SCC', 1887.
93 Anna Davin, 'Women in History' in Michelene Wandor (comp.), *The Body Politic*, Penguin, Hardmondsworth, 1972, p. 220.
94 Ann Curthoys, 'Towards a Feminist Labour History', in A. Curthoys *et al.*, *Women at Work*, Australian Society for the Study of Labour History, Canberra, 1975, p. 93.
95 Calculated from South Australian *Year Books* and *Report of Factories and Steam Boilers Department*.
96 CSCD 1923/456, 6.1.25, Deputy Commissioner, Repatriation Commission to SCC.
97 Daniels, *Women in Australia*. Vol. 1, p. 52, 'Minutes of the Girl's Industrial School'.
98 CSCD 1922/333, 19.4.22.
99 CSCD 1926/134, 18.2.26 re 'stealing'; 1922/502, 9.8.22 re 'finery'.
 1 Bonython, Lady Constance Jean, *I'm No Lady*, (C. Warren Bonython, ed.) Ch. 5.
 2 CCWPRD 1928/88, 17.3.28.
 3 R.J. Lawrence, *Professional Social Work in Australia*, ANU Press, Canberra, 1965, p. 18.
 4 Ibid., p. 28.
 5 A. Grenfell-Price, *Nursing in South Australia: The First Hundred Years*, Hunkin, Ellis & King, 1939.
 6 Edith S. Abbott, *Everybody's friend: The Inspiring Career of Kate Cocks*, M.B.E., Hassell Press, Adelaide, 1939, p. 9.
 7 CSCD 1926/330, 25.1.27.
 8 CSCD 1922/332, 1.6.22.
 9 CSCD 1924/114, 13.6.24.
10 CSCD 1924/119, 2.2.24, A.M. Kentish to Secretary.
11 CSCD 1927/433, 30.8.27.
12 CSCD 1901/460, n.d.
13 See Spence, *State Children*, p. 111.
14 CSCD 1923/248, 11.5.23.
15 CSCD 1921/218, 28.4.21.
16 CSCD 1923/452, 14.6.23.
17 CSCD 1922/360, 15.11.27.
18 CSCD 1918/51, 18.1.18.
19 It would be pointless to list Correspondence numbers for these. Examples are found throughout the files.
20 CSCD 1918/187, 15.2.18.
21 CSCD 1921/264, n.d.
22 CSCD 1918/229, 12.3.18, 'Surely man there is some spark of feeling left in you. Now just understand that if you do not straighten yourself up at once the children will be recalled and you summoned for their maintenance', Secretary to a father.
23 CSCD 1923/509, 24.7.23.
24 CSCD 1923/343, 16.6.23.

25 CSCD 1922/382, 30.6.22, E. Lee writing of a father who was an invalid.
26 CSCD 1919/922, 12.2.20.
27 Release Application 1919/17, 2.9.19.
28 Ibid.
29 CSCD 1921/218, 28.4.21.
20 Release Application 1919/23, 4.5.19.
31 Ibid., 1919/31, 8.4.27.
32 CSCD 1926/1368, 28.7.27.
33 CCWPRD 1927/448, 25.8.27.
34 CSCD 1919/121, 7.7.19.
35 CCWPRD 1927/409, 12.8.27, for example.
36 Release Application 1918/21, 14.3.18.
37 CSCD 1924/280, 7.7.27.
38 CSCD 1918/30, 20.7.18.
39 CSCD 1923/540, 16.8.23.
40 CSCD 1922/373, n.d.
41 CSCD 1918/229, 1.3.18.
42 F A. 9.2.37.
43 Lawrence, *Professional Social Work*, p. 29.
44 *Annual Report* of the CWPRD, 1946.
45 A.A. Edwards, Q. 5561, Royal Commission on Law Reform, 1926, p. 37.
46 Unpublished article by Suzanne Edgar.
47 PRG 104, South Australian Archives, Martha Crompton to Constance Davey, 9.7.56. Two members of the Davenport and Goode families had also held office on the SCC.
48 This had the power to order transfers to and from institutions; see p. 6 of 'Report of SCC', CSCD 1926/463.
49 South Australian Parliamentary Debates, 1923, p. 1028.
50 Royal Commission on Law Reform, 1923, p. 64, Q. 1413.
51 Ibid., p. 131, Q. 2519.
52 Ibid., 1926, p. 38, Q. 5560.
53 These charges were also made to the 1885 Royal Commission.
54 Royal Commission on Law Reform, 1926, p. 26. Q. 5391.
55 Ibid., Q. 5389. One probationary officer had to act as clerk.
56 Ibid., Q. 5318.
57 Ibid., Q. 5181.
58 Ibid., Q. 5179.
59 Ibid., Q. 5585.
60 Ibid., Q. 5664.
61 Ibid., Q. 5331.
62 Ibid., 1926, Q. 5535.
63 Ibid., Q. 5549.
64 Ibid., Q. 5551.
65 Kathleen M. Forwood, 'The Maintenance Act of 1926', Development of Social Work Essay, Flinders University, July 1980, deals with the bill in detail.
66 Miss Stirling, Mrs Goode, and Mrs Christophers had argued that women possessed 'innate' feminine sympathies that made training unnecessary.
67 Royal Commission on Law Reform, 1926, p. 41, Q. 5621.
68 Ibid., Q. 5605.

69 Ibid., Q. 5585.
70 Any sum was to cease on a child's fourteenth birthday except in special circumstances.
71 In 1940 they were still serving on the Board.
72 The members of the committee were Constance Davey, H.G. Alderman, H. Kenneth Fry, Wm. J. Adey, and Charlotte M. Leal.
73 By the time the report was printed war had intervened once again to displace idealism and innovation.
74 'Report of the Committee appointed by the Government to Inquire into Delinquent and other Children in the Care of the State', *South Australian Parliamentary Papers*, 1939, Vol. 2, No. 75, p. 8.
75 Ibid., p. 12.
76 Ibid.
77 Ibid.
78 Ibid., p. 14.
79 Ibid., p. 13.
80 Ibid., p. 15.
81 Ibid.
82 Ibid., p. 22.
83 Ibid., p. 23.
84 Ibid., p. 24.
85 Ibid., p. 41.

BIBLIOGRAPHY

Primary Sources

Unpublished material from the State Children's Department (located in the South Australian Archives)

Applications for the Release of Children from the Council's Control, 1914–21.

Applications to the State Children's Department for A Child to be Boarded-out or for Service, 1918–22.

Correspondence of the State Children's Department, 1887–1927.

Court Mandates committing Children to the Custody and Control of the Council, 1918–27.

Files relating to children under Departmental supervision and released in the 1940s and 1950s.

Ledgers of Children Boarded-Out, 1893, 1918–20.

Records of the visiting officer to licensed foster-mothers, 1890, 1898, 1909.

Reports and Correspondence concerning Foster-mothers and Applicants, 1918–28.

Returns of Children in the Care of the Department, 1927–28.

Published Reports and Official Papers

'Annual Reports of the State Children's Council and Children's Welfare and Public Relief Department', 1887–1940, *South Australian Parliamentary Papers*.

Australian Bureau of Statistics, *Persons under Guardianship and Children in Substitute Care*, June 1979, No. 4405.0.

'The Building Act Inquiry Committee, Second Progress Report', *South Australian Parliamentary Papers*, 1940, Vol. 2, Paper 32.

Census of the Commonwealth of Australia, 1901, 1911, 1921, 1947.

Children's Bureau of Australia, 'Families Helping Families', in Mary McLelland (ed.), *Proceedings of the Australian Foster Care Conference*, IYC, Sydney, 1979.

'The Destitute Commission Final Report, Part II, Children under the Care of the Government', *South Australian Parliamentary Papers*, 1885, Vol. 4, No. 228.

'Half-Yearly Reports of the Destitute Poor Board', 1860–87, *South Australian Government Gazette*.

Minutes of Evidence of the Royal Commission on the Basic Wage, Government Printer, Melbourne, 1920.

Printed Material and Regulations re Child Welfare 1895–1926. (Held by SAA.)

'Report of State Children's Council re Criticism by one of its Members', *South Australian Parliamentary Papers*, 1926, Vol. 2, No. 75.

'Report of the Committee appointed by the Government to Inquire into Delinquent and other Children in the Care of the State', *South Australian Parliamentary Papers*, 1939, Vol. 2, No. 75.

'Report of the Royal Commission on the Basic Wage', 1920, *Australian Parliamentary Papers*, 1920–21, Vol. 4, pp. 529–646.

'Report of the Select Committee of the Legislative Council on the Destitute Poor', *South Australian Parliamentary Papers*, 1867, Vol. 3, No. 91.

'Report of the Shops and Factories Commission together with minutes of proceedings, evidence and appendices', *South Australian Parliamentary Papers*, 1892, Vol. 2, No. 37.

Reports of the Society for the Supervision of Children Placed-out from the Magill Institution by the Destitute Board, 1872–86. (Held by SAA.)

'Reports on Lessening the Evils of Prostitution', *South Australian Parliamentary Papers*, 1867, Vol. 3, No. 86.

'The Royal Commission on Law Reform, Progress Reports, 1923–27', *South Australian Parliamentary Papers*.

'The Royal Commission on Penal and Prison Discipline, Third Report, Industrial and Reformatory Schools', *Victorian Parliamentary Papers*, 1872, Vol. 3, No. 55.

'The Secretary's Report of a Visit made by the President and himself to the Industrial and Reformatory Schools in Victoria and New South Wales', *South Australian Parliamentary Papers*, 1887, Vol. 3, No. 39.

'State Children's Council – Correspondence re Statement of Mr Ryan', *South Australian Parliamentary Papers*, 1915, Vol. 3, No. 113.

'State Children's Council Regulations', *South Australian Parliamentary Papers*, 1887, Vol. 3, No. 38.

Secondary Sources

Contemporary Books

ABBOTT, Edith S., *Everybody's Friend: the Inspiring Career of Kate Cocks MBE*, Hassell Press, Adelaide, 1939.

ACKERMANN, Jessie, *Australia from a Woman's Point of View*, Cassell, London, 1913.

BAYNTON, Barbara, *Human Toll*, Duckworth & Co., London, 1907.

BROWN, Louise, *et al.* (eds), *A Book of South Australia: Women in the First Hundred Years*, Women's Centenary Council of South Australia, Adelaide, 1936.

CAMBRIDGE, Ada, *Thirty Years in Australia*, Methuen, London, 1903.

CHANDLER, C.A., *Darkest Adelaide and Sidelights of City Life*, Adelaide, 1907.

COGHLAN, T.A., *Labour and Industry in Australia*, 4 vols, 1918, reprinted Macmillan, Melbourne, 1969.

ELDERSHAW, F.P. (ed.), *The Peaceful Army: a Memorial to the Pioneer Women of Australia, 1788–1938*, Women's Executive Committee and Advisory Council of Australia's 150th anniversary celebrations, Sydney, 1938.

HIGGINS, Henry Bournes, *A New Province for Law and Order*, Constable, London, 1922.

HILL, Florence Davenport, *Children of the State: the training of juvenile paupers*, Macmillan, London, 1868.

HILL, Florence and Hill, Rosamund, *Children of the State*, Macmillan, London, 1889.

HILL, Rosamund Davenport and Florence Davenport, *What We Saw in Australia*, Macmillan, London, 1875.
PIDDINGTON, A.B., *The Next Step: A Family Basic Income*, Macmillan, Melbourne, 1921.
PYKE, Lillian M., *Australian Etiquette*, The Specialty Press, Melbourne, 1931.
REEVES, Maud Pember, *Round About a Pound a Week*, Virago, London, 1979.
SPENCE, Catherine Helen, *An Autobiography*, W.K. Thomas, Co., Adelaide, 1910.
——, *Clara Morison*, Rigby, Adelaide 1971.
——, *State Children in Australia*, Vardon & Sons, Adelaide, 1907.
TROLLOPE, A., *Australia*, (P.D. Edwards & R.B. Joyce, eds), University of Queensland Press, St Lucia, 1967.
TWOPENY, Richard Earnest Nowell, *Town Life in Australia*, E. Stock, London, 1883.
YOUNG, Jeanne F., *Catherine Helen Spence*, The Lothian Publishing Co., Melbourne and Sydney, 1937.
——, *Dependent Children, Interstate Congress of Workers*, Adelaide, May 1909. (SAA)
——, *State Children's Convention*, Adelaide, 1907. (SAA)

Contemporary Articles

ALCOCK, F.A., 'Alice', *Lone Hand*, 1 April 1908.
ANDERSON, Maybanke, 'The Women's Movement', in Atkinson, M. (ed.), *Australia: Economic & Political Studies*, Macmillan, Melbourne, 1920.
COBBE, Frances Power, 'The Philosophy of the Poor Laws and the Report of the Committee on Poor Relief', *Frasers Magazine*, September 1864, pp. 373–94.
GARLAND, Tom, *The Slums of Adelaide*, 1942.
SPENCE, Catherine Helen, 'Heredity and Environment', Paper delivered before and printed at the request of the Criminological Society of South Australia, 23 October 1897.
——, *State Children's Council Administration also Description of Institutions controlled by the Council*, Adelaide, 1911. (SAA)

Modern Books

ARIES, Philippe, *Centuries of Childhood*, Penguin, Harmondsworth, 1960.
BARBALET, Margaret, *The Adelaide Children's Hospital 1876–1976*, Griffin Press, Adelaide, 1975.
BONHEUR, Leigh, *Hand Me Down: the autobiography of an illegitimate child*, Ure Smith, Sydney, 1971.
BONYTHON, Lady Constance Jean, *I'm No Lady*, Bonython, C. Warren (ed.), Adelaide, 1977.
BRANCA, Patricia, *Silent Sisterhood*, Croom Helm, London, 1975.
BRIGGS, A. and Saville, J. (eds), *Essays in Labour History*, Macmillan, London, 1960.
BROWN, Joan C., *'Poverty is not a crime': the development of social services in Tasmania 1803–1900*, Tasmanian Historical Research Association, Hobart, 1972.

BRUNO, Frank J., *Trends in Social Work 1874–1956*, Columbia University Press, New York, 1957.

BURNETT, John, *Useful Toil: autobiographies of working people from the 1820s to the 1920s*, Allen Lane, London, 1974.

COOPER, Janet, *Catherine Helen Spence*, Oxford University Press, Melbourne, 1972.

CURTHOYS, Ann, Eade, Susan, and Spearritt, Peter (eds), *Women at Work*, Australian Society for the Study of Labour History, Canberra, 1975.

DANIELS, Kay, *Women in Australia: An Annotated Guide to Records*, 2 vols, Australian Government Publishing Service, Canberra, 1977.

DAVEY, Constance M., *Children and their Lawmakers*, Griffin Press, Adelaide, 1956.

DAVIDOFF, Leonore, *The Best Circles*, Croom Helm, London, 1977.

DAWES, Francis Edwards, *Not in Front of the Servants: Domestic Service in England 1850–1939*, Wayland, London, 1973.

DEMAUSE, Lloyd (ed.), *The History of Childhood*, Psychohistory Press, New York, 1974.

DICKEY, Brian, *No Charity There*, Nelson, Melbourne, 1980.

DIXON, Miriam, *The Real Matilda: Woman and Identity in Australia 1788 to 1975*, Pelican, Ringwood, Vic., 1976.

DOMHOFF, G. William, *The Higher Circles*, Random House, New York, 1970.

FOAKES, Grace, *My Part of the River and Between High Walls*, Futura, London, 1976.

FRIED, A. and Elman, R.M., *Charles Booth's London*, Hutchinson, London, 1969.

GIALLOMBARDO, Rose, *The Social World of Imprisoned Girls*, John Wiley and Sons, New York, 1974.

HARTMAN, Mary and Banner, Lois (eds), *Clio's Consciousness Raised*, Harper & Row, New York, 1974.

HASLUCK, Alexandra, (ed.), *Audrey Tennyson's Vice-Regal Days*, National Library of Australia, Canberra, 1978.

HAWES, Joseph M., *Children in Urban Society: Juvenile Delinquency in Nineteenth Century America*, Oxford University Press, New York, 1971.

HAY, R.J., *The Origins of the Liberal Welfare Reforms 1906–1914*, Macmillan, London, 1975.

HECHT, J.J., *The Domestic Servant Class in Eighteenth Century England*, Routledge and Kegan Paul, London, 1956.

HENRY, F.S., *The Garden Suburb*, Library of the State Planning Office, Adelaide, 1942.

HICKS, Neville, *'This Sin and Scandal': Australia's Population Debate 1891–1911*, ANU Press, Canberra, 1978.

HIRST, J.B., *Adelaide and the Country 1870–1914: their Social and Political Relationship*, Melbourne University Press, 1973.

HORN, Pamela, *The Rise and Fall of the Victorian Servant*, Gill & Macmillan, Dublin, 1975.

HUGGETT, Frank, *Life Below Stairs: Domestic Servants in England from Victorian Times*, John Murray, London, 1977.

JENKINS, Shirley and Norman, Elaine, *Filial Deprivation and Foster Care*, Columbia University Press, New York and London, 1972.

JOHNSTON, George, *My Brother Jack*, Collins, London, 1964.

KEATING, M., *The Australian Workforce 1910–11 to 1960–61*, Progress Press, Canberra, 1973.

KEWLEY, T.J., *Social Security in Australia, 1900–1972*, Sydney University Press, 1965.

KINGSTON, Beverley, *My Wife, My Daughter and Poor Mary Ann*, Nelson, Melbourne, 1975.

——, *The World Moves Slowly: a documentary history of Australian women*, Cassell, Sydney, 1977.

LASCH, C., *Haven in a Heartless World: the Family Besieged*, Basic Books, New York, 1977.

——, *The New Radicalism in America 1889–1963: the intellectual as a social type*, Knopf, New York, 1965.

LAWRENCE, R.J., *Professional Social Work in Australia*, ANU Press, Canberra, 1965.

McBRIDE, Theresa, *The Domestic Revolution: the Modernisation of Household Service in England and France 1820–1920*, Holmes & Meier Publications Inc., New York, 1976.

MACKINOLTY, Judy (ed.), *In Pursuit of Justice*, Hale and Iremonger, Sydney, 1979.

MANSFIELD, Katherine, *Collected Stories*, Constable, London, 1964.

MATTINSON, Janet, *Marriage and Mental Handicap*, Duckworth, London, 1970.

MENDELSOHN, Ronald, *The Condition of the People: Social Welfare in Australia 1900–1975*, George Allen and Unwin, Sydney, 1979.

MERCER, Jan, *The Other Half: Women in Australian Society*, Penguin, Ringwood, Vic., 1975.

MIDDLETON, Nigel, *When Family Failed*, Gollancz, London, 1971.

MURNANE, Mary and Daniels, Kay (eds), *Uphill All the Way*, University of Queensland Press, St Lucia, 1980.

NATHAN, Edward Cohen, *Social Work in the American Tradition*, Amyden Press, New York, 1958.

OAKLEY, Ann, *Housewife*, Penguin, Harmondsworth, 1974.

——, *The Sociology of Housework*, Martin Robertson, London, 1974.

PLATT, Anthony M., *The Child Savers: the invention of delinquency*, University of Chicago Press, 1969.

PORTER, Hal, *The Watcher on the Cast-Iron Balcony*, Faber, London, 1963.

RADI, Heather and Spearritt, Peter (eds), *Jack Lang*, Hale & Iremonger, Sydney, 1977.

ROE, Jill (ed.), *Social Policy in Australia: some Perspectives 1901–1975*, Cassell, Sydney, 1976.

ROSE, Hilary and Steven (eds), *Political Economy of Science*, Macmillan, London, 1976.

ROSE, Michael E., *The Relief of Poverty 1834–1914*, Macmillan, London, 1972.

ROSEN, Ruth and Davidson, Sue (eds), *The Maimie Papers*, Virago, London, 1979.

ROVER, Constance, *Love, Morals and the Feminists*, Routledge & Kegan Paul, London, 1970.

ROWBOTHAM, Sheila, *Hidden from History*, Pluto Press, London, 1973.

ROWE, Janet, *Parents, Children and Adoption: a Handbook for Adoption Workers*, Routledge & Kegan Paul, London, 1966.

ROYSLAND, Dorothy, *A Pioneer Family on the Murray River*, Rigby, Adelaide, 1977.

RYAN, Edna and Conlon, Anne, *Gentle Invaders: Australian Women at Work 1788–1974*, Nelson, Melbourne, 1975.

SPEARRITT, Peter, *Sydney Since the Twenties*, Hale and Iremonger, Sydney, 1978.

SUMMERS, Anne, *Damned Whores and God's Police*, Penguin, Ringwood, Vic., 1975.

TEALE, Ruth, *Colonial Eve: Sources on Women in Australia 1788–1914*, Oxford University Press, Melbourne, 1978.

TOBIAS, J.J., *Crime and Industrial Society in the 19th Century*, David and Charles, London, 1967.

TOD, Robert (ed.), *Social Work in Foster Care: Collected Papers*, Longman, London, 1971.

TOWNSEND, Peter (ed.), *The Concept of Poverty*, Heinemann, London, 1970.

TREGENZA, John, *Professor of Democracy*, Melbourne University Press, 1968.

WALLACE, Judith, *Memories of a Country Childhood*, University of Queensland Press, St Lucia, 1977.

WHITELOCK, Derek, *Adelaide 1836–1976: a history of difference*, University of Queensland Press, St Lucia, 1977.

WILLIS, Sabine, *Women, Faith and Fetes*, Dove Publications, Melbourne, 1977.

WOODRUFFE, Kathleen, *From Charity to Social Work*, Routledge & Kegan Paul, London, 1962.

Modern Articles

ABEL-SMITH, Brian and Townsend, Peter, 'The Poor and the Poorest', *Occasional Papers on Social Administration*, No. 17, 1966.

ALEXANDER, Sally and Davin, Anna, 'Feminist History', *History Workshop 1*, Spring 1976.

ALEXANDER, Sally, 'Women's Work in nineteenth century London: a study of the years 1820–50', in Mitchell, Juliet, *The Rights and Wrongs of Women*, Penguin, Harmondsworth, 1976.

BRANCA, 'A New Perspective on Women's Work: a Comparative Typology', *Journal of Social History*, Vol. 9, Winter 1975.

BROWN, R.G., 'Poverty in Australia – The Evidence', *British Journal of Sociology*, Vol. XV, No. 2, June 1964.

BROWNE, Elspeth, 'Knowledge, Skills and the System', *Australian Social Work*, Vol. 29, No. 3, Sept. 1976. (A review of the Report of the Committee of Inquiry into the Care and Supervision Provided in Relation to Maria Colwell.)

CAMERON, Barbara, 'The Flappers and the Feminists: a Study of Women's Emancipation in the 1920's', *Women and Labour Conference Papers*, 1980.

CLAREY, J.J., 'Juvenile Crime: its treatment', *Australian Quarterly*, Vol. XI, No. 3, Sept. 1939.

COWAN, Ruth Schwartz, 'A case study of technological and social change: the washing machine and the working wife', in Hartman, M. and Banner, L., *Clio's Consciousness Raised*, Harper & Row, New York, 1974.

CURTHOYS, Ann, 'Towards a Feminist Labour History', in Curthoys, A., Eade, S. and Spearritt, P. (eds), *Women at Work*, Australian Society for the Study of Labour History, Canberra, 1975.

DAVIDOFF, Leonore, 'Landscape with Figures: Home and Community in English Society', in Mitchell, J. and Oakley, Anne (eds), *The Rights and Wrongs of Women*, Penguin, Harmondsworth, 1976.

——, 'The rationalization of housework', in Barber, Diana L. and Allen, Sheila (eds), *Dependence and Exploitation in Work and Marriage*, Longman, London, 1976.

——, 'Mastered for Life: Servant and Wife in Victorian England', *Journal of Social History*, Vol. 7, No. 4, June 1974.

DAVIN, Anna, 'Imperialism and Motherhood', *History Workshop*, Issue 5, Spring 1978.

——, 'Women and History', in Wandor, Michelene (comp.), *The Body Politic*, Stage 1, London, 1972.

DICKEY, Brian, 'Care for Deprived, Neglected and Delinquent Children in N.S.W. 1901–1915', *Journal of the Royal Australian Historical Society*, Vol. 63, Pt 3, Dec. 1977.

——, 'Evolution of care for Destitute Children in NSW 1875–1901', *Journal of Australian Studies*, No. 4, June 1979.

——, 'Health and the State in Australia 1788–1977', *Journal of Australian Studies*, No. 2, Nov 1977.

——, 'Industrial Schools and Reformatories in New South Wales 1850–1875', *Journal of the Royal Australian Historical Society*, Vol. 54, Pt 2, June 1968.

DUNNING, Becky, 'Being Poor and Female in Colonial Western Australia', *Hecate*, Vol. III, No. 2, July 1977.

GILBERT, Dorothy, 'Country Life in the Later Nineteenth Century: Reminiscences by Dorothy Gilbert', *South Australiana*, Vol. XII, No. 2.

GOLDNER, Hilary and Allen, Judith, 'Prostitution in New South Wales 1870–1932: Restructuring an Industry', *Refractory Girl*, Dec. 1979–Jan. 1980.

GORHAM, Deborah, 'Victorian Reform as a Family Business: The Hill Family', in Wohl, A.S. (ed.), *The Victorian Family: Structure and Stresses*, Croom Helm, London, 1978.

GOVAN, Elizabeth, S.L., 'A community program of foster-home care: NSW 1881', *Social Service Review*, Vol. XXV, No. 3, Sept. 1951.

HIMMELFARB, Gertrude, 'The Culture of Poverty', in Dyos, H.J. and Wolff, M., *The Victorian City: Images and Realities*, Routledge & Kegan Paul, London, 1973.

HORSBURGH, Michael, 'Child Care in NSW in 1870', *Australian Journal of Social Work*, Vol. 29, No. 1, March 1976.

——, 'Child Care in New South Wales in 1890', *Australian Social Work*, Vol. 30, No. 3, September 1977.

——, 'Randwick Asylum: Organisational Resistance to Social Change', *Australian Social Work*, Vol. 30, No. 1, March 1977.

——, 'Subsidy and Control: Social Welfare Activities of the New South Wales Government, 1858–1910', *Journal of Australian Studies*, No. 2, Nov. 1977.

——, 'The Apprenticing of Dependent Children in N.S.W. between 1850 and 1885', *Journal of Australian Studies*, No. 7, 1980.

HYSLOP, Anthea, 'Agents and Objects: Women and Social Reform in Melbourne, 1890 to 1914', *Women and Labour Conference Papers*, 1980.

KENNEDY, Sally, 'Australian Untouchables: domestic servants in W.A., 1920–40', *Hecate*, Vol. V, No. 2, 1979.

KINGSTON, Beverley, 'Poor Mary Ann: Domestic Service as a career for Girls in Australia during the Nineteenth Century', *Refractory Girl*, Summer 1974–75.

MACPHAIL, Janet and Taylor, Helen, 'Oral History: A Vital Dimension in the History of Women', *Women and Labour Conference Papers*, 1980.

BIBLIOGRAPHY

MAGAREY, Susan, 'The Invention of Juvenile Delinquency in early Nineteenth Century England', *Labour History*, No. 34, May 1978.

MARKEY, R., 'Women and Labour 1880–1900', *Women and Labour Conference Papers*, 1978.

MARKS, Pauline, 'Femininity in the Classroom: An Account of Changing Attitudes', in Mitchell, J. and Oakley, A. (eds), *The Rights and Wrongs of Women*, Penguin, Harmondsworth, 1976.

MILKMAN, Ruth, 'Women's Work and the Economic Crisis: Some Lessons from the Great Depression', *Review of Radical Political Economics*, Vol. 8, No. 1, Spring 1976.

MOZLEY, A., 'Oral History', *Historical Studies*, Vol. 12, No. 48, April 1967.

NANCE, Christopher, 'The Irish in South Australia during the Colony's First Four Decades', *Journal of the Historical Society of S.A.*, No. 5, 1978.

NEWBY, H., 'The Deferential Dialectic', *Comparative Studies in Society and History*, Vol. 17, No. 1, 1975.

POWER, Margaret, 'The Making of a Women's Occupation', *Hecate*, Vol. 1, No. 2, July 1975.

——, 'Women and Economic Crises: the great depression and the present crisis', *Women and Labour Conference Papers*, 1978.

PRITCHETT, V.S., 'The Culture of Hopelessness', *New Statesman*, 10 Dec. 1971.

RADI, Heather, 'Womens Work: Varieties of Drudgery', *Refractory Girl*, No. 10, March 1976.

RAMSLAND, J., 'The Development of Boarding-out Systems in Australia', *Journal of the Royal Australian Historical Society*, Vol. 60, Pt 3, Sept. 1974.

REIGER, Kereen, 'Women's Labour Redefined: child bearing and rearing advice in Australia, 1880–1930s', *Women and Labour Conference Papers*, 1978.

RITTER, Leonard, 'Boarding-out in N.S.W. and S.A.: Adoption, adaption or innovation', *Journal of the Royal Australian Historical Society*, Vol. 64, Pt 2, Sept. 1978.

ROE, Jill, 'What R & F Hill saw in Australia', *Women and History*, History Teachers Association of N.S.W., February 1976.

SOMMERVILLE, C. John, 'Towards a History of Childhood and Youth', *Journal of Interdisciplinary History*, Vol. 3, 1972.

SPEARRITT, Peter, 'The Kindergarten Movement: tradition and change', in Edgar, D.E. (ed.), *Social Change in Australia: Readings in Sociology*, Cheshire, Melbourne, 1974.

SUMMERS, Anne, 'A home from home – Women's philanthropic work in the nineteenth century', in Burman, Sandra (ed.), *Fit Work for Women*, Croom Helm, London, 1979.

TAY, F., 'The Administration of Social Service Provisions for Underprivileged Children in Western Australia 1947–54', in Roe, Jill (ed.), *Social Policy in Australia*, Cassell, Melbourne, 1976.

THOMPSON, E.P., 'Patrician Society, Plebian Culture', *Journal of Social History*, Vol. 7, No. 4, Summer 1974.

THOMPSON, Janna, 'Housework and Technological Change', *Women and Labour Conference Papers*, 1978.

TRUDGILL, Eric, 'Prostitution and Paterfamilias', in Dyos, H.J. and Wolff, M. (eds), *The Victorian City: Images and Realities*, Routledge & Kegan Paul, London, 1973.

WALKOWITZ, Judith R. and Daniel, J., '"We are not Beasts of the Field": Prostitution and the Poor in Plymouth and Southampton under the Contagious Diseases Acts', in Hartman, Mary and Banner, Lois (eds), *Clio's Consciousness Raised*, Harper & Row, New York, 1974.

WIMSHURST, Kerry, 'Child labour and school attendance in South Australia 1890–1915', *Historical Studies*, Vol. 19, No. 76, April 1981.

WINDSCHUTTLE, Elizabeth, 'The Public Role of Ruling Class Women in Colonial Australia, 1788–1850', *Women and Labour Conference Papers*, 1978.

WORSLEY, P., 'Britain – Unknown Country', *The New Reasoner*, No. 5, Summer 1958.

Theses

ADAMSON, P.D., 'Attitudes to Law-breakers and discharged prisoners', BA Hons thesis, Adelaide University, 1972.

BARBALET, Margaret, 'State Children: Theory and Practice in South Australia 1918–1928', MA thesis, Adelaide University, 1973.

BOWES, K.R., 'The 1890 Maritime Strike in SA', MA thesis, Adelaide University, 1957.

BRUESCH, Helen, 'Childhood as an Ideological Construct: the Official Definitions of Childhood in the Colony of NSW 1788–1825', BA Hons thesis, Australian National University, Canberra, 1978.

BYERLEY, Rosemary, 'The Treatment of Children in State Institutions', BA Hons thesis, Adelaide University, 1967.

CHINNER, Christine, '"Earthly Paradise": A Social History of Adelaide in the early 1890s', BA Hons thesis, Adelaide University, 1960.

COTTLE, A.R., 'A study of the rich of Woollahra during the Great Depression', BA Hons thesis, University of New South Wales, 1976.

DAVIES, Catherine, M., 'Women in Industry: the development in the employment of women in South Australia from 1900–1954', BA Hons thesis, Adelaide University, 1956.

DE VRIES, G.D., 'The Conditions of Child Birth in Adelaide', BA Hons thesis, Adelaide University, 1963.

FIELDING, Jane, 'The Social Control of Female Delinquency: Occupational Ideologies of Policewomen, Welfare Workers and Magistrates', BA Hons thesis, Australian National University, Canberra, 1975.

FORWOOD, Kathleen M., 'The Maintenance Act of 1926', Development of Social Work Essay, Flinders University, Adelaide, 1980.

HALLADAY, Allan Edwin, 'Poverty and the Large Family in Sydney 1968–69: a Study of Living Conditions and Social Policy', PhD thesis, Australian National University, 1971.

HENRY, Judith, 'The Establishment of Children's Courts in Victoria 1899–1906', BA Hons thesis, Monash University, Melbourne, 1971.

HORAN, Susan, M. '"More Sinned Against than Sinning": Prostitution in South Australia, 1836–1914', BA Hons thesis, Flinders University, 1977–78.

KIEK, L.E., 'The History of the South Australian Labour Unions', MA thesis, Adelaide University, 1948.

LOVELL, S.F., 'A City's Crime: Juveniles and Crime, Hobart 1860–1890', BA Hons thesis, University of Tasmania, Hobart, 1973.

MAGAREY, Susan, 'The Reclaimers: A study of the reformatory movement in England and Wales 1846–1893', PhD thesis, Australian National University, 1975.

——, 'A Study of Catherine Helen Spence', MA thesis, Australian National University, 1971.

MARKS, W. 'The Establishment of the Children's Court in New South Wales', BA Hons thesis, University of Melbourne, 1972.

MILGROM, Karen, 'Domestic Service in Australia 1860–1920', BA Hons thesis, Monash University, Melbourne, 1975.

PEAKE, Andrew, 'The State Children's Council, 1886–1895: Welfare Development – Innovation or Imitation?', Development of Social Work Essay, Flinders University, Adelaide, 1980.

WALTHER, Cora, 'Child Welfare, Delinquency and the Law in New South Wales 1896–1914', BA Hons thesis, University of New South Wales, 1968.

WIMSHURST, Kerry, 'Street Children and School Attendance in South Australia 1890–1915', M Ed thesis, Flinders University, 1979.

WORDEN, M.A., 'Some Social Attitudes in South Australia 1836–57', BA Hons thesis, Adelaide University, 1964.

ZWECK, Wayne, 'The Relief of the Poor in the Depression', BA Hons thesis, Adelaide University, 1964.

INDEX

SOURCES OF ILLUSTRATIONS

Cover: National Library of Australia.
  2: Gundagai, C.I. Bell Collection, National Library of Australia.
  4: *Annual Report of the State Children's Council*, 1914.
  13: *Annual Report of the State Children's Council*, 1913.
  18: Dorothy Roysland, *A Pioneer Family on the River Murray*, Rigby, 1978.
  24: South Australian State Library.
  29: South Australian State Library.
  31: Marshall's 'Lily White Washer' in *Cyclopaedia of New South Wales*, 1907, National Library of Australia.
  42: Advertisement from the *Australasian Ironmonger*, 1901, National Library of Australia.
  54: *1908 Handbook of South Australia*, C.E. Bristow, Government Printer, Adelaide.
  61: National Library of Australia.
  64: Correspondence of the State Children's Department.
  79: *Annual Report of the State Children's Council*, 1913.
  91: South Australian State Library.
  108: *Annual Report of the State Children's Council*, 1912.
  116: *Building Act Inquiry Committee, 1940*, South Australian Parliamentary Papers, Vol. 2, No. 32, 1940.
  118: *Annual Report of the State Children's Council*, 1913.
  135: *Cyclopaedia of South Australia*, 1907, National Library of Australia.
  168: Bathurst Historical Society, National Library of Australia.
  174: *Annual Report of the State Children's Council*, 1914.
  185: South Australian State Library.
  189: C.H. Spence, *State Children in Australia*, Vardon & Sons, Adelaide, 1907.
  192: C.H. Spence, *State Children in Australia*, Vardon & Sons, Adelaide, 1907.
  206: C.H. Spence, *State Children in Australia*, Vardon & Sons, Adelaide, 1907.
  213: *Annual Report of the State Children's Council*, 1914.
  217: Correspondence of the State Children's Department.